~~IM~~PERFECT

This is an IndieMosh book

brought to you by MoshPit Publishing
an imprint of Mosher's Business Support Pty Ltd

PO Box 4363
Penrith NSW 2750

indiemosh.com.au

Copyright © Holly Carr 2021

The moral right of the author has been asserted in accordance with the Copyright Amendment (Moral Rights) Act 2000.

All rights reserved. Except as permitted under the Australian Copyright Act 1968 (for example, fair dealing for the purposes of study, research, criticism or review) no part of this publication may be reproduced, stored in a retrieval system, or transmitted in any form or by any means, electronic, mechanical, photocopying, recording or otherwise, without the written permission of the publisher.

A catalogue record for this work is available from the National Library of Australia

https://www.nla.gov.au/collections

Title:	Imperfect
Author:	Carr, Holly (1981–)
ISBNs:	9781922628671 (paperback) 9781922628688 (ebook – epub) 9781922628695 (ebook – Kindle)
Subjects:	FICTION/Romance/General; Suspense; Workplace; Mystery & Detective/Cozy/

This story is entirely a work of fiction. No character in this story is taken from real life. Any resemblance to any person or persons living or dead is accidental and unintentional. The author, their agents and publishers cannot be held responsible for any claim otherwise and take no responsibility for any such coincidence.

Cover concept by Holly Carr. Cover layout by Ally Mosher at allymosher.com. Cover image used under licence from Adobe Stock

I~~M~~PERFECT

Love can leave a scar.
So can other things.

Holly Carr

This book is dedicated to my son, Taylor, who I imagine to be the pizza delivery guy in chapter 28.

Contents

Chapter 1 – Wow 1
Chapter 2 – Problems 10
Chapter 3 – Progress 19
Chapter 4 – A Night with the Boys 27
Chapter 5 – Chivalry and Injury 33
Chapter 6 – Denial 41
Chapter 7 – Dinner and Diligence 47
Chapter 8 – Um, What? 55
Chapter 9 – Escape 62
Chapter 10 – Meetings and Greetings 70
Chapter 11 – Booze and Near Misses 80
Chapter 12 – Behind Enemy Lines 88
Chapter 13 – Faking It 97
Chapter 14 – A Surprise Encounter 103
Chapter 15 – Confessions from the Murky Past 109
Chapter 16 – Honeytrap 116
Chapter 17 – Her New Demands 125
Chapter 18 – Building a Backbone 132
Chapter 19 – Legal Advice 141
Chapter 20 – Some Hard Truths 149
Chapter 21 – An Unexpected Betrayal 157
Chapter 22 – Sex and Drugs 164
Chapter 23 – More Sex and Drugs 173
Chapter 24 – Lies and Mistakes 183
Chapter 25 – Revelations 189
Chapter 26 – The Verdict 198

Chapter 27 – Should I, Shouldn't I?...............................204

Chapter 28 – Clarity..212

Chapter 29 – Some Welcome Assistance......................220

Chapter 30 – Ding! Round Two....................................229

Chapter 31 – A Spider in the Spotlight 238

Chapter 32 – A Faint Prayer 248

Chapter 33 – A Fateful Night 254

Chapter 34 – Oops 265

About the Author 273

Chapter 1 – Wow

Sam knew exactly where she'd gone wrong. In hindsight, it was obvious. They should never have been left unsupervised. Her notoriously erratic friends couldn't be trusted to make a collective decision on a pizza topping, let alone anything more complicated.

There must have been a hundred new messages in the group chat, all alarmingly off topic. She had innocently sent off a suggestion before bedtime, hoping to lock in a girls' night out and force herself out of the house for once. She'd forgotten her friends required a firm, guiding hand to shield them from the bounty of distracted boyfriend memes and cat gifs at their fingertips.

This is what I get for going to bed early, she thought, scrolling through the excess during breakfast.

They were no closer to locking in a date or location than before she'd closed the chat. Sam had articulated her availability before muting the notifications, assuming they weren't far off sleep as well. Clearly, she'd been mistaken.

You guys could talk the hind legs off a donkey, she typed. *Shouldn't at least some of you have been busy pleasuring your husbands?*

Not waiting for a reply, she gulped the last of her tea and left for work.

She arrived in the car park at the same time as her colleague Clarice, who nodded pointedly towards Sam's suspiciously tanned legs.

'I don't know why you bother with that stuff in winter. It looks like a lot of work.'

Sam laughed as the two made their way towards the building's entrance. 'Not all of us are naturally bronzed Greek goddesses,' she replied, referring to Clarice's Mediterranean olive skin tone. 'Without a layer of the fake stuff, some of us look like muscular, uncooked scone dough. Besides, being brown makes me feel warmer in this miserable weather.'

Clarice rolled her eyes. 'It'll warm up soon enough. And I bet Tristan would love to slather jam and cream on you,' she suggested, nodding towards the womaniser in the product development team as he pulled into a parking space. 'No matter what colour you are.'

Sam gave her a long-suffering look as she held the office door open. 'Hard pass. Thirty-seven is too old to be putting up with self-absorbed pseudo-playboys with commitment issues. Even if I'm pretty sure he thinks I'm younger.'

They chuckled softly, lapsing into silence while Sam peeked into the boss' office. Her new job had started two months ago, but she was only meeting Alex in person for the first time today. He wasn't there yet, so they moved to the tiny office kitchen to continue their Tristan bashing.

'He was flirting with Rebecca again the other day,' said Clarice, frowning at the ancient coffee machine. 'She was eating it up. I think I need to chat to her again.'

'Maybe I should start flirting back,' Sam joked, carefully pouring milk into her tea. 'Take one for the team, keep him off the girls that don't know any better.'

Clarice stirred sugar into her mug with a thoughtful expression. 'That's actually not a bad idea,' she mused. 'At least it might convince poor Rebecca he'll jump on anything with a decent chest circumference.'

Sam grimaced as they left the kitchen, careful not to spill her tea as she threaded her way through the cramped desks. She wasn't even sure she remembered how to flirt. Firmly single for almost three years, she'd been with her husband for ten more before that. Her skills were decidedly rusty. Any flirting in recent times had been for laughs. Finding the right mix between alluring and aloof wasn't a consideration when the real objective was to tease your friend's 'alpha-male' type husbands. She just stuck to making vaguely threatening suggestions about handcuffing them and putting things up their asses. There wasn't any enticement in that. She hoped not, anyway.

With a faint smile, she turned her attention to work matters and opened her email program. There was an update from the boss there.

Morning Samantha,

Looks like I probably won't be in today after all — it's 4am and my plane has just landed. We were delayed taking off, and we've been circling for two hours. I'm heading home to bed.

Alex

Sam sighed. She'd been looking forward to their meeting to break up the monotony. Since she'd started working here, it had become abundantly clear that Alex's previous assistant was either unbelievably slow or just incredibly good at hiding how little of her activity was work related. Bored, she'd tried to coax Alex into giving her a few more tasks at the beginning, but to no avail. She suspected her predecessor's incompetence had something to do with his reluctance.

Alex's distrust was frustrating. She'd taken a step backwards, career-wise, because the toxic, stifling atmosphere at her last workplace had gotten so bad she'd been approaching a nervous breakdown. Her last employer had characterised her attempts to improve things as 'pushy'. Taking on a less demanding role had been a calculated move to trick herself into a more relaxed frame of mind, but it had turned out to just be irritating. *Seems like I need more 'stimulation' than 'relaxation',* she reflected.

She'd given up on her plan to take a backseat within two weeks of starting here. Preserving the status quo wasn't in her nature. She looked for projects even when she wasn't trying to, and this office had them in abundance. Assuming she could convince Alex to give her the go-ahead.

Maybe I am pushy, she mused. *Surely there's a nicer word for that. Assertive? Strong-willed?*

Overbearing, whispered a voice in her head. *Domineering, bossy …*

She smiled ruefully, trying to rationalise the big ideas she had up her sleeve. Even if her meddling was evidence of a personality defect, no one could deny that the company needed a serious overhaul.

Owing to a lack of adequate heating and cooling, roughly half of the building complex wasn't in use. Everyone was crammed into a central area or a few offices either side. With no room for new colleagues, most people were overworked. Plus, the car park, kitchen, and washroom facilities were almost scandalously inadequate. Modifying the space was her top priority. Her well-researched plans were just waiting for Alex's approval.

In addition to that, her employer completed an eye-popping amount of work she could easily be doing for him. She prayed daily that his distrust was related to her inept predecessor, and not just indicative of his general nature. Being micromanaged was one of her biggest pet peeves, and she was anxiously awaiting an opportunity to feel him out.

In the meantime, she'd spent her tedious days doing what she could to make the existing space more comfortable and professional. All the ridiculously old reading material in reception had been replaced with subscriptions to industry-specific magazines, and she'd swapped out the uglier pieces of artwork on the walls. Best of all, there was now a 'records room' in one of the disused wings. The abundance of rarely used shelves and filing cabinets littering the main wing had been moved in there, making much-needed space. Not a huge accomplishment, but it'd still been the talk of the office for a week.

As she reflected on her small achievements, Sam checked over her plans for the umpteenth time. Without much to occupy her, the proposal had grown quite detailed. She hoped Alex would go for it, otherwise she anticipated a lot of dull days ahead.

By two pm, she was completely fed up. This had been happening on and off since she'd started working here, and it was driving her crazy. Just because she didn't have a high workload, it didn't mean she needed to put up with this level of inefficiency.

'Who do I have to open my legs for around here to get a mouse that works?' she complained quietly, furiously clicking the buttons to get it to register.

Someone behind her cleared their throat.

'Lauren in IT should be able to help with that,' said an amused voice.

She froze. She hadn't heard anyone approach. No one was supposed to overhear her crude remark. She was just venting.

'She's already paid a sufficient wage for providing that service though, so a polite "thank you" should be adequate compensation,' the speaker added, sounding suspiciously like he was fighting back laughter.

Sam had only spoken to him on the phone a few times, but the deep voice was familiar.

'Please don't be Alex,' she begged, her plea barely audible. She turned to face the owner of the amused voice, steeling herself for the worst.

Her new employer held out his hand for her to shake. 'It's nice to finally meet you in person, Samantha,' Alex said, still smiling at her gaffe.

Oh, crap, she thought. *That's beyond embarrassing.*

She prayed he wasn't the type to take advantage of her insinuation. He'd seemed thoroughly professional in all their exchanges so far, so probably not. Although the longer she looked at him, the more she suspected it wouldn't be such an onerous chore.

Embodying the classic 'tall, dark and handsome' profile, he also possessed broad shoulders, perfect bone structure (only partly hidden by a short beard), and intense green eyes framed by the sort of lashes women envied. Even the scar from a long-healed face wound didn't detract from the effect. If anything, it gave him a more masculine beauty.

Swallowing her shock, she hastily reminded herself that: a) hormonal response aside, she was very emphatically not interested in romance, and b) developing a crush on your boss was the worst kind of pathetic.

Making a momentous effort, she arranged her features into an apologetic smile and stood, taking Alex's proffered hand. It was warm and strong, shaking hers firmly.

'It's really nice to meet you too,' she began. 'I'm so sorry for that. I honestly didn't think anyone would hear me, but obviously I shouldn't be saying it anyway. I just let my frustration get the better of me …' she trailed off, realising she'd been babbling.

'I'm really sorry,' she repeated. 'It won't happen again.'

Alex waived magnanimously to reassure her, mirth still dancing in his eyes. 'It's fine,' he said. 'Honestly, it's been a crappy day; I was glad for the comic relief.'

Still not past it, Sam spoke again. 'I hope you don't think that I would actually …' She wasn't quite sure how to complete that attempt to restore her reputation. Not without saying things she shouldn't again, anyway.

Alex chuckled as he answered. 'Don't stress about it,' he assured her. 'You obviously didn't mean it literally. Don't censor yourself around me just because I own the company. A laugh once in a while will keep things from getting too boring.'

Sam smiled and nodded to show she'd calmed. Outwardly, at least. Gorgeous, nice, and makes allowances for her big mouth? This could be a problem.

Get it together, she told herself sternly, *don't be ridiculous.* She was probably just jumpy because he'd caught her off guard. And she hadn't expected him to be so good-looking. Or maybe this tightening in her downstairs area just meant she needed to pee.

'How about you go chat to Lauren about your mouse while I catch up with Dave?' suggested Alex. 'I'll meet you in my office a bit later, and we can get acquainted.'

Sam agreed, and Alex smiled at her again before walking towards the boardroom. She caught herself peeking at his behind as he walked away. *Not a good sign.* Maybe it wasn't just her lack of preparedness causing her heart to beat like this. She should really give Clarice a talking to for not warning her the boss looked like the male lead in a rom-com.

Realising she was still staring at his butt, Sam sat down and deliberately angled her gaze at the computer screen.

Hmmm.

This was unexpected. It'd been a long time since meeting a man had affected her so suddenly. Probably about thirteen years, come to think of it, when she'd met her husband. She'd dropped her drink when he smiled, and Logan had somehow gained Superman-like reflexes to catch it before it hit the ground. He didn't even spill anything, declaring months later that his dexterity had been fuelled by love at first sight.

It wasn't like she hadn't considered that a new man could be in her future during the three years she'd spent without him, but this had hit her without warning. She'd assumed attraction would be something that happened gradually, not a cheap infatuation produced by her undersexed libido.

But now wasn't the time to have a breakdown about it, so she mentally shook herself and refocused. *Work now, overanalyse later.* She foresaw a glass of wine and a quiet giggle at her idiocy tonight. In the present, she was going to see Lauren about her mouse, as suggested.

But first, crush aside, she had to talk to someone about the situation who would appreciate it.

OMG you guys, she typed into the group chat, *just met my new boss in person for the first time. He's so good-looking I had to squeeze my legs together to stop my underwear from dropping to the floor.*

For good measure, she also wrote a message to Clarice. *You could have warned me!*

A response in the group chat made her phone vibrate, and she quickly flicked back to read the reply. *Sounds like a workplace hazard. You'll have to stop wearing knickers, so you don't trip over them,* she read.

Sam laughed softly and typed a response. *I could just wear pants, I guess.*

The answers were swift.

I'd stick with the skirt. It'll be so much more efficient when he bends you over his desk. Think how impressed he'll be when he doesn't have to deal with your granny panties, one said.

That kind of foresight and planning sounds like grounds for a promotion to me, chimed in someone else.

Sam rolled her eyes and decided to respond later. It'd give the girls a chance to really work themselves into a frenzy, of course, but she didn't have time to do the topic justice.

With that thought, she purposefully strode over to Lauren to talk about her malfunctioning mouse.

Half an hour later, Sam followed Alex into his office, where he stopped with surprise. She quickly explained about the new records room. The cacophony of filing cabinets that had previously graced his wall was now housed (much less precipitously) in a different section of the office.

'But if it's inconvenient for you, I can move it back. Most of the documents looked to be quite old, so I didn't think you'd be referring to them often,' she said.

Alex shook his head. 'No, no. It's great. I was just berating myself for not considering the empty wings as a storage option. I never look at those files. The accounts team started keeping them in here years ago,' he said. 'And they rarely look at them either, truth be told,' he added, gesturing for her to sit.

Relieved, she sat in front of Alex's far too small desk, being careful not to disturb any of the piles of paper precariously stacked atop it. 'I suppose you've become too used to not thinking about the disused space,' she speculated. 'It needed some fresh eyes.'

Alex nodded, taking off his suit jacket and hanging it over his chair. She was careful not to let her eyes linger too long over the broad, muscular chest now revealed. The suit didn't need to create an illusion of a good body. It just enhanced his natural athleticism.

'Feel free to speak up if your fresh eyes spot any other genius suggestions,' he said while taking a seat.

Before she even had a chance to evaluate if this were rhetorical or not, he changed the subject. 'I'm sorry I scared you earlier,' he began. 'I know you weren't expecting me in today. I thought I'd pass out as soon as my head hit the pillow after that flight from hell, but apparently it just wired me too tight to sleep.'

Sam nodded. 'If you'd stayed in bed much longer, you probably wouldn't have slept tonight anyway,' she pointed out.

'So here I am, ruining your day instead,' he agreed, grinning at her.

She laughed, relaxing a little. Crush or no crush, she could get on board with a sense of humour. 'And I thought the mouse was going to be the worst of my problems,' she replied cheekily.

Satisfied they were both on the same wavelength, the conversation turned to work-related matters. Sam wisely decided it was too soon to bring up her drastic plans to make the office more liveable. People tended to be stubborn when they were tired, and she didn't want to risk him digging in his heels for no logical reason. For all she knew, Alex had an emotional attachment to the way things were. He might even be unaware of the magnitude of friction it seemed to cause everyone. Locked away in this shoebox of an office all day, it wasn't hard to believe he'd be out of touch.

As she stood up to leave the office after their chat, Sam was already planning how best to present her plans. She'd let him settle back in today, allowing him to catch up with things before she disturbed his equilibrium.

Soon though, there is going to be some upheaval, she promised herself.

Chapter 2 – Problems

Distracted by a laugh in the main office, Alex looked up from his screen. Sam pushed her hair behind her ear as Clarice spoke, her profile coming into better view without the obstruction. She wore little pearl studs in her earlobes today. Their iridescent shimmer had caught his attention a few times.

Sam answered Clarice enthusiastically, using her whole body to illustrate her response. Alex smiled; he wasn't close enough to hear what they spoke about but enjoyed her energy.

His new assistant was quite a character. It had only taken him the length of an afternoon to note how well liked she was. Now, at the end of that same week, he marvelled that she'd somehow become the heart and soul of his office in such a short space of time. He wasn't the only one who watched her unconscious performance.

True, many of the onlookers were men, probably charmed by more than her sense of humour. There had to be more to her allure than aesthetics though. His last assistant had a similarly attractive face and enticing curves, and she hadn't managed to engage with the office the way Sam did.

He realised his eyes had strayed down to those curves, and almost recoiled in shock. *Calm down,* he told himself. It had been unconscious, his thoughts affecting his line of sight. He wasn't attracted to Sam like other men seemed to be, but that didn't mean he wasn't objectively aware of her appeal. She was hard to ignore.

He was certainly trying though. There was so much work to get through, but his gaze kept drifting in her direction. And it didn't help that her desk was right outside his office. His ears had become so attuned to her voice that he found himself listening every time she answered the phone. Her magnetism was maddening.

And she'd gotten to him again, he realised. His eyes had been trained on Sam for several minutes.

Annoyed at himself, he got up and closed his office door, resolving to finish his task with no further distractions. There was a meeting scheduled with the sales team in half an hour and he needed to prepare. He intended to make sense of the odd numbers in last quarter's sales figures.

A while later, Alex sat in the boardroom listening to Dave, the sales manager. The numbers were down across their whole range, and this meeting was intended to determine what the common denominator was. Multiple clients had ordered less stock, or not at all.

There was no downturn in the dash camera industry itself — they'd been getting more and more popular since he'd gone into business — so something had to be happening internally. Or not. It could just be bad luck, a coincidence. Clients sometimes overstocked, after all, and the subsequent months were often leaner for their suppliers. The quarter before had been solid, so this did lend credence to that particular theory.

In fact, it wasn't just the preceding quarter that'd seen growth. The last few years had been spectacular across the board. Alex reminded himself he should consider some pay rises for the umpteenth time. His team were superstars and deserved to be rewarded for their efforts.

But had they dropped the ball this time? It hadn't just been one or two people. There was a steady downturn across the whole department. His research this afternoon had shown that.

This led him to conclude it wasn't related to the staff, but he just couldn't see any other reason for it. There was no obvious explanation for why they should be experiencing a slump.

If indeed it was just a slump. This quarter was looking fishy too, although the sales reps had assured him it was early days yet. Many people didn't order until the last minute, and things could change at the drop of a hat.

After an hour, Alex realised they were going around in circles and adjourned the meeting. Time was better spent looking after this quarter's numbers than speculating about the previous one. The company's cash position was still looking optimistic overall. They could afford a few lean months. He decided to stop obsessing and just keep a close eye on it for now.

Dave followed him into his office as he walked back, promptly negating his resolution to not give his concerns any more attention. They chatted quietly, both aware of the open door and the closeness of the staff outside.

'Do you think there's something going on we don't know about?' asked Alex directly, now they didn't have to censor themselves.

Dave paused, a thoughtful look marring his otherwise genial face as he considered his answer. 'Look,' he began, 'I don't know for certain. There are problems within the company, for sure, but I know my staff. None of them would be deliberately slacking off. They're hard workers, too hard probably, and we're lucky to have them. If there was any way I could promote a couple of them, I'd do it in a heartbeat.'

Something in his tone caused Alex to wait him out rather than respond straight away.

Dave paused too, clearly unsure if he should continue.

'But?' Alex prompted, eliciting a sheepish smile from Dave. Not much got past Alex.

'But they're overworked,' he admitted. 'And I think we can both sympathise with that. The bigger we get, the bigger the workload, with the same amount of people to tackle it. It's possible they've just collectively let things slip. I've been telling you for ages we need more staff.'

Alex sighed, rubbing his temples. If this was the reason, he needed to figure out somewhere to put another sales rep and fast. The longer the team coasted by on a subpar performance, the more ingrained mediocrity would be. No matter how many people he hired.

Dave left shortly after, and Alex followed him to the door, looking out at the office. He mentally moved desks, trying to figure out a way to squeeze in another without it becoming a fire hazard.

His attention was inevitably drawn to Sam when her phone rang. She cheerfully answered, while he absentmindedly looked over the contents of her desk. It housed a weird collection of things, giving an insight into the woman who had made it her own. The magnets from various foreign countries proclaimed her well-travelled and didn't seem out of place, but the exceedingly old troll doll and a few 'magic' crystals made a strange juxtaposition with the general professional feel. *I wonder if she thinks those rocks have any use beyond decoration,* he mused.

He listened as she spoke, appreciating the light pleasantness of her tone. It sounded like she was speaking to their office stationery supplier, who was a difficult contact. His previous assistant had often argued with them, although he blamed Tiffany's attitude for that. Her phone manner wasn't as endearing as Sam's.

He chastised himself for the unfair thought. His low tolerance for Tiffany's antics was likely coloured by his dislike of her in general. Sam's conversation seemed to indicate she was having issues too, so Tiffany's personal failings weren't entirely to blame. Sam kept her cool though, turning away from her screen to give the conversation her full attention.

She blinked, looking surprised to find Alex standing behind her, but continued her conversation with no misstep. Flashing him a smile, she quirked an enquiring eyebrow his way.

Flustered, he fought his embarrassment. Sam was probably used to the attention she attracted; he didn't want her thinking he was another admirer. Waving dismissively, he turned to walk back to his desk.

Looking at the time, he resolved to make a phone call of his own so he wouldn't have to come up with an excuse for staring at her when she finished hers. She was scheduled to clock out soon and had developed a tradition of popping her head in to wish him a good night before she left.

Sure enough, ten minutes later, Sam leaned inside his door, coat on and handbag hung off her elbow. She smiled and mouthed 'have a good weekend' before turning to leave.

Alex watched her go, trying to ignore the niggling feeling of having forgotten … to ask her something? To do something? He wasn't sure what, but anxiety nagged at him, and he itched to call her back and figure out why he needed her.

Arriving at home later that night, he was met by his frowning daughter.

'Dad,' said Stacey reproachfully, 'it's Friday.'

Alex looked up at the clock, noting it was almost eight-thirty. He opened his mouth to explain what had kept him at work so late, but then closed it resignedly. She was right, after all. It was Friday, and there was always some excuse for his workaholic nature. 'I'm sorry,' he said contritely, accepting his plate of reheated dinner.

To his surprise, she wasn't content to just shake her head at him and head for the TV tonight. Instead, she sat at the counter next to him with a stern look on her face. 'We need to talk,' she said.

He swallowed his first mouthful a little too quickly, having to cough so he didn't choke on mashed potato. 'This isn't about my working too much again, is it?' he asked warily, scooping a forkful of peas into his mouth. He'd just realised he was starving.

Stacey rolled her eyes at him. 'Yes, actually. It is,' she said. 'We both know you'd be sleeping on the couch in your office if you didn't have me to come home to. And in a couple of years, that might just be the case. Who knows where I'll end up after I finish high school?'

She'd said as much before, but Alex was trying not to think about it. No parent was comfortable with the idea of their fifteen-year-old talking about moving away in the foreseeable future. Even if she was almost sixteen — and going on forty, if the way she spoke to her father was any indication.

'You've said so before,' he answered, trying to look more engrossed in his dinner. Maybe she'd lose interest if she didn't have his full attention. 'I've told you; I'll take care of myself. No sleeping at the office, no working round the clock. Scout's honour.'

She snorted. 'You can make promises till you're blue in the face, but that doesn't mean it'll play out that way,' she said. 'I know you mean it, but I also know what you're like. Something will come up, it'll be important, and you'll convince yourself it's just once … before you know it, you'll be waking up there more mornings than not.'

He waved a fork at her in protest, but he couldn't interrupt her lecture with his mouth full.

'Besides, it's not just about that,' she continued. 'You have no life. You go to work, you come home to me, you go to the gym, rinse and repeat.'

'That's not true,' he protested, finally managing to swallow the mouthful of pork chops. 'I go out with my brothers sometimes. And I see my friends once in a while …'

Actually, come to think of it, I don't remember the last time I saw someone other than family or work colleagues. Best not to dwell on that. He tried to skate past it, but Stacey cut in ruthlessly.

'You go out once a month, if that,' she countered. 'For a couple of hours, tops. Almost always with the uncles, and they still complain because you're always the first to leave. We keep talking about this,' she continued, exasperated, 'and you keep promising you'll do better. I've tried everything I can think of, but you just won't —' She stopped her sentence prematurely, the words appearing to elude her amid her frustration.

It made him feel guilty. Mostly because she was right. They'd talked about this more times than he cared to count, and it always ended with some vague (but emphatic) promises on his part. He'd get to it — when work calmed down.

Not that it ever calmed down, which was likely the problem. He needed to do something about that. One day. *One day soon,* he promised himself, with about as much conviction as normal. He had only just arrived home from two months overseas, after all. There were plenty of things needing his attention before he could give it a serious go.

Stacey though … she deserved more reassurances than that. While he'd spent the first six weeks of his time away working, he'd met with his daughter and the rest of their family for a two-week holiday at the end. Their time together had highlighted her own problems, and he'd been wondering if his rampant workaholism was a part of it.

He thought furiously while he chewed, turning to her after he swallowed. 'All right,' he conceded. 'You have a point. I've made promises before, and I've not delivered. I'm not going to do that again,' he said, noting her sceptical look, 'but you'll have to give me some time.'

She frowned, opening her mouth (to argue, no doubt).

'Three months,' he said, heading her off. 'Give me three months, and I'll get back to you about what I'm going to do. Tangible stuff. That's more than you've gotten before.'

She still looked suspicious, probably wondering if he was stalling for time.

'I can't make these changes overnight,' he said exasperatedly. 'The business would fall apart. I need some time to figure out what I can change, and how soon I can put it into place. I'm not guaranteeing everything will be different right at that moment, mind you,' he warned, 'just that I'll have a plan.'

Stacey gave him a long, level look, her expression unreadable as he chewed innocently. He truly did intend to come up with something. His daughter had made her point before, and the aftereffects of their trip had spoken even louder than she had. He felt … better. Rested. Relaxed.

The change of scenery was long overdue. He'd still been working for the first six weeks of course, planning his business meetings to line up nicely with the holiday his family had badgered him into joining them on. He'd worked even harder than usual, if he were honest. Stacey had stayed with his parents for that month and a half, so he'd had all that time without her to really throw himself in the deep end. Maybe she had a point about her presence tempering his enthusiasm.

His mother obviously agreed with her. He knew very well the reason why the autocratic matriarch had insisted they book a yacht instead of a hotel was due to the lack of Wi-Fi. He'd been completely out of touch with the office the entire time.

Stacey had been as unhappy about this as him. Two whole weeks of no social media, no talking to her friends, and enforced close quarters with her Babushka, whom she'd already had enough of in the preceding month and a half. Eva had lectured her teenage granddaughter on everything from her life plans to her taste in clothes.

Alex hadn't been spared the scrutiny either, but Eva's gripes with her son were of a completely different genre.

'You have evaded women for too long,' she'd scolded, her Russian accent adding an authoritative edge to her words. 'Look how Anastasia avoids those of her own sex. She even dresses like a boy, to hide her woman's body.'

'She's just a tomboy, Mama,' he'd explained, attempting nonchalance. 'Not everyone has the femininity of a ballet dancer, and it's normal for teenagers to be awkward about puberty. Leave her be.'

She'd snorted in response, driving her point home with some well-chosen follow-up words. 'You know I am right. Even when she was little, you kept her in a world of men. Her nanny was even a man, because of you and your silly prejudices. She takes no joy in her gender, and she has no comfort in herself. Look at her cousins, see how they bloom in confidence as they grow. Do you not want that for your daughter?'

The conversation had gone downhill from there. Privately, Alex agreed with some of her points. Stacey's sense of belonging might benefit from a more regular feminine influence, although he didn't rate the socially constructed trappings of womanhood his mother valued. And he'd be damned if he agreed a new wife was the best way to tackle the problem.

He came back to the present when his plate was almost clear, breathing a sigh of relief when Stacey agreed to his proposal. She might be awkward with the general public, but she wasn't shy around him. If anyone was going to force him back into some semblance of a life, it was her.

Chapter 3 – Progress

Almost two weeks after their first meeting, Sam was slowly coming to accept that her first half an hour with Alex was an anomaly. They hadn't shared more than five consecutive minutes alone since then.

He'd clearly been working for some time when she arrived in the mornings and showed no sign of leaving when she departed in the evenings. Even lunch didn't slow him down. The man seemed to subsist primarily on coffee and protein bars. If he wasn't in a meeting, he was on the phone, or had closed his office door to avoid interruptions.

Sam hadn't even managed to talk to him about her lack of work, let alone present anything so ambitious as a total overhaul of the office. No wonder his last assistant's inactivity went undetected. Alex's disinterest in her was so pronounced he probably wouldn't notice if she spent most of her time liberating office supplies to sell on eBay.

Her phone dinged, and she reached for it eagerly. Anything to break up the monotony of another boring day.

Will you call the parentals already? They're driving me nuts.

Ugh. Anything but that.

It was from her brother, and he was right. She hadn't spoken to them in over a week, and they were probably getting worried again.

Tonight, she typed back. *Sorry, time got away with me.*

He'd know it was more than forgetfulness, but it couldn't be helped. It wasn't that she didn't love her parents, they just took a lot out of her. Come to think of it, she was having drinks with Clarice tonight and probably wouldn't have time to give them the requisite exuberance to avoid concerned follow-up calls.

Tomorrow, actually, she typed into a new message. *I'm busy tonight.*

She looked up when a flash of movement caught her eye to find an angsty-looking teenage girl with fire engine red hair at her desk. The young woman gestured to the closed office door. 'Is he in a meeting or something?' she asked with a frown, adjusting the backpack hanging from her hunched shoulders.

Wondering how on earth a random teen had manoeuvred her way through the whole office without being questioned, chaperoned or at least announced, Sam hesitated before answering. 'He's not available at the moment, I'm sorry. Can I take a message?'

The young woman frowned deeper and swung her backpack down, opening it to pull out handfuls of pale blue chiffon and satin. The fabrics looked vaguely luxurious, but she didn't seem too impressed. Not if the force of her yanking was any indication. 'Just give him this, and tell him to do something about his mother,' she instructed, thrusting the dress at Sam and stalking off. She almost mowed down Clarice in her haste.

Bemused, Sam watched the girl manoeuvre her way back through the desks again.

'What's up with Stacey?' asked Clarice as she arrived at Sam's desk.

Sam looked up at her friend, bewildered. 'I have no idea. She seems unhappy with Alex's mother though. Who is she?' queried Sam.

'Oh, have you not met her yet?' asked Clarice. 'That was Alex's daughter. She's usually all right, just a bit quiet. Typical teenage moodiness, you know.'

Sam panicked. 'Oh crap, should I have interrupted Alex? I had no idea he even had a daughter! I told her he was busy,' she explained anxiously.

Clarice shrugged. 'Don't stress. If he hasn't taken the time to tell you about her, he can hardly expect you to know what to do when she shows up,' she soothed.

Somewhat mollified, but still a little rattled, Sam stood up. 'I'd probably better let him know she was here anyway,' she said, shaking out the blue fabric (which turned out to be a dress). She moved towards Alex's door without further ado.

'Don't forget drinks tonight,' Clarice reminded her as she walked away.

After knocking briefly, Sam opened the office door and tilted her head in. 'Sorry to interrupt, Alex,' she said hesitantly.

Her handsome employer looked up from his screen and smiled, softening the frown lines that had been prominent a moment before. 'That's fine, Sam,' he said, leaning away from his desk. 'What's up?'

'I'm so sorry,' she said again, moving into the office. 'Apparently, I just turned your daughter away. I had no idea who she was until Clarice explained, and didn't think I should be interrupting you while your door was closed.'

Alex's frown lines had returned when he noticed the dress she held. 'I'm guessing she left that with you,' he said.

'Uh, yes, actually,' Sam answered, holding it up for him to peruse. 'And instructions for you to "do something about your mother".'

He smiled resignedly and nodded. 'My parents' fiftieth wedding anniversary is next weekend,' he explained. 'My mother has decided the accompanying celebration is to be a black-tie event. Her and Stacey don't see eye to eye on the subject of Stacey's wardrobe. She's decreed that "Anastasia will conform to the dress code, or"… well, or nothing. My mother isn't one to give ultimatums. She just gives orders and expects they'll be carried out,' he finished with a shrug.

'Not the best way to get through to a teenager,' noted Sam.

'Sending a dress is her idea of being helpful,' he explained, nodding at Sam's assessment. 'She thinks that as she's saved Stacey the indignity of dress shopping, she's the good guy.'

'I don't think Stacey sees it that way,' said Sam.

'You're not wrong,' agreed Alex.

'I'm guessing your mother's concession to her tastes is to make it blue instead of pink?' Sam asked, frowning at the offending dress.

Admittedly, it was quite nice, but her brief introduction to Alex's daughter had illustrated it was categorically not the dress for Stacey. Blue didn't automatically make it less girly.

'That sounds about right,' agreed Alex.

'Not exactly meeting in the middle, but she tried, I guess,' Sam said tactfully.

Alex shrugged noncommittally and looked willing to dismiss the subject. Sam wasn't letting it go so easily. A fond note in his voice made it obvious he loved both his daughter and his mother very much, but the man seemed clueless about his role in this little dance.

'To be honest, I don't know what your mother was thinking,' she said, cunningly steering the conversation where she needed it to go. 'That blue is going to clash horribly with her hair. She'd look much better in black, or a dark green even.'

'She only dyed it a couple of days ago. My mother doesn't even know about it yet,' explained Alex. 'Actually, she's probably going to have conniptions when she sees it.'

'Honestly, her hairdresser didn't do the greatest job,' said Sam. 'I didn't see it for very long, but it looks a bit uneven.'

'I think she did it herself,' said Alex. 'If the state of her bathroom sink was any indication.'

Sam unsuccessfully attempted to hide her look of alarm. Alex looked at her questioningly.

'That's a drastic colour to be doing on your own,' she explained. 'There's some real potential to ruin your hair, and it's not easy to get it right. She seems to have done an okay job, but I'd still book her into the hairdresser to have a look. We don't want her hair to start falling out, and maybe they can even things out a little too.'

It was Alex's turn to look panicked.

Correctly intuiting his look of anxiety, and silently thanking her lucky stars for the opportunity to give the poor girl a voice, Sam offered to make an appointment for Stacey with her own hairdresser. 'And I'll see if I can find an outfit she might be more comfortable in,' she added.

Alex's expression turned to surprise, obviously unsure what to make of her self-appointed role. 'I'd be happy to have the help of someone who knows what they're talking about,' he began cautiously, 'but I don't want to add to your workload. You didn't sign up to be my daughter's personal shopper.'

Sam wasn't getting a better opening than this. 'Actually, Alex,' she said brightly, 'I've been trying to get a moment to speak with you about my workload since you got back. Quite frankly, I don't have enough to do.'

Alex was obviously taken aback and opened his mouth to respond, but Sam kept going before he had a chance to speak. 'I'm hesitant to talk my way out of a job, but I also don't want to be dishonest. Plus, I'm bored. You're paying me to do a job I can get done before my lunchbreak. I've been trying to put the extra time to good use — that's why all the little changes in the office have happened — but most of the things I'd like to work on really need your input. Or at least your approval.'

Alex had stopped looking confused, nodding along during this speech. He used her pause to speak up. 'I'm so sorry, Sam. My last assistant always seemed so busy. I was convinced the rumours of her laziness were false. She wasn't the most likable person.' He grimaced, and Sam wondered what the woman had done to get on his bad side. 'I probably should've understood when you were offering to do things for me while I was overseas. I'd dismissed it as an attempt to look good for the new boss,' he continued. 'I'll definitely start throwing more work your way.'

This was a great start, but Sam wasn't content to leave it with vague promises. She wanted something tangible. 'Just give me a sec,' she said, backing out of the office. 'I have a few specific things to ask you about, but I need to send you some related figures and things.'

Before Alex had a chance to object, she skipped to her computer and hit 'send' on the three emails sitting in her draft folder, just waiting for her to give them a proper introduction.

Coming back into the office, she began talking before Alex had a chance to either start reading the emails or to suggest they do this another time. She'd revised her plan of attack a few days ago. He probably wouldn't give her time to get through her original pitch, so she had to give it to him straight. *Which suits me just fine,* she admitted. *If I'm going to be 'pushy', may as well push in the right direction.*

'I've been here just over a month and I've been keeping my eyes and ears open,' Sam began. 'I'm not going to sugar-coat it: your employees are seriously unhappy. I'm not naming any names, but I know of three people actively looking for new jobs. At least two of them would be a serious loss — the kind of loss that would stress everyone out even more and snowball to more people leaving. And keep firmly in mind,' she continued, 'this is just the staff I know about. I haven't worked here long. Not everyone is confiding in me.'

Alex's face changed from resigned tolerance to genuine concern as she continued talking, outlining the specific complaints, and taking the time to present irrefutable evidence.

'So basically, our problems can be divided into three categories. The office is too crowded, there aren't enough staff, and there's no room for career advancement,' she finished.

Alex was silent for a bit, sitting back in his chair looking overwhelmed. She wondered if she should launch into her proposed solutions or if she should give him a moment to acclimatise. She was about to get started when he sat forward and rubbed his eyes.

'This is a lot to take in,' he began, leaning on his elbows to rest his chin on steepled fingers. His shirt sleeves were rolled up, and she had a tantalising view of his muscled forearms. 'I knew things weren't perfect. Dave and I were discussing something similar last week, but I hadn't realised how dire it was. To be honest, I've been meaning to sort out the rest of the building and hire a few new people for years. I've just never had the time to do the research.' He shook his head dejectedly. 'I guess I'll have to make it a priority if I don't want to be the captain of a sinking ship,' he finished, looking tired at the prospect of more work.

Sam heard him mumble something about Stacey being unhappy, while he glanced mournfully at the piles of documents on his desk.

Perfect. He'd arrived right where she needed him to.

'Actually, Alex,' she said earnestly, 'I've already done that for you.'

The look of surprise on his face was almost comical. Sam got the impression he'd been doing everything on his own for so long that it had never occurred to him to delegate. She directed him to the first of her three emails, which included several quotes, as well as a proposed layout for the refurbished space.

'Obviously, some of this will be influenced by how many staff you want in that particular department,' finished Sam. 'The second email includes recommendations about specific staff needed, based on what people are telling me, and on what I've calculated will be acceptable cost and profit. I also popped in an idea about a small restructure. It would give you opportunities to promote deserving staff members. I know I've overstepped the boundaries a bit there,' she continued, belatedly acknowledging her boldness, 'but I had all this information at my fingertips. It didn't make any sense to let it go to waste. Of course, you're going to understand our staff needs better than I am. This is based purely on the information I had available.'

Alex had been opening the attachments as she spoke. 'Don't apologise, Sam, I'm grateful for your initiative. And impressed,' he added, looking up from his screen. 'I've never had the time to explore this, and now I can make the decisions I need to make. I've been putting it off for years, and you come and drop it all in my lap, tied up in a metaphorical ribbon. I've had the cash for the refurbish for years now,' he continued. 'Just not the time to do anything about it. All that money has been burning a hole in my pocket, and it's not doing great things for me at tax time.'

Sam was elated. She'd thought getting him to spend the cash would be the hardest part, but he had the money ready to go! And he'd characterised her overzealousness as 'taking initiative'. That was a relief.

Alex smiled at her, and her stomach did a somersault.

He is far too good-looking, she thought distractedly.

'I'm almost too scared to ask, but what's the third email for?' he asked.

She laughed, feeling a bit giddy from how well this was all going. 'That one is a little tamer. It's some suggestions for things you're doing yourself that I could be doing for you.'

Alex nodded, looking relieved. 'If you want to take on more, that's great. Especially after the resourcefulness you've just shown. Let me look it over, and I'll get back to you with answers on Monday.'

Recognising a dismissal, Sam stood and smiled at him. 'I'll go find Stacey an outfit, and then we'll really finish our Friday on a high note,' she said excitedly.

Chapter 4 – A Night with the Boys

Pausing before seating himself at the table with his brothers, Alex surveyed the remnants of their meal. A plate bereft of tortilla chips but still smeared with salsa, guacamole and cheese indicated it had once housed nachos. Other dishes held the cold remains of sauce from some chicken wings, a few crumbs from some potato wedges, and something he had to assume was a garnish. There was no way his brothers had ordered something where lettuce was the main ingredient.

The addition of a couple of rounds of empty glasses was testament to how overworked the bar was. Evidently, none of the staff had been around to clear the table yet. Or maybe their designated server was an attractive woman, busy avoiding his younger brothers.

None of them had ever had much difficulty gaining the attention of a woman, and Erik and Noah applied their talents generously. Their mother's influence saved them from being total degenerates, but Alex still pitied the women that crossed their paths. If it had only been the two of them, he wouldn't have come tonight. His interest in their escapades extended only to their ability to distract the women that pursued him.

Fortunately, his older brothers were much more pleasant company. James and Christian were both happily married and subsequently posed little threat to the feminine population of the bar tonight. Their presence ensured Alex wouldn't be abandoned in favour of chasing a potential conquest.

Greeting them and ignoring their good-natured ribbing about his tardiness, Alex indicated he'd go order the next round before he sat down. He made his way to the bar, trying to decide what to order for dinner while he was there, and promptly lost his train of thought as the woman in front of him turned around.

'Sam!' he said. Caught off guard, his eyes travelled down her body, taking in that she'd changed to higher heels and a shorter dress since leaving the office a few hours ago. The loose cut of her outfit caused it to hang off one shoulder and quite low over the other, curving invitingly downwards at her cleavage. Alex determinedly fixed his eyes on her face.

'Alex!' said Sam, clearly also surprised. 'Long time, no see.'

It was a crappy joke, but he laughed all the same. He'd noticed that Sam loved a good quip. It'd seemed like a grab for popularity at first, but further observation had proved she wasn't above making a fool of herself. She was just naturally affable.

She was also scrutinising his attire, a small frown marring her friendly face.

'You've just left the office, haven't you?' she asked, a bit sternly.

Alex laughed again, sheepishly this time. He only had a handful of women in his life (and most of them were related to him), but they all seemed to think him incapable of caring for himself.

That's one more for the list, he thought ruefully. *And an unexpected one at that. Aren't I supposed to be in charge here?*

Sam was shaking her head, but her smile softened her rebuke. 'Alex, you work too hard,' she admonished. 'And you never eat anything. I have no idea how you manage to keep yourself so buff.'

She eyed him up and down while she spoke, and Alex suspected his incredulity was written all over his face. As refreshing as he found her tendency to speak her mind, he wasn't yet used to it. *No filters for this one,* he thought, *she'll blurt it all out no matter who's on the receiving end.*

'Sorry, that may have been a little inappropriate,' she apologised. She held up two glasses of wine. 'This is our third round, and I'm a cheap drunk.'

Alex belatedly realised someone was probably waiting on that other glass of wine. He'd held her up long enough. 'It's fine. I'm about to start catching up,' he said with a chuckle, gesturing towards the bar. 'If you watch closely, you might even see me eat something.'

Sam laughed too as they parted ways.

Alex felt a bit off-centre after running into her, struggling to focus. He almost forgot to order his burger. He played back their conversation from this afternoon as he paid, still elated at his realisation that her plans would help him keep his promise to Stacey.

His brothers stared at him as he made his way back to the table, various degrees of shock and curiosity evident on their faces.

Alex stared back blankly. 'What?' he finally asked.

Christian was the first to speak. 'You laughed,' he said, wonder colouring his voice.

'With a strange girl,' added Erik excitedly.

'A GOOD-LOOKING strange girl,' emphasised Noah.

'Three times,' concluded James with a hopeful grin.

Alex's confusion cleared. He shook his head, smiling tolerantly. It must have looked like he was trying to chat up a strange woman. No wonder they were so stunned. 'That's my new assistant, Sam,' he explained, looking over at her table, where he also noticed Clarice.

Both women looked at him as Clarice talked, and Sam smiled warmly. Alex smiled back, nodding at Clarice by way of a greeting. Turning back to his brothers, he realised they were still gawking at him like he'd grown another head. His smile turned to confusion. 'You all know about her. I'm sure I mentioned her while we were away,' he said.

James opened his mouth to speak, but Christian cut him off with a warning look. His oldest brother didn't often take the lead in a conversation, only doing so when he thought the subject matter required a more delicate touch. Alex eyed him warily, preparing to sift through some subtext.

'It seems like you two are getting along really well,' Christian began. 'Has it worked out okay? Especially considering you did all the interviewing over the phone. I remember you were worried about that.'

Alex could hear the deliberate casualness in his voice. Most people wouldn't notice, but a lifetime of dealing with Christian's cunning had primed him to be suspicious. He took a drink to give himself some thinking time. The liquor was strong, but it did nothing to mask the taste of apprehension growing in him. 'She's very good at her job,' he said eventually.

Christian nodded, sipping nonchalantly from his own drink. 'It seems like she has a great sense of humour too,' he said. 'You don't laugh easily. We've talked about you needing to lighten up for years now.'

Annoyed the conversation had turned so psychoanalytical, Alex couldn't keep the irritation from his voice. 'Maybe she's just funnier than you,' he countered. 'Why do you care? Are you looking for a side piece? I hadn't realised that was part of the criteria. She's probably a bit young for you under normal circumstances, but if we're in mid-life crisis territory, I'd say she's just about right.' He spoke antagonistically on purpose, needling his brother to provide an outlet for his exasperation. He realised he was still frowning as he glanced at Sam again, so he quickly smoothed his face. He didn't want her to think she was the source of his aggravation.

'It's you that likes the young ones,' chimed in Erik with a laugh.

Christian shot him a dirty look. 'It's the young ones that like him,' he said to Erik pointedly. 'That's what I'm getting at,' he directed at Alex. 'Sam seems nice, and a lot less predatory than your last assistant. I know how uncomfortable you were when she started making eyes at you.'

Oh, Alex thought, *that.*

He relaxed now that he understood why they were so concerned. While the situation with Tiffany wasn't public knowledge, he didn't really keep many things from his brothers. She'd begun flirting with him towards the end of her employment, standing too close and finding excuses to touch him. Her fake smiles and laughter had made him uneasy, and her attempts to 'subtly' bend over and display her cleavage had been laughably obvious.

Alex hadn't found any part of the situation remotely funny. He'd become increasingly more uncomfortable, unsure what to do. He wasn't a stranger to women making a play for his attention, but he usually avoided them until they lost interest. Or set Erik and Noah onto them.

Avoidance and distraction hadn't been possible on this occasion. He had to walk past Tiffany every time he so much as entered or exited his office. Instead, he'd moved the start date of his trip abroad forward, expanding his existing plans to work away.

Unfortunately, this tactic had driven her to desperate measures. Working late the night before flying out, he'd returned from a trip to the bathroom to find her draped across his desk, clad only in lingerie. He'd fired her on the spot, none too gently, and no one in the office had seen or heard from her since.

Pulling his attention back to the present, Alex responded, 'She's attracted a bit of attention around the office, but I don't think she's interested in any of it. If they're respectful, she tolerates it, but she doesn't show any special attention to anyone. She's just nice.' He shrugged, glancing her way again. 'A good find, really. She's come up with some great ideas,' he added, enthusiastically outlining everything they'd talked about that afternoon.

His brothers nodded along and asked all the right questions, but something was off. Alex couldn't shake his suspicion that they were thinking about something else.

A few drinks later, the topic of conversation had changed. Noah was entertaining them by going into far too much detail about his latest conquest. As he mentioned her long, toned legs, Alex's gaze strayed back to Sam's table again, noticing Clarice was sitting there by herself. Where had Sam gone? He frowned, eyeing the room with vague urgency, until he spotted her leaving the ladies' room. She saw him looking and began to smile.

Her expression died as she was unceremoniously shoved sideways. A large man had staggered into her as she skirted the dance floor. She caught herself against the wall as Alex realised the man had been reeling from a punch, and the noise level rose as a fight broke out.

His peripheral vision vanished as he stood, knocking over his chair. Hurrying towards her, Alex watched Sam trying to dodge the men being pushed and knocked her way. The fight had quickly escalated into an all-out brawl, with multiple participants.

Just as he reached her, he heard glass crashing and saw the gleam of a broken bottle.

Chapter 5 – Chivalry and Injury

Sam barely had time to register the full implications of the noises around her before Alex was there. His arms encircled her, his broad shoulders shielding her as they moved out of the centre of the maelstrom. They reached the corner of the room, and Alex positioned himself so she was in a protective triangle, with two walls to her sides and himself in front, his arms solid around her.

She looked up as he shouted at her, too shocked by the rapidly escalating situation to take in his words. Someone collided with his back and he grimaced, but held still, his strength combined with his elbows wedged against the walls preventing any of the impact reaching her.

'Turn around!' he shouted again.

She obliged this time, realising she was probably safer with her back to the brawl. Alex's arms tightened around her, and she felt his body, muscled and hard, pushed firmly against her back now. His presence was reassuring, and she relaxed enough to enjoy a guilty moment of pleasure at their closeness.

She wasn't reassured enough to totally block out their surroundings though. The solid wall he made between her and the fight did nothing to mute the crashes and grunts, and the unpleasant smell of spilled alcohol wasn't quite strong enough to mask the imagined scent of her fear.

Suddenly, Alex stiffened and swore.

Sam instinctively tried to turn and identify the problem.

He tightened one arm around her waist as he admonished her. 'Stay still! Security is breaking it up, you can move soon,' he said through gritted teeth.

He was right. Sam could hear the noise dying down, and she sensed the flurry of movement also dissipating. Alex loosened his grip on her and stepped back so she could turn around. The group of men he'd been sitting with were approaching with mildly concerned looks on their faces, and she followed their gazes to the subject of their attention.

Alex was bleeding.

She hadn't even noticed the bottle before he'd cut her off from the fight. It appeared to have gone in the back of his arm, and a large piece of glass was still embedded deep in the muscle. It was slowly oozing blood and would undoubtedly need stitches.

'Who says chivalry is dead?' asked one of the men as they arrived, to no one in particular. The others laughed as he reached over to pull the glass out.

'No, don't,' said Sam, moving to stop him.

The man winked at her and made no move to step back. 'It's all right,' he explained. 'Heroes like Alex aren't worried about a little pain. He can take it.'

Sam rolled her eyes. *So ... it's going to be like that.*

'I'm not worried about his pain threshold. If you take it out, you risk doing more damage. At the very least, you'll be making the wound bleed heavier. Leave it where it is until a professional can get to it,' she admonished.

Chastised, the man held up his hands and let Sam take over. Remembering her first aid training, she appropriated a towel from the kitchen and applied pressure either side of the glass, wincing in sympathy as she saw it hurt Alex. To keep his mind occupied, she had him introduce her to the men, who turned out to be his brothers. They were all as handsome as he was, but with the addition of varying degrees of cockiness.

Must be a good-looking dad, she mused to herself. *Or several good-looking postmen.*

She was relieved when the ambulance arrived. The amount of blood Alex had lost was surely approaching the serious end of the scale, but the paramedics didn't seem too worried. He was a big guy, so she supposed he could afford to lose a little blood. Alex also didn't seem concerned. On the contrary, he seemed annoyed at the attention, and even more annoyed at his brothers' continued jibes.

A short while later, Sam sat in a hospital cubicle with Alex and his brothers, waiting for Alex to get some stitches. A doctor had managed to carefully pull the glass out, but they were yet to finish the job. Various doctors and nurses were occupied with seeing to the participants of a pretty decent bus vs truck crash, from what she'd overheard.

Alex's brothers were vying for her attention while they took turns teasing him. He eventually kicked them out, under the pretence of getting him some coffee, although Sam suspected it was more because a couple of them had started flirting with her than out of any wish for the ensuing peace.

She hadn't said much since they'd arrived. This was partly because it was difficult to get a word in with Alex's brothers around. They were obviously close to one another and had also imbibed maybe a couple of drinks too many. Sam could see how Alex had come by his easy-going nature. He'd need it to put up with that level of sass.

Alex also hadn't said much since arriving, but he had shot several concerned looks Sam's way.

'Are you all right, Sam?' he asked when they were alone.

She looked over at him in the hospital bed, noting the towel from the bar still wrapped around his arm, and blood on his clothes. His obvious worry seemed so out of place that she laughed out loud. 'Surely I should be asking you that,' she answered, getting out of the chair his brothers had chivalrously insisted she take. She paused at his bedside.

Throwing caution to the wind, she sat on the edge of the bed and took the hand from his uninjured arm in hers. *Screw propriety,* she thought. *He must need a bit of comfort.*

Alex appeared taken aback at her affection, but he didn't protest or pull away. 'I just meant you've been unusually close-mouthed since the ambulance arrived,' he said, grimacing again at the word 'ambulance'.

Sam chuckled again at his expression, correctly interpreting it as a distaste for having a fuss made over him. 'You're really bothered by that ambulance ride, aren't you?' she asked.

Alex shrugged, and winced as he moved his wound. She squeezed his hand gently in sympathy.

'You're familiar with my brothers now. Can you see any scenario in which I will live that down?' he pointed out.

'I think they're more focused on your heroics at the bar than the ambulance ride,' mused Sam, looking at Alex thoughtfully. 'I haven't properly thanked you for that yet.'

Alex went to move his injured arm as if to wave off her thanks, wincing again as the wound was disturbed. 'No thanks necessary,' he said.

As she opened her mouth to protest, he added, 'Really, it might seem like they think I'm an idiot for jumping in, but this is exactly what any of them would've done if they'd seen it first. They'd think a lot less of me if I hadn't, and so would I. The teasing is technically a compliment.'

Sam frowned and tried to thank him again, but he cut her off, visibly uncomfortable with the subject. 'You haven't answered my question yet. Are you okay? I can't imagine you've had a front row seat to a lot of bar fights,' he said with a concerned look.

She gave up on trying to show her appreciation. She'd write him a card or something. 'I'm okay,' she said. 'I tend to go into overdrive when there's an emergency, but I'm always at a bit of a loss when I have to calm down. The adrenaline wears off, I guess.'

Alex nodded and absentmindedly curled his fingers around her hand. He seemed to have moved past the shock of her casual familiarity quite quickly.

'What about you? Are you okay?' she asked him. 'I mean, I know you're not in the best shape, but ...' she trailed off, unsure how to convey she was concerned about his emotional state.

It wasn't every day you received a stab wound, and Sam hadn't known him long enough to determine if he was the type to shrug this off. He seemed fine so far (if a little surly with his brothers), but she didn't need him to put on a brave face for her benefit.

Alex nodded and squeezed her hand again. 'This isn't my finest moment,' he admitted, stroking her fingers with his thumb. 'But I've definitely been in worse shape.'

Sam reached up without thinking, intending to run her finger down the scar on his cheek, which was just visible for a couple of inches above his beard. She hadn't asked him about it yet, and no one at the office had mentioned anything. At this point, it could be a childhood misdeed or attempted murder, for all she knew. He flinched when she made contact, his hand freezing in hers, and she quickly pulled away. 'Sorry,' she apologised, feeling herself blush. 'I didn't mean to startle you. I just realised you probably meant it literally, and my stupid hand moved independently of my brain.'

Oh crap, she thought, cringing internally. *That was extra dumb. Boundaries, Sam. BOUNDARIES.*

For the briefest second, Alex looked so frightened she wasn't sure what to do. Even stranger, he gained control of his features so quickly she thought she might have imagined it. His gritted teeth and resolutely blank expression shut her out from what he may be feeling, and she wondered that he still didn't pull his hand from hers.

His rigid stillness lasted just long enough for her to fear she might soon be unemployed. Eventually, he relaxed his jaw, exhaling slowly. Sam breathed a little easier too. She watched as he parted his lips and hesitated, as if he were debating on saying something.

What a perfect moment for a first kiss, she thought.

It was a silly thing to consider. She wasn't even sure she was emotionally prepared for that kind of intimacy. Forcibly reminding herself of how unlikely it was, she tried to quash her hope.

Still, her imagination was her own domain. And with the curtains drawn to give the illusion of privacy, his hand curled around hers while she stroked his fingers instead now, she could believe a little. All he'd have to do was let go of her hand, gently brush back her hair, draw her chin towards him ...

Sam snapped out of it when she noticed she'd inadvertently leaned forward half an inch. *Slick,* she thought. Her imagination might be her own domain, but she shouldn't visit that particular dreamland right in front of him. She pretended to be resettling her weight on the bed, hoping he hadn't spotted her idiocy.

Her fantasy hadn't taken long, and Alex was still poised to speak as she pushed it aside. Whatever he almost said, she didn't get to find out. Instead, the curtain opened, and his brothers strode back into the cubicle.

Alex swiftly pulled his hand from hers, although not quickly enough for the one in front — Christian? — to miss. He grinned, and Sam wondered if her face looked as guilty as Alex's did. She didn't know why they should be embarrassed. It was just some innocent affection. Besides, they were both adults. Even if they'd been living out her first kiss fantasy, they were allowed. Right?

'Coffee!' announced Christian. 'And a muffin for the bleeder,' he added, handing over both to Alex, muffin balanced precariously on the coffee cup.

Alex took it and drank with enthusiasm, leaving the muffin abandoned in his lap for now.

Noah beamed at Sam and handed her a coffee too. 'I'm not sure how you take it, sorry, but I'm far too much of a gentleman to let you go without,' he said gallantly, making the dimple in his left cheek dance.

Sam took the drink awkwardly, unsure how to refuse it without seeming unappreciative.

'Sam doesn't drink coffee,' said Alex helpfully. 'Tea, isn't it?'

She nodded and smiled apologetically. 'I appreciate the thought, though,' she said to Noah.

Noah looked disappointed and glanced at Erik, who triumphantly handed Sam another cup.

'You just won me $100,' he said, pulling little containers of milk and sugar out of his pocket and proffering them too. He had the dimple as well.

Quickly realising she was all out of hands, coffee in one, tea in the other, Erik gestured peremptorily for Noah to take the coffee away.

Sam knew she shouldn't encourage them, but she laughed anyway. 'Glad I could help,' she said.

'I think you deserve to benefit from the winnings,' Erik said. 'I'll take you to dinner and we'll spend Noah's hard-earned cash.'

She 'noped' out of that as quickly as she could. 'Oh, that's okay,' she said. 'The tea is all the spoils I need. You earned it; you enjoy it.'

Evidently not one to give up easily, Erik tried to protest. Deciding now was a perfect time for a bathroom break, Sam put down her tea and excused herself.

Looking at herself in the mirror, she grimaced. Fluorescent lighting was not kind. She hoped the lighting in the hospital room was nicer. Actually, considering how Erik and Noah were behaving, it was safe to bet it was at least passable. No harm taking the time to freshen up though.

She quickly brushed her hair and touched up her makeup, her thoughts turning to Alex. Her frown turned to a faint smile, and butterflies stirred inside her. She tried to quash them, reminding herself she shouldn't read too much into the affection he'd shown when holding her hand. They were both likely a bit vulnerable tonight. There was every chance he just needed the emotional support her warm hand on his provided, which was exactly why she'd instigated it. His brothers weren't exactly the type to provide reassurance. Sure, there was a sense of camaraderie between them, but she couldn't see them saying anything directly sympathetic.

Besides, she was still undecided on her own feelings. She was attracted to the guy, absolutely. He was gorgeous; he didn't seem bothered by her occasional tendency to put her foot in her mouth, and he had a likeable personality. And they appeared to be compatible enough to conceivably be happy together. Assuming one of them made a move, which was unlikely. Alex was her employer, after all. And she had her own problems. Well, just the one really. But Logan took up a sizable chunk of her heart, so he could hardly be considered trivial.

Finishing her lip gloss, she decided none of it mattered.

So what if I like him, she thought. *I'm allowed to look at a nice man. It doesn't have to mean anything. I can just leave it at that.*

Lost in thought, she made a wrong turn on her way back to the cubicle. She ended up approaching the closed curtains from the opposite direction, instead of back through the gap she left on her way out. Her name floated through the thin material and she hesitated, not wanting to eavesdrop, but also wanting to be sure they weren't saying anything that would be awkward if they knew she'd overheard.

'Back to my original topic,' Alex was saying. 'Stop cracking onto Sam. I don't need her angry at me because one of my brothers hit it and quit it. She's off limits.'

Yup, it's going to be a tricky one.

Sam wondered if she should retrace her steps and go back around the other way. She was still debating when the conversation started getting good.

Chapter 6 – Denial

Tired, emotional and bleeding, Alex probably hadn't approached this topic with an appropriate amount of guile. His request that Noah and Erik leave Sam alone had been met with increasingly frustrating sexual innuendo. In addition to this annoyance, his pronouncement she was 'off limits' had probably just spurred them on. While mostly friendly, the rivalry among the five of them was the bane of their mother's existence. Noah and Erik viewed his objection as a challenge.

Clearly not content with watching the battle between Alex, Noah and Erik play out, James had also begun to put his two cents in. 'You know what they're like,' he said, gesturing expansively. 'You can't stop them. Besides, she's a grown woman. If she's interested in either of these two idiots, it's not like you have any authority to stop her.'

'I'm not worried about *her* interest,' said Alex. He thought she had more sense than that. 'I just don't want her putting up with Casanova and Don Juan here for my sake. I know exactly what they're like. They'll start dropping by the office to flirt with her, and she won't be able to get away from them.'

Not that she'd put up with it if they were bugging her too much, he thought smugly. *She certainly doesn't seem like the type to hide her true feelings, but she shouldn't be put in that situation to begin with.*

Christian hadn't said much yet but finally cleared his throat, drawing the attention of the room as he assumed a serious expression.

Alex immediately clamped down on his panic, trying to keep it from his face. He was unsure how much Christian had seen when he'd arrived back from the cafeteria.

'Are you sure you don't just want her for yourself?' his brother asked, confirming Alex's worst fears and throwing a whole new angle for contention into the conversation.

The others went quiet with obvious shock, and not a little excitement. This was completely taboo. Sure, they'd danced around the subject at the bar earlier, but Christian's forthright confrontation was different. The issue of Alex and women wasn't something they discussed. Ever. That was strictly their mother's domain, and they knew Alex's willingness to discuss it with even her was limited. If she'd been any less domineering, he probably wouldn't have tolerated it.

And precisely because their mother was so overbearing, they'd all privately agreed to not join her crusade. Oh, she'd tried getting them on board. Many times. Many, MANY times. Mama devotedly believed happiness only came in twos, and she wasn't shy about expressing herself. Fortunately for Alex, her sons had closed ranks against her time and time again. Erik and Noah had both taken one for the team on many an occasion. They usually flipped a coin to decide who would seduce the woman their mother had intended for their stubbornly celibate brother.

Alex froze, feeling like a deer caught in the headlights of an approaching car. He'd already quashed this theory earlier in the night, but it was different now. Now it was risky. He couldn't quite pinpoint what had changed. Was it the shared experience of danger? The intimacy of their private moment in the hospital? The combination of booze and blood loss affecting his equilibrium?

'I saw you holding her hand when we came back in the room,' explained Christian with no hint of the teasing Alex expected to hear. 'Did something happen while we were gone?'

James let out a low whistle. He looked like he'd been hit by a truck packed with fireworks and puppies: unsure whether to celebrate or to notify the authorities. Erik froze as solidly as Alex had, mouth open and arms paused in the act of folding his hands behind his head. Noah's coffee started sliding out of his hand, requiring a catch so awkward it would have been cause for immediate mockery during any other conversation.

Alex shook his head forcefully, not making eye contact with any of his brothers. He didn't want to be having this conversation, and he definitely didn't want to be feeling this vulnerable. 'No, nothing happened,' he explained, a bit too quickly. 'She instigated that. Nothing amorous about it; I think she's just the type of person who soothes herself by soothing others.'

Feeling dangerously cornered, Alex struggled to keep his emotions from his face. He knew they'd infer he was hiding something if he fired up, so he needed to keep calm. There was no reason for them to jump to conclusions. He hadn't touched a woman in eleven years, and he had thought they understood why. This just wasn't on the cards for him. Surely over a decade of abstinence counted for much more than his warmth towards one woman.

Christian hesitated before pressing his agenda. 'Look, I get where you're coming from. I think if that were all it was, I'd probably have never said anything. And honestly, I'm still tempted to drop it. I don't want to hassle you about something that is such a big issue for you. We've always been on your side in Mama's quest to get you paired up with someone, but you're different with this girl,' he explained. 'Even before you'd put your cape on and flew to her rescue, there was something off. We already pointed out how weird it was to see you laughing so much with her,' he said.

Alex tried to remind them they'd already dismissed that, but was forestalled when James chimed in.

'Normally you've got your guard up around women, but not with her. You're comfortable. That's why we thought it was bizarre in the first place.'

'You were looking over at her every minute or so while we were at the bar,' added Erik enthusiastically. 'We were all nudging each other under the table every time you looked again.'

Momentarily stumped, Alex opened and closed his mouth as the panic started to take over. Didn't they understand he didn't want to be talking about this? They'd only known this girl an hour and a half, yet they were all jumping on the romance bandwagon.

Consciously unclenching his fist, he tried to construct a sentence that would make sense. 'I don't … you guys know I don't …' he stuttered. 'I mean, I understand why you'd get that impression,' he tried again. 'Objectively, she's perf —' He stopped mid-word, shaking his head violently to rid it of the word 'perfect', and began his response again. 'Look, I get it. She's kind, smart, funny, beautiful, and a whole lot of other things. But since Victoria …' His voice faltered over the rarely spoken name, and then picked up again. 'Since Victoria, I don't go in for that life. Zero interest. You all know I haven't even looked at a woman in years. It's not even difficult for me. No woman, no matter how lovely, could tempt me to break that streak now,' he finished.

They were all silent for a moment, the quiet only punctuated by the footsteps of someone walking down the hallway.

Finally, Christian spoke. 'Maybe you should,' he said softly.

Into this tense atmosphere, a doctor finally strode in to take care of Alex's stiches, effectively ending their conversation.

Sam returned a short while later, only to be ejected into the waiting room down the hall with his brothers. Alex was trying not to think about her while the doctor sewed him up, especially as the tugging and pulling of the thread reminded him of all his previous encounters with having his flesh sewn back together. He surreptitiously touched his chest with his good hand, where the scar beginning on his face deepened. Mercifully, he'd been unconscious for those stiches, but they'd itched like a beast while they were healing.

By the time he finally got home that night, he was exhausted. Aside from the physical exertion of the adrenaline-fueled bar fight and injury, he was emotionally drained from trying to not think about Sam.

To their credit, his brothers hadn't said another word about her since Christian's suggestion. Erik and Noah had also stopped hitting on her though, and he wasn't sure how he felt about that. He absolutely didn't want them anywhere near her, but they were acting like he had a prior claim to her attention. He could feel them scrutinising his every interaction with her and was almost rude in his haste to get home once he'd finally been discharged, barely even saying 'goodbye'.

Injured arm angled away from the faucet, he stood under the shower and tried to capture a little of the calm usually invoked by the flow of water. Desperately exercising a habit formed long ago, he pictured all the tensions of the day washing down the drain with the sweat and grime. His knowledge that more than a little blood and spilled alcohol were also being purged kept intruding on his thoughts though, making tranquillity impossible.

Memories of Sam also kept clamouring for attention. Her skilled rebuttal of Erik's advances was already a treasured memory; one of the few that brought a smile. He just wasn't sure how he felt about the other scenes playing out in his mind. Her hands, tiny and gentle, but strong and unselfconscious on his. The curve of her neck, and how her bare skin shone, uninterrupted over her shoulders and décolletage in the dress she'd worn. Her body pressed against his in the corner of the bar while the fight raged behind him ...

Alex cringed when he remembered how he'd frightened her when she touched his face. Sometimes he forgot about his disfigurement, but that was just the way he liked it. He'd grown the beard to camouflage it. When the scar was new, he'd been worried he would always need to explain its presence, but it usually made other people even more uncomfortable than him. To his relief, he was rarely asked about it.

Sam's easy acceptance, her willingness to so casually *touch* something he'd erected an invisible barrier around, left him feeling off balance. He didn't even touch it himself if he could help it. It hadn't felt like a part of him for years. Even his family didn't mention it.

Thinking of his family reminded him of Noah and Erik's interest again. They'd been giving Sam appreciative looks long before the hospital. His request they get him some coffee had largely been a way to keep her out of their line of sight for a while. Otherwise, he might have done something out of character to keep them apart, and further incriminated himself.

Not that their suspicions have any merit, he quickly reminded himself. He had zero interest in a romantic or sexual relationship. The idea that any of what had transpired tonight was the result of an unrequited attraction made his chest ache.

Realising his breathing had become shallow and he was clenching his jaw, Alex deliberately opened his mouth and took a deep breath. He looked up, stretching his neck out, and then down doing the same. The sight that met him was so unexpected he gaped.

Okay, he eventually thought. *Maybe there is some truth to their talk after all.*

Intellectually, he might not want any romantic involvement. Emotionally, the idea might scare the stuffing out of him. But his body had certainly responded to memories of her touch and exposed skin. It had been a long time since any woman had roused this kind of reaction in him. James was right about one thing — he was undeniably more relaxed around her than he'd been around a woman in a long time.

Chapter 7 – Dinner and Diligence

Lying in bed Saturday morning, Alex decided to be a little distant with Sam next week. Not rude, just subtly putting some space between them. The lines had been blurred last night. Between the scene at the bar, their strange intimacy at the hospital, and the completely unexpected conversation with his brothers (not to mention his obvious physical reaction to her in the shower last night), he was left feeling very guarded. Thing needed to go back the way they belonged before he lost control of the situation.

This resolution had lasted less than a minute into her phone call later that morning, checking how he was doing. He'd needed to hide his excitement from Stacey when he saw who was ringing him. It'd taken iron self-control to not leave the room like a secretive teenager.

Even then, he'd hoped he could still distance himself from her, but Sam had been so sweet, so concerned, and so grateful that he couldn't bring himself to disappoint her. He didn't want her to think he was mad because he'd been hurt. After trying his hardest to reassure her, he eventually caved to her insistence she cook dinner for him and Stacey that night. She'd been alarmingly persuasive.

Maybe that's what the draw is, he thought as they ended the call. *I've always liked a strong woman.*

He shied away from the memory of where that weakness had left him, trying to focus on Sam's less intimidating qualities instead. *Confidence isn't a crime*, he reminded himself. *You can come across high-handed and still be caring.*

The nuances of her personality weren't really the issue anyway. The real cause for concern was that she seemed to be slotting into his life too easily. He had no objection to a friendship with her. He loved being around her. His brothers were right about that. She made him laugh often, and her presence reminded him to relax his habitually tensed muscles. Enjoying himself came naturally for the first time in years. For a man who had spent so long needing to actively prompt himself to have fun, it was a novelty.

No, friendship wasn't the problem. The problem was, he could no longer deny to himself that he was genuinely attracted to her. Their forthcoming dinner plans were an equal source of dread and excitement.

He took a deep, calming breath before opening the door for her that night. It didn't do him much good though, as the sight of her standing on his porch in tight jeans caused the next breath to catch in his throat. He literally choked on air, managing to cover it (he hoped) with a cough.

'How's the arm?' Sam asked as he showed her to the kitchen. She had adamantly refused to let him help with the bags she carried, making him feel a little redundant.

'Not so painful I can't carry a bag of groceries with the other one,' Alex grumbled.

She laughed as she put the bags down on the bench. 'There are two bags, and I have two arms. Two good arms, to be specific,' she amended. 'Even if you were at full strength, it'd be unnecessary.'

Alex let it go with good grace, but mostly because he was distracted by the way she had taken charge of his kitchen. Completely at home, Sam began unpacking the food without a second thought while they chatted. She refused to let him help, so he sat awkwardly on a barstool and tried not to watch too intently.

Pulling out a bottle of wine, she located the appropriate glasses and poured them a drink before starting her preparations. Alex was thankful she took the lead in the conversation. He was too distracted by her presence to contribute much. Stacey had been out most of the afternoon and hadn't returned home yet, so it was just the two of them for now. Hyperaware of the privacy this afforded them, he struggled to control his thoughts. Imagined sensations kept clamouring for his attention: the smell of her skin as he kissed her neck, the taste of her mouth as it moved against his own, the feel of her skin after he removed her top …

He came back to reality when his imaginary Sam was down to her underwear. He couldn't get her naked without also undressing himself, and the thought shocked him out of his waking dream. There was no way he could be intimate with a woman without her being sickened and turned off by his scars, and that thought was like a kick in the balls. Not going to happen.

Stacey came home a short while later, and they all enjoyed the dinner together. In hindsight, Alex didn't know why he was so worried about the visit. He and Sam had an easy rapport, and Stacey had been won over the moment Sam pulled out a black jumpsuit and offered to lend it to her for his parents' anniversary dinner. The two quickly bonded while shopping online for matching footwear with an express shipping option. Alex had seen the shoes, and his mother wasn't going to like them. Chunky, metallic boots weren't her idea of formal wear, but they appeared to make his daughter happy, so he didn't say anything.

After dinner and shoe shopping, Stacey made herself scarce, and Alex found himself talking to Sam about work. He'd been impressed by her resourcefulness so far and was keen to pick her brain some more.

They eventually got onto the subject of the new staff she'd suggested.

'So, obviously we need to do something about the office space before you start bringing them in by the truckload, but I think you could get away with hiring a receptionist now,' she said thoughtfully. 'No one sits at the front desk because they don't want to be stuck greeting all the visitors, so there's room. The accounts team will be ecstatic. They won't have to answer the phones anymore.'

Alex nodded, distracted by the elegant gestures she made to go along with her words.

'You could also have the newbie look after the enquiries inbox,' she added. 'Sales have been doing it, but they're too busy to be prompt about it.'

Alex nodded again, surprised at the depth of Sam's knowledge. He hadn't even known the sales team were responsible for the inbox, let alone that they were doing a bad job of it.

'I'll advertise on Monday,' he agreed. 'As you're looking for more work, any chance you want to take over those emails in the meantime? I'll get someone hired ASAP, so it shouldn't be for long.'

'That's fine,' agreed Sam. 'Then I can train the new receptionist. It'll be a good place to learn about the business before starting to answer the phone.'

Excited to be doing something productive, and relieved to be speaking to Sam about a comfortable topic, Alex gradually relaxed enough to enjoy their conversation. He even felt calm enough for some banter when the topic shifted to rehoming the product development team. The PD 'Boys Club' made up the bulk of her admirers, and most of them were as aggravating as Tristan. Because they were such a source of friction, it made sense they be the first to relocate to a new wing.

'Won't you miss your fan club when we lock PD so far away?' Alex teased. The irony that he privately understood their interest wasn't lost on him, but he hoped drawing attention to her other suitors would mask his fascination. He was concerned she would pick up on the changes in his demeanour. Intellectually, Alex knew she'd never take advantage of his weakness for her, but emotionally … he couldn't stand the thought of her knowing the silly power she had over him.

Sam rolled her eyes in response to his jest, shaking her head with a smile. 'Honestly, you can move them to another building for all I care. In fact, it's my birthday soon. How about you move them to another country for me?' she joked.

'That'd be quite a commute,' said Alex, pretending to consider the idea. 'But at least I wouldn't have them distracting you so often. I heard Tristan hinting about taking you to dinner the other day. Don't want you getting a big head from all the attention,' he said cheekily.

Rolling her eyes again, Sam corrected him. 'He wasn't so much inviting me to dinner as hinting about how he'd like to have *me* for dinner,' she explained. 'And trust me, if I could arrange for an unattractively giant head to scare him off, I would.'

Suddenly feeling protective, Alex frowned. Tristan's efforts sounded a lot less innocuous than he originally thought. 'I'm sorry, Sam, I shouldn't be joking this way,' he said seriously. 'I didn't know it went beyond an innocent attempt to gain your attention. You don't have to put up with that. I'll talk to him on Monday. Do you want to put in a sexual harassment complaint?'

She shook her head, and the green-eyed monster in his chest growled. He'd never been a particularly possessive man, but his staunch celibacy in recent years hadn't prepared him for this turn of events.

'It's fine,' she said. 'To be honest, I'm low-key trying to keep his interest, so he stays away from Rebecca. Clarice and I are worried that she's not sophisticated enough to see past the fact that he's cute and occasionally funny. It might not work though,' she continued with a frown. 'I'm not doing enough to *encourage* him. I'm just also not doing anything to *dissuade* him. I have a feeling that it's not enough to keep him interested in just one woman. He's still keeping her on the hook.'

Alex didn't like it one bit, but if she weren't going to formally complain, he couldn't really do much. Unless he overheard something. He resolved to keep his office door open more frequently, and consciously relaxed his fists when his injured arm began to ache. Feeling a little abashed at his jealousy, he unsuccessfully tried to suppress his happiness Tristan was botching things so badly. He was determined to quash his own romantic fancies, but that didn't mean he welcomed the idea someone else might interest her. Especially someone as unworthy as Tristan.

This was a thought that kept him awake until late into the night, his body and mind craving Sam's undivided attention. The possibility of rivals beyond the inept efforts of his brothers and employees caused him a fair amount of anxiety. He kept picturing her smiling and laughing with a faceless man who cared for her in a way he could never bring himself to.

He tried to imagine happiness for her in this scenario. She was undeniably deserving of the love and joy he envisioned, but the thought of her with someone else left him feeling despondent, frantic to attract her interest himself. He was too broken to try, but a man could dream, couldn't he?

By the time Monday rolled around, Alex's injury was mending nicely. He'd always been a fast healer and was grateful his movement was no longer impeded after a couple of days rest. Clarice wasn't exactly known for her discretion, so it was a given the entire office would hear about their Friday evening adventure sooner or later. It would be a lot easier to downplay it without an obvious token of the damage. A visibly amused Sam had agreed to be vague about the specifics to the other staff.

As the week progressed, Alex noticed they were really beginning to work well together. He was starting to relax into this strange new dynamic. Allowing himself to trust her with more responsibility went against his instincts, but it produced great results.

It also brought other underutilised staff to his attention. He had a great team of people working for him, and his attempts to micromanage them were probably more of a hinderance than anything. There was always so much to do, and he never had time to do it. His involvement in every inconsequential decision just meant people had to wait on him instead of getting on with the best course of action.

This was especially the case with Dave, who was almost always on the same page as him. Sam's plans for new hires hadn't included a general manager, but Alex was sure this would be a good move. Aside from rewarding Dave's loyalty, it was practical. His sales manager knew the company almost as well as himself and could take some work off his hands. Stacey would be ecstatic.

While he was working on this plan Thursday afternoon, Sam walked through his door, pausing just past the threshold.

'Knock, knock,' she said with a smile.

She was particularly beautiful today, her long hair swept up in an elegant ponytail, and her décolletage visible above the wide neck of her dress. Long, toned legs were discretely displayed through a tasteful split to the knee of the skirt.

'Come in, Sam,' he said, hiding his eagerness to hear how her day was going. 'What have you fixed for me now?' he joked. He was still trying not to panic every time he looked at his practically bare email inbox.

Sam smiled briefly but didn't engage in his attempt at banter. 'Actually, Alex, I'm not even sure this is worth mentioning. It's just a weird trend I've noticed since I started looking over the enquires inbox,' she said with a frown.

Intrigued, Alex sat forward and gestured for her to continue.

'It's the emails I forward onto the sales team. Most of the clients email their rep directly, but a few contact the enquiries address and I just forward them on. I don't know if this is normal, but there seem to be several people indicating they've been offered similar products from one of our competitors, for slightly under our pricing,' she said worriedly. 'My understanding is the figures on our contracts are confidential. It seems odd so many of them are undercut just enough to catch the client's attention.'

Alex listened intently as she gave details about who and how much, frowning as he put the pieces into place. 'Just them?' he clarified. 'There aren't other companies undercutting us?'

Sam shook her head. 'No, just them. If it were multiple companies, I'd have just assumed it was business as usual,' she confirmed.

Sitting back thoughtfully, Alex paused a moment before commenting. 'I'd already noticed we'd lost a lot of business recently,' he mused. 'I was wondering what was going on.'

'Is someone leaking information?' asked Sam tentatively, giving voice to Alex's unspoken fear.

He didn't answer out loud, just gave her a grim look.

'Do you want me to do up a spreadsheet?' suggested Sam sensibly. 'We can look for trends, maybe get a bit of clarity.'

Agreeing, Alex asked her to prioritise this so he could look it over asap. He wouldn't have a chance tomorrow, because he'd be out of the office in meetings all day.

As Sam turned to leave the room, he allowed himself a small sigh at the sight of her retreating. Three whole days away from her. He'd have to be content with whatever memories he managed to store up before then.

Chapter 8 – Um, What?

'Okay, Mum, gotta go!' Sam said with false cheeriness as she parked her car. 'I'm at the gym now.'

Her mother nattered on for another few minutes before Sam finally got rid of her, and she breathed a sigh of relief. *Why are they still like this?*

She was seriously tempted to back out again and just drive home. Surely keeping her mother entertained for the fifteen-minute drive here counted as a workout. Besides, there was ice cream in her freezer.

She snorted, rolling her eyes.

I do this every time, she thought. *Why do I still need to psyche myself up?*

Getting out of the car, she reflected her Thursday indecision was especially useless because she knew she had to go. One of her favourite bargaining chips was 'you can always work out tomorrow'. But she never came to the gym on a Friday night, because her Friday night bargaining chip was 'it's Friday! Go start your weekend!', and it inevitably won because … it was Friday, and she wanted to start her weekend. Ergo, Thursday was a non-negotiable gym night.

Walking towards the entrance, she told herself it was stupid to try and get out of it anyway. She enjoyed the gym. She just couldn't quite convince herself of that before the exercise endorphins hit.

Strangely, a man in her peripheral vision had exited his car at the same time as she had. This normally wouldn't have bothered her, but he didn't seem to be dressed for the gym and was only carrying a document satchel that plainly didn't have room for clothes and shoes.

Frowning, she also noted he wasn't headed for the doors. He was walking at an angle that would intercept her path instead.

Normally a hive of activity this time of night, her concern grew when she noticed there didn't seem to be any other people in the large, twilit carpark. She considered slowing down to fiddle with a shoe or something, testing to see if the worrying stranger continued walking his same path.

This left her vulnerable if he was planning to attack though, so she dismissed the idea. Perhaps she should sprint it instead? The man would probably think she was an idiot, running scared from what was likely non-existent danger.

She settled for walking faster, faking a concerned look at her phone. If his intentions were innocent, he'd just think she was running late or something.

To her chagrin, he also sped up. He was closer now, and even if she started running, there was a fair chance he'd catch her. She estimated the distance to the entrance and the odds someone would hear her screaming.

'Samantha?' he called.

Shocked, Sam hesitated on the brink of breaking into a run, trying to get a better look at the man in the semi-darkness.

'Samantha Faulkner?' he asked again, smiling as he angled directly for her.

Sam nodded warily, unsure if she should be frightened the strange man knew her name. She must have looked like she was on the verge of flight, as he stopped at a roomy distance, holding up his hands in a placating gesture.

'My name is Richard Holland,' he said apologetically. 'I'm sorry if I startled you. I didn't consider the connotations of approaching a woman alone at twilight.'

Richard attempted a reassuring smile at the end of his introduction.

Sam purposefully relaxed her stance, more so he'd think she let her guard down than anything. She certainly didn't feel any more comfortable. The tactic was aimed at speeding up this unexpected meeting so she could get inside where it was safe.

Clearly realising Sam wasn't going to offer anything to the conversation just yet, the stranger continued talking. 'I understand this is completely unexpected, and you have no reason to trust me, but I have a proposition you might find enticing,' he said, smiling again.

It wasn't a nice smile. His whole demeanour screamed 'used-car salesman'. Not the kind trying to make an honest living, either. The kind that ripped off little old ladies.

When she still didn't speak, he tried again. 'The deal would involve a significant cash pay-out,' he tried. 'And I assure you, your part wouldn't be too taxing.'

He gestured to the little restaurant across the street, conveniently placed to cater for the gym patrons that couldn't be bothered cooking after their workout. 'Can I buy you a coffee and we'll go over the details?' he asked.

Sam glanced at the cafe, then back at Richard, and hesitated. 'Significant cash pay-out' wasn't an easy phrase to ignore, but she still didn't trust the guy.

Visibly struggling to not show his impatience, Richard made another attempt to reassure her. 'Look, I know I've startled you, and being so secretive probably hasn't engendered a lot of trust, but I promise I mean no harm. You'll feel safer in the restaurant than you do out here in any case. I'll tell you what, I'll go in now and you can watch me sit at one of the tables up near the window. Then you can come join me, so I'm not walking behind you,' he tried.

She thought about this for a moment, eventually nodding. He was right, she would feel safer in the restaurant. It was well lit and there would be witnesses if he tried anything funny.

Seemingly satisfied, the suspicious man adjusted his satchel and walked towards the door. He turned a couple of times before he reached the entrance, obviously checking Sam was still there. Disappearing briefly to order at the counter, she eventually saw him seat himself in the window, as promised.

She watched him do all this, thinking furiously. Her life had become genuinely interesting of late. Saved from a bar fight last week by her gorgeous boss, now approached by a mysterious stranger with a cryptic offer. *It's probably a joke.*

No longer concerned about her immediate safety, she walked towards the restaurant while considering what his proposal might entail. Seating herself across from her would-be benefactor, she began talking without preamble. 'I'm not doing anything illegal for any amount of money, so if that's a part of it, we may as well go our separate ways now,' she said.

Richard smiled, failing to hide his predatory satisfaction at her curiosity. 'I can confirm you won't be asked to do anything illegal,' he said reassuringly. 'The task we require of you is perfectly lawful and happens all the time, it just isn't usually instigated at the behest of a third party. I doubt you'll even find it unpleasant. And there's the pay-out to consider,' he added, still grinning shiftily. 'If you complete the task set for you, you'll receive a payment of $50,000 cash.'

'Cash?' Sam asked cautiously, more wary of this condition than impressed by the amount.

'Yes,' he said, again smiling his horrible smile. She wished he'd stop with it already. 'No need to involve the tax man in this.' He laughed at this statement, a short, sharp bark that reverberated among the tables.

The staff and the few patrons clustered in the takeaway waiting area looked over at them curiously, but soon went back to their work and aggressive phone scrolling.

'Okay,' said Sam shortly. 'What do you need me to do, and I'll consider it.'

'Actually,' Richard replied, opening his satchel. 'We just have to take care of this first.' He slid a document out, facing it towards her and handing her a pen. 'This is a non-disclosure agreement,' he explained. 'I'll give you the rest of the details after you've signed it.'

Sam visibly baulked at this, and he quickly did his best to downplay the seriousness of the request.

'It's just a formality — pretty standard,' Richard explained nonchalantly. 'I can't see any reason why you'd need to tell anyone about it. Like I said, it's all perfectly legal. The only unusual part of the operation is that it didn't originate organically.'

'And that I'll be getting paid for it, of course,' said Sam, trying to not let her sarcasm shine too brightly.

Richard laughed again, making her cringe and shuffle back in her seat. To keep him quiet for a bit, she cast her eyes down and pretended to look over the document, thinking furiously.

She could probably rule out that he was working for some sort of criminal organisation *(Wow, overreact much?)*. While she didn't know a lot about non-disclosure agreements, she was pretty sure he couldn't use it to stop her reporting a crime. They also wouldn't want the paper trail if there was any chance of her going to the police.

This put to rest her fears he was going to bump her off if she refused, but it did nothing to allay her concern she would want to tell someone. Richard's reassurance meant nothing. If this undertaking included information that she felt someone else needed to know about, she'd be riddled with guilt if she couldn't tell them.

Fifty grand was a lot of money though. Dollar signs practically swam before her eyes as a dark, greedy place in her soul tried to drown out her conscience.

She needed more information. As the waitress finished putting two coffees down in front of them (which Sam promptly ignored), she threw out a question. 'Who's the second party?' she asked. Busy reaching for the sugar, Richard looked confused, so she clarified. 'You referred to yourself and your associates as the third party, and I assume I'm the first party, but this implies the existence of a second party. Who is the second party?' she asked again.

Looking surprised, he replied while spooning exactly five sugars into his cup.

'Their identity can't be revealed until after you've signed the NDA.'

Sam saw the exact moment Richard realised he should have dodged her question. He stopped stirring, his face became shinier, and he looked annoyed. His response had nominally confirmed a second party did indeed exist.

He quickly covered it and took a sip, but this was enough information to confirm Sam's fears she may be in a moral conundrum here. She needed more time to think, and she needed some practical advice. Watching Richard carefully in case his reaction gave her more information, she took him on a little emotional rollercoaster ride.

'This all sounds pretty straightforward. To be clear, I sign this agreement, and you then outline a job you want completed. I have your assurances it's legal, and I'll be compensated to the tune of $50,000, tax free, if I complete it. I'm assuming you decided cash so there is no paper trail?' she asked.

Richard nodded, and then made as if to speak, but Sam continued before he could start. 'In that case, I need to speak to my lawyer before I sign this,' she said, watching for some alarm in his reaction.

He looked more taken aback than anything, evidently not anticipating this turn of events. 'I'm confused,' Richard said, setting his cup down and beginning to gesture in earnest. 'Is the deal not to your liking? $50,000 is a lot of money, especially for a task that isn't at all onerous. You have my assurances this is above board. My intentions are clear and honest.'

Sam laughed at this, startling him, and belying her secret, selfish temptation. *Damn, this is too good to be true ...* 'Your intentions are anything but clear and honest. You refuse to give me any details, and you're proposing tax evasion. There's no clarity or honesty in these deeds,' she pointed out.

If the look on his face was any indication, it seemed like Richard had expected this transaction to be a slam dunk. The little angel on her shoulder gained a distinct advantage over the devil on the other. It was fun keeping him unsettled.

'I'm not saying no,' she said soothingly. 'But let's face the facts. Even if there aren't any moral or legal consequences to your mystery chore, and I'm happy to perform it with gusto, I have no way of ensuring you're going to pay up. This NDA is the only paperwork. I want advice from my lawyer before I get in any further.'

No matter how tempted she was, that was the crux of it. She couldn't afford to be so reckless without any kind of reassurances.

A reluctant understanding showed on Richard's face, and he sat back to think furiously, his ridiculously sweet coffee forgotten for the moment. Sam watched, wondering what other information she might shake from him in his vulnerable state.

'Would you excuse me a moment?' he asked, his turn to surprise her. 'I just need to make a phone call.'

Nodding, she watched as he got up from the table and walked outside. His phone call was quickly answered, and he spent a few minutes frowning and gesturing. He seemed to be arguing with whoever was on the other end. Finally finishing the conversation, he smiled and gave her a thumbs up before walking back inside.

Sitting down, he triumphantly shared his exciting news, like a child showing off a captured frog. 'I've been authorised to promise you $3000 upfront if you agree,' he said.

Sam barely paused before answering. 'Half,' she said, not bothering to waste any more words on her counteroffer. He'd never agree. She was just shaking the tree to see what other interesting information fell out.

'Half?' he exclaimed. 'It's not certain you'll be able to do it, even if you agree to try. There's no wa —' The last words of this sentence were cut off, as it seemingly dawned on Richard that he'd accidentally given away information again.

Nothing prior to this had questioned Sam's ability to achieve a positive result. It had been presented like completion was a given.

Now visibly annoyed with either her or himself, Sam couldn't tell which, Richard stood up and collected his satchel. '$5000 upfront, final offer, the other $45,000 if you're successful. Talk to your lawyer if you're that paranoid, and I'll be in touch shortly,' he said stiffly.

Sam nodded, not fazed by his thinly veiled derision. 'Give me your card and I'll call you after I've made a decision,' she tried, hoping to glean more information from his employment details.

'I'll be in touch,' he snapped again, leaving her alone, half a coffee left abandoned next to her untouched cup.

Chapter 9 – Escape

Fighting his impatience, Alex endured the bare minimum of polite conversation before excusing himself to an imaginary errand. His mother had really outdone herself this time. The woman he was seated next to for dinner was attractive and charming, but her predatory attempts to gain his attention were achieving nothing but his frustration.

She kept touching him, patting his arm like he was a skittish horse she was trying to tame. She pushed her hair back every few minutes or so, running her fingertips over her exposed décolletage and grazing her cleavage. It was a ludicrously obvious attempt to get his gaze to follow.

It didn't work, and Alex couldn't understand why she kept trying. Surely, she had some other moves? As a distraction, he had committed to a private drinking game in which he took a sip of wine every time she caressed herself. It was no good though. If he kept it up, he was going to end up drunk as a monkey before the first course was served, hence the need to extricate himself.

Resolving to delay his return for as long as possible, he slipped a $50 note to the function coordinator and was promptly escorted to an out of way corner in the kitchen. After explaining his predicament, the good-natured catering staff laughed uproariously and gave him a plate of food to eat while he hid.

Stacey found him there about a half hour later, enjoying the banter of the staff around him. He took a moment to appreciate the miracle that his daughter looked comfortable and confident dressed in her finery. The black jumpsuit Sam had lent her was sleekly tailored, tapering down her legs to the boots his mother had detested so much. It was fairly plain in comparison to the other attire on display that night, but her hair and the intricately patterned boots added a certain 'pizazz'.

Sam's hairdresser had spent Thursday afternoon doing something to Stacey's long tresses — he didn't know what — but her hair looked much nicer now. Still shockingly red, but healthier, more stylish, and a lot less trashy. As she almost always wore it up, he'd forgotten it was nearly waist length. Her cousins had spent some time delightedly straightening it for her this afternoon, and she wore it hanging loose down her back. She honestly looked stunning. Alex suspected this fact was all that kept his mother from protesting her fashion choices too voraciously.

'Babushka sent me to find out why you've abandoned your date,' she said, rolling her eyes. They both knew his mother would never be so obvious as to use the word 'date', but Stacey had correctly interpreted her meaning.

'I left to preserve her modesty,' said Alex cheekily, already a little tipsy. 'I was afraid if I didn't start flirting back, she was going to pull out her breasts and wave them in my face.'

'That's a shame,' said Stacey seriously, playing along. 'I think the uncles would've enjoyed that. Unkind of you to put her feelings before theirs.'

Alex laughed, abandoning the charade, and patting the bench next to him. His daughter considered the height thoughtfully, a bit more of a jump for her than it had been for her much taller father.

A helpful young dishwasher quickly moved a stool over for her, and she flashed him a smile in thanks. The young man's answering grin was a little warmer than entirely necessary, his gaze lingering appreciatively as she hopped up next to Alex.

Stacey gave no indication she'd noticed, but she did push her hair back a little self-consciously as she settled on the bench. 'So, are you planning to stay in here all night?' she asked her father.

I wish I could, he thought. For a start, the food was probably better so close to the source. Freshly plated, no cooling while the rest of the tables scattered around the ballroom finished the prior course. And of course, the added advantage of no one aggressively flaunting themselves at him.

'I think I might be written out of the will if I do,' he said. 'Actually, it might be worth it.'

Stacey smiled and opened her mouth to reply but was forestalled when her grandmother swept into the room. The straight-backed figure paused, frowning when she noticed them perched on a disused workbench with the kitchen staff flowing smoothly around them. Alex wasn't surprised when their activity level seemed to double. His mother was an imposing figure, even slight as she was, and her mere presence often encouraged new heights of industry.

Picking up her long skirt, she made her way towards them with a look on her face that suggested a lecture was about to begin.

Experienced at diverting her, Alex immediately pulled out the best weapon in his arsenal. 'Mama, how is it you manage to look so elegant and graceful walking through such a mundane setting?' he asked, fondly noting he wasn't even lying.

He wasn't sure if she did it on purpose or if all the ballet training in Russia had been instilled in her bones. Every move was like a dance. Even approaching eighty, eyes followed her appreciatively across the room.

'I know what you're doing, and it's not working,' she said, the accent she still had more than fifty years after leaving the former Soviet Union adding an exotic flair to her speech.

'What do you mean?' asked Alex, feigning surprise.

She waved a hand peremptorily, dismissing his attempt to distract her.

Oh well, he thought. *It was worth a try.*

'Why are you in here, hiding? My handsome son should not be closeted in the kitchen. He should be at the party, entertaining my guests. You are not cooking the dinner, no?' she finished sarcastically.

'I'm sorry, Mama,' Alex lied smoothly. 'I went to check a few things with the event coordinator and the chef, and then got talking to Stacey when she came to find me. I didn't realise so much time had passed.' He got down from the bench as he spoke, turning to help Stacey do the same.

By the time he faced his mother again, she was scowling at him but didn't seem inclined to press the issue. He took her arm, and the three of them went to rejoin the party. Stacey and the attentive dishwasher shared a covert smile on the way out.

Walking back towards their table, Alex spotted Noah now occupying his chair, engaged in conversation with his bosomy neighbour. Trying to hide his relief, he took his brother's seat further down the table instead.

Now comfortably ensconced between his sisters-in-law, he glanced up to see his mother scowling at the new seating arrangement. There wasn't much she could say without causing a scene, but she wasn't known for her subtlety. He quickly turned to Christian's wife and struck up a conversation, hoping the lack of attention would thwart her. 'The food is excellent, isn't it?' he said to Rose, hoping she'd understand and indulge his lame conversation attempt.

Visibly amused, she ignored his question and instead reassured him. 'It's all right, your father distracted her. I think you're safe for now,' she said, picking up her wine glass. 'And how would you know about the food, anyway? You missed the first course.'

'The chef let me taste a few things,' Alex said shiftily, unwilling to admit he'd paid $50 for the questionable privilege of eating out of his lap in the stuffy kitchen.

'What's your escape plan if Erik and Noah ever settle down?' Rose asked, discreetly nodding towards Noah and his new lady friend.

'God in heaven, I don't wish that on any woman,' he said. 'Even Captain Cleavage deserves better than that. Although she seems to be signing up for at least one night of Noah's undivided attention.'

Capturing the eye of a passing waiter, Alex had Noah's disused wine glass filled for himself and took a bigger mouthful than was probably polite. Thus fortified, he turned back to Rose and noticed her looking at Stacey. 'She looks happy tonight, doesn't she?' he said fondly.

His daughter's uncharacteristic cheeriness and poise were unmistakable. Normally she'd be hunched and defensive, but tonight she laughed and joked, joining in on the universal disgust at her cousin Leo's inside-out eyelids trick.

'She does,' agreed Rose. 'I thought the outfit Eva chose was blue, though? Don't tell me Stacey actually took herself shopping for something that wasn't ripped jeans.'

'No shopping,' agreed Alex. 'My new assistant loaned that to her,' he added, attempting nonchalance but feeling his stomach flutter at the thought of Sam. Wary of his brothers' gossip, he watched Rose carefully for a reaction.

She didn't disappoint. He could see she was trying hard to keep a neutral face, but a knowing smile kept dancing around the corners of her mouth. Rose was a locked vault when you told her a secret, but she was hopelessly inept at lying. Because of this, you always knew when she was hiding something, even if you usually had no clue what it was.

Not this time. Alex had a fair idea what his brothers had been saying. He briefly considered spilling the beans on everything he'd been feeling this past week. Rose would keep it to herself, and it might be good for him to get it out. Cathartic, maybe. Lancing the poison of his unwanted infatuation.

Rose would be squarely in the 'make a move' camp though, so he decided against it. He couldn't give into his attraction. He didn't want to. The repercussions would be too far reaching, affecting his life and Stacey's in ways he didn't want to consider. And that was assuming he managed to miraculously succeed in gaining Sam's affections. His vulnerability and embarrassment at her probable rejection was another story entirely.

Because he was primed to see it, Alex realised how strategic Rose's next words were.

'Christian mentioned you two were getting along well,' she said, deliberately casual. 'I didn't know she was so close to Stacey though. How did they meet?'

Choosing to play along, he answered just as nonchalantly. 'Funnily enough, they met the day the blue dress arrived,' he said. 'Stacey showed up at the office, angry at the presumption, and stormed out when Sam told her I wasn't available. Sam took pity on her when I explained, and she found something more suited to her tastes.'

Rose nodded along with his synopsis, her artifice poorly hidden. 'Lending an outfit to her boss' teenager is generous,' she commented. 'I don't even like lending things to Daisy, and she's my daughter. They too often come back with buttons missing or stitching undone. I hope Stacey was grateful.'

Alex nodded, pretending to still watch his daughter so he didn't have to meet Rose's eyes. 'She was ecstatic when Sam bought it over,' he confirmed. 'They spent about an hour on our couch searching for the shoes to go with it.' Realising he'd inadvertently admitted she visited them at home, Alex quickly took another swallow of wine to cover his guilty face. Luckily, he was spared further questioning by the arrival of the second course.

He cemented the end of the conversation by turning to speak with Valentina on his other side instead. Like his mother, James' wife was a big talker, and he could participate in the conversation without too much effort.

The main course and speeches passed without incident (unless you counted his father gesturing a bit too emphatically during his time with the microphone and throwing half a scotch and coke over one of his grandchildren), and Alex soon found himself wondering where the time had gone as he left the hotel bathroom. One minute he'd been deftly avoiding undesirable conversations, the next he was twirling Stacey about the dance floor. His shy daughter had been mortified, escaping after only one song. He'd last seen her chatting to her new dishwashing friend in a quiet corner of the room and had wisely decided not to interrupt.

Making his way back through the lobby towards the function room, he was almost mown over by someone exiting the hotel bar.

'... told you, no! I'm not interested. Leave me alone or I'm getting security involved!' the woman exclaimed, looking over her shoulder at the man following her out.

Alex thought he looked vaguely familiar but wasn't really paying enough attention to the chastised man to be sure. The indignant lady was a more welcome sight.

Sam literally walked straight into him, dropping her bag and swearing as the contents went everywhere. 'I'm so sorry,' she said. 'I wasn't watching ... Oh!' she exclaimed, finally realising who she had run into. 'Alex!' she said, as surprised to see him as he was to see her.

They both crouched to collect the contents of her bag, and Alex belatedly realised the man had disappeared. 'Is everything all right?' he asked, concerned. 'Should I go after him?'

Standing and closing her bag, Sam shook her head.

She didn't seem upset, and he cautiously relaxed, his eyes drinking in the sight of her dressed to impress. 'Overenthusiastic suitor?' he asked, his remaining concern warring with his happiness at seeing her.

She shook her head more forcefully as she answered. 'No, nothing like that. I met him the other day and he ...' she trailed off, looking a little dazed. 'Actually, it's a long and weird story. I don't even properly understand it myself. What are you doing here?' she asked, changing the subject abruptly. 'I mean ... that didn't come out right. Let me start again. What a surprise to run into you! What brings you out tonight? I thought you had your parents' anniversary party?'

Classic Sam, Alex thought. *A little awkward, but always kind.*

'The party is in the function room,' he said, gesturing back to the other end of the lobby.

'Oh, I'm sorry!' she exclaimed. 'I didn't mean to keep you from it. I was just trying to get rid of that snake. Ignore me, go back to your family.'

Alex had been shaking his head since she apologised. 'It's fine,' he said. 'They won't miss me just yet. I'm trying to avoid my mother, truth be told.' He paused, before again voicing his concern. 'Are you sure you're okay? Who was that guy?' he asked.

Sam sighed, shrugging helplessly. 'It's a long story,' she said again, gesturing invitingly to some chairs a short way down the room.

As Alex sat opposite her, he calculated how long he could keep her to himself before someone came looking for him. Running into Sam two weekends in a row was an unexpected treat, and he planned to indulge his guilty pleasure.

Chapter 10 – Meetings and Greetings

'So, after he left, I ditched the gym and called my lawyer friend, Pearl, instead,' explained Sam. 'Who is walking towards us,' she added belatedly.

'Where the fuck have you been?' asked Pearl, a little louder than was probably appropriate.

Her companion, Candice, rolled her eyes and tried to quiet the boisterous woman.

'Don't you shush me!' Pearl exclaimed. 'It's a girl's night. There's no ditching for men. Even a hot one,' she finished, eyeing Alex appreciatively.

Candice shook her head in mock dejection and shot Sam a tortured look. 'Lucky I'm not the jealous type,' she mumbled, just loud enough to be heard. She flopped onto a couch and held out her arms to Pearl, who happily snuggled in next to her.

Sam watched Alex take this in with bemusement. Her friends were a colourful bunch even when sober. She wasn't entirely sure introducing her boss to them on a boozy night out was the best career move, but she didn't have much of a choice. At least they were solid enough not to mention her confession from earlier in the evening, detailing how her feelings for this man just kept deepening.

Introductions over, Sam went back to the topic at hand. 'I was just catching up Alex on what happened Thursday night,' she said.

'Oh yeah, what happened with your mystery weirdo tonight?' asked Candice. 'I didn't see where you went after he pulled you off for a chat.'

'You should have brought me with you,' said Pearl with a frown. 'I don't trust him. He's so oily you could fry chips in his asshole.'

Clearly struggling not to laugh at Pearl's frank assessment, Alex appeared to have a hard time injecting the appropriate amount of concern into his next statement. 'You went off alone with a strange man?' he asked Sam.

'Not ALONE alone,' assured Sam. 'Just to the other side of the bar. Away from my loudmouth friends so I could actually hear him.'

'You should have at least brought your lawyer,' grumbled Pearl.

'My lawyer is drunk,' pointed out Sam.

'Better a drunk lawyer than no lawyer at all,' retorted Pearl.

'He followed you here?' interrupted Alex with a frown.

Sam shrugged. She had no idea how their paths had crossed tonight, and Richard hadn't seemed inclined to answer questions.

'Considering his reaction, I'm guessing you decided not to sign the NDA?' asked Alex.

Sam nodded. 'I'd already spoken to Pearl on Thursday night, and she thought it sounded pretty shady,' she began.

'It was ludicrous,' interrupted Pearl. 'The scope of it wasn't even defined. I get that he wanted to protect his secrets, but you can't go signing something as broad as that. You could be setting yourself up for a hellish lawsuit.'

'Anyway,' said Sam forcefully, glaring at an uncaring Pearl, 'he showed up tonight, and he wasn't happy when I told him my lawyer had advised against it.'

Pearl opened her mouth (probably to describe how little she cared about Richard's happiness) but was forestalled when Candice put a hand over her lips.

'To be honest,' continued Sam, 'I got the impression he was surprised I'd actually followed through and gone to one. He must have thought I was bluffing. He was pretty insistent I was passing up the opportunity of a lifetime and my lawyer didn't know what she was talking about.'

'What I want to know is why he's so desperate he's found you twice out in public,' said Candice. 'Is he following you? Is someone close to you telling him your schedule?'

'Maybe you should start following him instead, Sherlock,' said Pearl rudely, having disentangled herself from her wife's grasp.

Laughing, Sam explained to Alex that Candice was a private investigator and probably in a better position to find the answers to her questions than anybody else. Pearl often used her services in her more troublesome cases. She had a knack for uncovering things people would rather keep quiet.

Alex had been frowning through much of this and finally spoke when Sam fell silent. 'I only saw him briefly, but I thought I recognised him,' he said, to her surprise. 'I wonder if this has anything to do with the concerns we were discussing on Thursday.'

Sam couldn't believe she hadn't already considered this. It fit perfectly. Richard wanted information about the company, probably information his current source couldn't retrieve. She had access to pretty much everything, and she was a new employee. He probably assumed she hadn't developed a strong loyalty just yet.

Watching Alex as they discussed this possibility, Sam reflected on how wrong her mysterious harasser was — she'd never betray Alex. She'd never looked forward to her workday as much as she had this last week. The overheard conversation at the hospital created as many questions as it answered, but she just couldn't get his brothers' encouraging words out of her head.

Her offer to cook him dinner last weekend had been a shamefully calculated move. Scared the surreal night of bar fights and serious family chats would push them further apart, Sam had resolved to cultivate a relationship with him outside of work. She was still almost as hesitant to move things to a romantic level as he seemed to be, but it couldn't hurt to lay in some groundwork. Just in case.

Funny how fate has thrown us together two weekends in a row, she thought.

Maybe there was hope for them if she was patient. Everything she'd overheard indicated he was resisting at best, but completely appalled by the idea at worst. It wasn't much to go on really, but she was drawn to him all the same.

Alex was staring at Sam with a speculative look on his face. 'Any chance you're free this Friday?' he asked, catching her completely off guard. 'It's fine if you're not,' he added hastily, 'it's just that the company I suspect he's working for is having a product launch party that night. They've invited me and a guest to attend.'

Sam frowned. 'Why on earth is a competitor inviting you to their party? Isn't that a little weird?'

Alex nodded, grimacing. 'The owner, Dimitri, is a family friend. Sort of. "Frenemy" is how Stacey would describe it, I think. I'm surprised he's not at my parent's party tonight, actually. I'd bet good money that he was invited. Mama's one of those "keep your friends close, and your enemies closer" type of people.'

Sam nodded slowly. 'Still, seems weird inviting you to work stuff, doesn't it? I mean, friendly rivalry is all well and good, but ...' She shrugged, not convinced it all added up.

Alex snorted. 'To be honest, I'm pretty sure he's in love with my mother. Or at least, he used to be. He's just obsessed with staying on her radar now, or maybe getting his revenge for her marrying Dad. Any opportunity to ask about her, or to show off how much money he's making. Dad thinks he used to hope Mama would leave him when she got a whiff of Dimitri's millions. Which is dumb, really. It's not like Dad's ever been shy of a dollar.' He shook his head ruefully.

'That's even weirder,' objected Sam. 'Why are your parents friendly with him if he's trying to break up their marriage?'

Alex laughed at this. 'You have to know my dad to understand. There isn't a jealous bone in his body, but he does have a perverted sense of "justice". He's always extra affectionate with my mother when Dimitri is around, just to show him what he missed out on.'

Sam and her friends chuckled, starting to get it.

'Your dad sounds like a character,' commend Sam.

'He is,' agreed Alex. 'And he'd be pleased if I caught Dimitri in something shady. So, do you want to come help? The party's at their head office, so it might be a good opportunity to ferret out some information.'

Candice frowned at his words, and Sam braced herself for the lecture.

'Don't go snooping,' she admonished. 'There's no harm in seeing if you run into your mysterious new chum, but don't go riffling through the filing cabinets or anything. It's not worth the consequences.'

Candice had too often had to deal with the fallout from someone's poor attempt at doing her job. By the time they called her, the other party was so suspicious it made her efforts almost worthless. Sam was surprised she'd even allow them this much freedom, and assumed her friend was about to start a sales pitch to get herself hired.

Alex's speculative look had moved from Sam to Candice. Trying to quash the jealousy that flared, Sam forcefully reminded herself that Candice was far too loyal to Pearl to be a rival.

'You're a private investigator?' confirmed Alex.

This was all it took for Candice to become all business.

While they talked, Pearl yawned rudely and got up from the couch. 'I'm going to get drinks,' she announced, before flouncing back towards the bar.

Candice got up too, handing Alex her business card. 'I better make sure she doesn't get herself kicked out,' she said. 'Give me a call and we'll go over the details next week.' With that, she hurried after Pearl, leaving Sam and Alex alone again. As she walked away, Candice gave Sam a quick wink behind Alex's back.

Correctly interpreting this as evidence she was leaving them alone on purpose, Sam reflected that drunk or sober, her friends always looked out for her. Feeling a protective rush of affection, she quickly defended Pearl's drunken antics. 'Pearl's a kick-ass lawyer,' she said, 'she's just not a frequent drinker, which pairs really badly with tequila.'

'Tequila is the devil,' agreed Alex. 'I've avoided it since my twenty-first birthday. I woke up the day after it with a large penis and testicles shaved into my left calf.'

Sam laughed incredulously, unable to picture Alex this young, this drunk, or this carefree. 'Please tell me you lost a bet or something, and didn't just do it on a whim,' she implored, struggling to contain her mirth.

'I didn't do it myself,' he explained. 'It was one of my brothers, after I passed out. To this day, none of them will own up to it. I assumed my mother would shake it from them, but she just told me it was my own fault for scorning the drink of my countrymen.'

'The drink of your countrymen?' repeated Sam curiously.

'Vodka,' he explained. 'Hard to tell when my surname is Whitaker, but I'm half Russian. My first name is Aleksander,' he said, spelling it for her, 'and because of the way Russian nicknames are composed, my mother usually calls me "Sasha".'

Surprised, she protested, 'But you write it as 'A-L-E-X.'

He nodded and explained. 'I got sick of it being misspelled in high school, so just decided to embrace it. Christian took it a step further and legally changed the spelling from 'K-H-R-I-S-T-J-A-N',' he added. 'We shouldn't complain though. Erik and Noah have it easy, but James' first name is "Zdravko". Our mother is a traditionalist, so he's named after our grandfather, but our father refused to use it day to day. Russian people don't usually have arbitrary middle names, just a patronymic, but he insisted James have something easily pronounceable in the mix.'

'Speak of the devil and he doth appear,' quoted Sam, nodding towards the ballroom entrance.

James had just appeared with a statuesque, dusky beauty by his side. He grinned broadly when he recognised Sam, saying something quietly to the unknown woman. She beamed and bore down on them with eagerness.

'You are Samantha!' she said enthusiastically, her accent hinting at South American origins. 'My husband has told me so much of you. I am Valentina,' she finished, kissing Sam's cheek as she stood to meet them.

Sam liked her immediately and beamed right back while answering. 'It's lovely to meet you,' she said.

'Nice to see you again, Sam,' said James, striving to not be overlooked.

'Good to see you too, Zdravko,' she said, struggling to keep a straight face and not ruin the effect. She'd sensed from the get-go that Alex's brothers were best kept off balance.

It worked as intended, a hard frown immediately crossing his face, which he directed at Alex while saying something in Russian.

Struggling through his laughter, Alex answered, also in Russian, and James made a rude hand gesture.

'I think,' began Valentina, 'they are name-calling. My Russian is not so good. Bah! We shall ignore them. You will come to have a drink with myself and Rose?' she asked, rolling the 'R' for Rose pleasantly. It wasn't quite a question, as she didn't wait for an answer, pulling Sam towards the ballroom.

A short while later, Rose distracted Valentina long enough for Sam to quickly text Candice. She suspected the quieter woman had taken pity on her. Valentina was … overwhelming. She let her friend know she was just having a drink with Alex's family and would return to the bar soon, before turning her attention back to the pair she sat with. Valentina was still in the middle of her story when the answering text arrived.

Don't bother, said Candice. *Audrey and Annie have already left, and Lil's just about asleep where she stands. I'm ordering an Uber before Pearl gets any drunker and vomits in it.*

Another text popped in while Sam was reading the first one.

Get to know your future in-laws, and text me when you get home, followed by the wink-faced emoji.

Valentina noticed Sam checking her phone and her face fell. 'You are leaving us already?' she asked.

'Actually, no,' said Sam. 'It looks like my friends have decided to call it a night, so I have nowhere to be. Are you sure I'm not imposing though?' she asked, concerned she was crashing the party.

'Of course not!' Valentina exclaimed, beaming at her. 'Any friend of Alex is welcome,' she reassured her, before inexplicably exclaiming 'Eva! Bernard!' and waving frantically over Sam's head.

Sam turned to see an older woman approaching, impeccably dressed and impossibly graceful. The lines age had imprinted on her face somehow enhanced her loveliness, her cheekbones and eyes still prominent and upswept. She looked severe, but not unkind, and Sam belatedly realised this must be Alex's mother.

The man following was obviously her husband. The resemblance to his sons was striking, and Sam had a sudden vision of how Alex would look in thirty years or so. Much the same really, just with deeper laugh lines and iron-grey hair.

She shot a panicked look at Rose, who smiled reassuringly. Sam relaxed a little. Even though the unassuming woman hadn't managed to say much so far, Sam had correctly intuited that Rose was a kind and trustworthy soul. Evidentially, Alex's brothers had excellent taste in women.

She was introduced to Eva and Bernard, who were delighted to learn who the strange uninvited guest at their party was. Eva shook Sam's hand firmly and assured her she was indeed welcome, while Bernard grinned rakishly. 'Another pretty girl for me to flirt with is never a problem,' he told her, winking at Valentina and Rose.

Eva swatted at him and rolled her eyes when he mimed a grievous injury, turning her attention back to Sam.

'You have been making my Sasha very happy in his work,' she said lovingly, 'but he works far too hard. You must send him home early some nights, so he can come visit his mother.'

Sam laughed easily. It seemed she wasn't the only one keen to get Alex out of the office on time for once. 'I'm trying,' she promised. 'We're working on expanding the office so he can hire some more staff. I'm hoping it will help to lighten his workload.'

'Praise the Lord!' said Valentina. 'He hasn't had a social life since I have known him, but James tells me he was the life of the party before he married.'

Intrigued, Sam wondered if she was about to learn more about the mysterious Victoria. Was she Alex's ex-wife? The only time Sam had ever heard her mentioned was when she overheard Alex and his brothers, but they hadn't gone into much detail. She still didn't know if his reluctance was due to a messy divorce or a lost love. Sam belatedly wondered if he was a widower, surprised she hadn't considered he may be in mourning.

Eva quickly disabused her of this notion, making a superstitious hand gesture before responding. 'We will not discuss his marriage to that witch at my party,' she declared, a frown marring her strong features. She turned to look at Alex approaching them. 'Sasha!' she said imperiously. 'Go to the bar and get us some Vodka … Please, darling,' she added, softening her demand.

Having already been chased off once by his sisters-in-law, Sam saw Alex try hard not to look too put out with this request. He shot Sam a worried look, which she responded to with as reassuring a smile as she could muster. He also looked quickly at Rose, who nodded. The quiet girl's support seemed to placate him as he turned to complete the errand without protest.

By the time he returned, a bottle of Vodka and six glasses on a tray, his mother was busy inviting Sam to their next family dinner. Sam was flattered but sure her attendance would just freak Alex out, so she was attempting to refuse politely.

'Mama!' scolded Alex as he sat in the chair his father had vacated so he could be next to Sam. 'Leave Samantha be. She doesn't want to be having dinner with her boss' family. She puts up with enough of me at the office.'

'Oh no!' protested Sam as he began to pour. 'It's not that. I just think I've imposed too much already. I'm not even supposed to be here right now. We just keep running into each other, and you're going to get sick of me.'

'Sick of you?' exclaimed Valentina (clearly on Eva's side), just as Bernard snorted. 'You are being silly now. He will love to have you at dinner, won't you, Alex?'

Alex sighed theatrically as he handed out the drinks. 'Sorry, Sam, I tried to get you out of it,' he said cheekily. 'You'll just have to put up with them.'

Sam laughed and capitulated with good grace. It may never eventuate, and if it did, she could always make up an excuse if he seemed uncomfortable. Sipping her Vodka while the conversation flowed around her, she reflected that even if she hadn't been smitten with Alex, she could never get enough of this family. Their easy camaraderie reminded her of her own relationship with her parents, before the Logan situation had changed everything.

Alex leaned forward and spoke quietly, for her ears alone. 'I could never get sick of you,' he whispered.

Sam stared at him, surprised by the intimacy of his statement. He looked back at her, and she smiled slowly at the genuine warmth and sincerity in his eyes.

Chapter 11 – Booze and Near Misses

Alex was drunk. So was everyone else though, so he wasn't too worried about that. Most of the party guests had long since left, including his mother with his daughter, his nieces and nephews, and his father, who would probably regret his last few drinks tomorrow. His brothers, Sam, Valentina and Rose had stayed at the bar drinking and laughing.

The exception was Noah, who had disappeared around the same time as they moved from ballroom to bar. According to reports, he'd not left alone, so they didn't expect to hear from him until tomorrow. Or later today, technically.

The bar gradually emptied of patrons as it got later and later, but no one gave any serious thought to leaving until someone suggested food. Suddenly they were all starving, and to the relief of the bar staff, they began putting on coats and exiting for last-minute trips to the bathroom.

Their destination was a small burger place only a couple of streets away, and so they decided to walk it. Alex fell a little behind the group, preoccupied by an unreadable text message on his phone. He was unsure if the illegibility was due to his state of intoxication, or if advancing age was affecting his vision.

Giving up, he soon found himself staring at Sam's silhouette. The coat she wore was thick and fluffy but tapered in at her waist where she'd tied it closed. It stopped at mid-calf, and he contemplated the small amount of shapely leg and ankle he could see, her tiny feet enclosed in some strappy heels. He could well understand why the sight of some ankle was a cause for excitement in days long gone. With the rest of her so thoroughly covered, the exposure seemed almost illicit.

Pull yourself together, you pervert, he thought. *This is how fetishes start.*

Almost echoing his thoughts, an amused voice sounded beside him.

'Please tell me the reason you haven't touched a woman in so long isn't because you've been busy masturbating to pictures of feet on the internet this whole time,' said Noah.

Alex had jumped at his first words. Noah had a habit of sneaking up behind people, and a long time ago, he'd perfected walking soundlessly on pretty much any surface. It was an annoying trait Alex had never really made peace with. 'Where have you been? Tired of your new friend already?' he asked, ignoring Noah's statement.

'She fell asleep after the first round,' his little brother answered casually. 'She wasn't so good that I felt it necessary to wake her for a second session, so I had a shower and came to find you guys. I saw you walking away from the hotel and decided to catch up.'

'Fell asleep?' queried Alex. 'How have you had time to go home, wear out a woman, shower and come back in? You live almost an hour away.'

'I got a hotel room,' said Noah nonchalantly.

'You got a *hotel room,*' repeated Alex incredulously. 'To have sex with a woman who probably would've let you screw her in the bathroom. And you're not even sleeping in it.'

His brother shrugged, clearly not fussed by the situation. 'Mama doesn't like it when Erik and I fish from the pond she's created for you. She looks for any excuse to give us a talking to. I'm sick of getting in trouble when she hears about whatever hidey-hole I've taken a woman to this time. I figure she can't get mad about this,' he reasoned.

Alex laughed, amused by his naivety. 'You think you're not getting in trouble for abandoning her in a hotel room?' he asked. 'You don't actually have to sleep with them, you know. I appreciate you getting tonight's predator of choice off my back, but if you're worried about the repercussions, you could've just ditched her at the end of the night.'

'Technically, I did ditch her at the end of the night,' commented Noah with a salacious grin. 'I just collected my reward for being such a great brother first.'

Alex shook his head with mock disappointment as they caught up to the group. Sam's heel slipped on the wet cobblestones as she turned to greet Noah, and she started to fall. Alex was walking close enough that he caught her easily, thrilled at the feeling of his arms around her, even this briefly.

She looked directly into his eyes as she warmly thanked him, and he felt his heart thump faster and his breath catch in his throat.

Beautiful, he thought disjointedly. *Too beautiful.*

The short break in forward movement had put them a little behind the rest of the group. Sam didn't seem in a hurry to catch up, and Alex wondered if he could get away with touching her again. Everyone else faced forward, so they didn't have an audience to see any uncharacteristic affection on his part.

He drunkenly reasoned Sam had been demonstrative enough that she wouldn't think too much of a companionable arm around her shoulders, reaching for her before he could chicken out. She not only allowed this but put her arm around his waist in response. They walked in silence, slowing getting further and further from the rest of the group until they were half a block behind.

This time, Alex was the one to trip. He accidentally pushed Sam into a wall, his hand letting go of her shoulder and smacking against the bare stone to break his fall. His other arm automatically went to her waist to help break her impact, and they ended up face to face.

She looked up at him, their mouths inches apart, her hands on his chest, and he forgot everything. He forgot all the reasons why he avoided women, the things that had been done to him, the possible repercussions of acting on his feelings. All he could think of was the ache in his chest, the curve of Sam's parted lips, and the warmth of their shared body heat. Poised to kiss her, he drunkenly wondered if she wanted this as much as he.

A car slammed on its brakes behind them, the tyres skidding on the wet road. He broke away from Sam and turned just in time to see two vehicles narrowly avoid an accident. As he watched, they righted themselves and continued their respective journeys.

The moment was lost, and Alex felt himself close to panic as he grasped that he'd almost capitulated. He forcefully reminded himself he didn't want this, and nothing had transpired that he needed to be too concerned about. It all happened so quickly. As far as Sam knew, he had clumsily stumbled into her and that was that. Any pause in the time it took him to back away could be explained by inebriated reflexes.

'That was intense,' commented Sam.

Alex's panic flared again. Had she noticed his blunder after all?

He confirmed with relief that she was looking at the cars still moving into the distance. She'd been talking about the traffic near-miss. Breathing a little easier, he picked up the pace so they could catch up to his family.

'Stupid to drive so recklessly in the wet,' he agreed tonelessly, secretly thanking his lucky stars for the distraction.

Without it, he'd potentially still be kissing Sam right now. His hands caressing the curves of her body. His tongue tasting hers. Her embrace pulling him tight against her, reckless with her desire to have him closer still, breaking the kiss to suggest they move to a more private location …

Or she could be making awkward excuses as to why she was leaving. He could be embarrassed beyond measure, contemplating a sexual harassment lawsuit. Sam could be minutes away from calling her friends to laugh at him for being so presumptuous, because how could she possibly want him? Women didn't want him. Sure, some of them wanted his money, but Sam wasn't like that.

She would never laugh at him either, he had to admit. She was far too nice for that. He'd know what she was thinking though. He had to stop letting his guard down around her. It was too easy to be comfortable in her presence, too easy to forget why he couldn't be with her.

As they approached their destination, Alex realised there was a commotion happening. They had missed closing time by ten minutes. Everyone was arguing about where to try next.

Rallying himself from his depressed funk, Alex suggested they go to his place. He had plenty of food, and more drinks. Everyone enthusiastically agreed (probably because of the drinks more than the food), and they summoned a couple of Ubers.

Remembering his resolution to avoid more intimate situations with Sam, he went for the front door of the car when it pulled up. Erik just beat him to it, so against his better judgement he ended up in the backseat next to Sam.

His brothers kept the conversation alive through the short trip back to his place. Sam interjected occasionally, but Alex mostly stayed quiet, struggling with his temptation. Sam had removed her coat before getting in and now had it draped over her lap and a little of his. It would be so easy to slide his hand under the pile of fabric and 'accidentally' touch her half-bared leg, currently pressed against his in the too small backseat. His brothers wouldn't see under the coat, and she'd been drinking too heavily to notice the forbidden grope.

And what's next? Are you going to 'slip' and grab her breasts? Get a grip, he admonished himself. If he was going to fantasise about touching her intimately, he may as well fantasise she knew about it and wanted it.

But he could enjoy the closeness of the backseat while it lasted.

A couple of hours later, and drunker still, Alex sat back to survey the scene around him. The remains of food, glasses, and bottles (both empty and still in use), and various discarded footwear and clothing littered the room. They provided a relaxed backdrop to a night that kept getting louder and funnier.

James was passed out in an armchair, wearing five bow ties and no shirt or shoes. Valentina (also barefoot, wearing James' shirt in place of her dress) was trying to teach Rose and Sam how to Samba. She was impeded by Erik and Noah, who had acquired the ladies' shoes and were participating in the lesson with ridiculously over the top gusto.

Rose had given up on the lesson and was sitting in Christian's lap, whispering in his ear. He didn't know if her topic were endearments or complaints, but they'd be in bed soon either way.

Alex had been trying to not watch the Samba lesson too closely. Watching Sam's hips shimmy and roll had been mesmerising. She was quite good, really. He had to look away periodically, so she didn't catch him staring.

Because he was deliberately not looking, Alex was surprised when Sam sat down on the couch next to him. His arm had been draped across the back of the couch, and she now sat in the space it made. She tucked her legs up, tilting her knees across his lap and laying her head across his outstretched arm.

Without thinking, he reached up and touched his finger to the tip of her nose. It was a silly move, done more out of intoxication than affection. She giggled and took a hold of the offending hand, pulling it down into her lap. He was uncomfortably aware they weren't alone, but he didn't want her to let go.

'You look tired,' she commented.

Sam looked a little sleepy herself, but he wasn't about to risk offending her. 'I've been trying to go to bed for the last half an hour, but I just can't seem to get my legs to work,' he answered.

Startling him, she swiftly stood and tugged on his hand. 'I'll help,' she announced.

'We're going to turn in too,' said Rose, pulling Christian up behind her.

The sleeping arrangements long since decided, the happy couple went off towards Stacey's empty room. They left behind Valentina trying to wake James so they could go to another bedroom. Erik and

Noah, not yet ready for their dancing lesson to be over, did their best to hinder this. Alex saw Sam give them an assessing look and privately suspected she would 'forget' to wish them goodnight on her way to her own room.

Bemused at the picture they painted, he allowed her to lead him to his room by the hand. He was too far gone in drink and fatigue to be concerned at the connotations of being alone in his bedroom with her.

His eyes fluttered closed as she pushed him to sit on the bed. Her lips pressed to his forehead briefly, and he anticipated that the next place her mouth would gently brush would be his lips.

When it came, Sam's kiss was so light, so gentle, he almost couldn't feel it. Her hand skimmed his body so softly that it was nothing more than a prickling of his skin where her fingertips grazed outside his shirt.

His eyes flew open when he felt a tugging on his foot, confused until he realised that he'd fantasised so vividly, he'd imagined her kisses and caresses were real. Disappointed, he lifted his foot to help her remove his shoes and socks.

As she stood, her smile turned to concern, and Alex realised he was still pining for her so desperately it must have shown in his expression. He forced a smile, and she stroked his face once, before moving her hands to his shirt buttons. Panic flared in him and he grabbed her hands, shaking his head. He couldn't let her see his scars.

'Shirt and pants staying on? Won't you be uncomfortable? Or do you just want me to leave first?' she asked.

'Pants can come off,' he mumbled. 'Shirt stays on.'

She looked confused, and he belatedly realised this was an odd request by normal standards. Oh well, too late now.

She pushed him back to lie on the bed, undoing his belt and pants. Sliding the pants off, he was amused to note she ensured his underwear stayed up. He also suspected she kept his shirt tails over his groin. He'd probably be thankful for this tomorrow, but right now he kind of wanted her to get a look at the outline of his package. It wasn't fair he be the only one wondering what it would be like if they made love. He considered 'accidentally' moving the shirt and peeking to see if she was impressed, but quickly dismissed the idea as too juvenile.

Sam tugged on his hands and he stood up with her encouragement, moving a couple of steps before getting into the bed properly. The room spun as she placed the covers over him and kissed his forehead again. 'Sweet dreams,' she whispered.

Stay, he thought disjointedly.

He was far too drunk for anything serious to happen, but the idea of holding her while they slept was extraordinarily comforting. He idly wondered what she would wear, deciding to offer her a T-shirt. Ignoring the voice in his head telling him he'd regret this tomorrow, he uttered his invitation again, out loud this time. 'Stay,' he begged.

He hadn't intended to plead. It was meant to sound confident. She was supposed to stay because she wanted to, not because she felt sorry for him. Opening his eyes, he struggled to compose a sentence that would make his suggestion sound more inviting.

The room was empty. He'd left it too long, and he was alone. As he finally lost the battle and slipped into unconsciousness, Alex bitterly wondered if his tardiness was a precursor to their future together.

Chapter 12 – Behind Enemy Lines

The next week passed in a blur of inconvenience. Most of the staff were carpooling, as construction of a new car park necessitated the existing one be partially closed off. The added inconvenience only proved to highlight how cramped they were. If it weren't for the obvious plans to make ready one of the disused wings, everyone would have had a much harder time reigning in their tempers.

The building works were progressing rapidly, to the general excitement of pretty much everyone. The first new wing would house the PD team in generous comfort, and their old equipment room would become a staff break room, thereby benefitting everyone. The unspoken cherry on top was that the rest of the office would soon not have to share close quarters with guys like Tristan.

Sam and Alex hadn't talked about the weekend for most part. She didn't know what had possessed her to undress him. Well, that was a lie. Vodka and lust were a potent combination. Unfortunately, Alex now seemed to be having a hard time looking her in the eye. She had a sneaking suspicion he was avoiding her.

In hindsight, she was glad she'd snuck out early on Sunday morning. Waking with the sun, it only took one trip to the bathroom to decide there was no way she was letting Alex see her like that. Hungover with messy hair, last night's makeup, and last night's outfit, she was the poster girl for the 'walk of shame'. All she lacked was her underwear stuffed into her bag. She'd quietly gathered her things and hightailed out of there.

While her survival instincts could take the credit for her well-timed exit, the opportunity to avoid an awkward 'morning after' conversation couldn't be discounted. She'd texted instead. After apologising for slipping out, she'd deliberately downplayed her memories of the previous evening, intuitively understanding it was probably best if she didn't officially remember much.

This had been a good move but hadn't cancelled out the night altogether, as Alex obviously remembered plenty. His family's insistence that she join the party was enough to blur the boundaries of a solid work-based friendship, but she thought he could have dealt with that. Add in multiple affectionate moments, his brother's comments at the hospital the week before, and the intimacy of her putting him to bed … well, Sam wasn't surprised there had been repercussions.

She mourned the undoing of their easy friendship, dreading their attendance together at the rival product launch event on Friday night. It was awkward at the office all week, and they could get away with not being alone for decent periods there. At a party where she didn't know anyone but him, it was going to be hell.

Alex picked her up that morning before work — her carpool buddy for the day. They were to leave for the party straight from the office, so it made sense to arrange it this way when she'd agreed to come. Of course, when they'd made the plans, they were still on friendly terms.

She couldn't deal with the strain anymore. It was time to act.

'I read this article once,' she began cautiously, 'that said it was easier to have uncomfortable conversations with people in a car because you didn't have to be face to face. Plus, neither of you can really get out of it once you've started.'

She deliberately didn't look to see how he reacted to this statement, nervous about signs he didn't welcome her pending honesty.

'We were pretty well liquored up last weekend,' Sam said. 'I don't know about you, but I'm an affectionate drunk. You seemed okay at the time, but I'm getting the impression you're uncomfortable with it now.'

Alex was silent as she finished speaking, and she took the opportunity to peek at him. He was staring at the road, no change in his expression. A muscle in his cheek twitched, and he looked over at her briefly, but still didn't say anything.

'Any thoughts?' she asked, fishing for a response.

He smiled at this, and she wondered if there was hope for them after all.

'I get the feeling your affection is not so much augmented by your intoxication as it is hobbled by your sobriety,' he said, still smiling.

Sam stayed silent, sure this couldn't be his only comment. Alex seemed reluctant to continue talking though, and she decided to wait him out.

Finally turning to see her staring at him stubbornly, he seemed to give up. 'Okay, look,' he said, half-letting go of the wheel to run one frustrated hand through his hair. 'Saturday night was weird for me. You might be comfortable with near strangers, but I struggle to relax around my own family. I haven't made a new friend in years, and I've been fine with that.'

Sam watched him looking out the window at the traffic and marvelled that the article had been right. This was a more in-depth response than anticipated.

'Yes, I was okay with everything at the time,' he continued, acknowledging her point. 'A willing participant even. But in the cold light of day …' he trailed off, sighing again, and not finishing the thought out loud. 'Look, my problem is not with you. You were your usual charming, cheeky self, just a little more so. My problem is me. I'm not usually like that, and it's difficult to adapt,' he said ruefully.

'So, you're not mad at me?' asked Sam, finally giving voice to her real fear.

He smiled again, looking over at her briefly. 'No, I'm not mad. Just struggling with the repercussions of a new friend, who also happens to be a beautiful woman, which I normally avoid like the plague,' he said, startling her with the casual compliment.

'Alex,' she began hesitantly, 'I wasn't coming onto you or anything, I just —'

He interrupted her, shaking his head forcefully. 'I know, I know. I wasn't suggesting that. I just meant … well, I'd never think you'd be interested in me anyway. I'm sure you could do far better than a boring, scarred old man. I just meant I have trust issues with attractive women,' he finished agitatedly.

She was as surprised at his self-assessment as she was flattered by his earlier compliment. Frowning, she resolved to disabuse him of his ridiculous notions. 'Boring, scarred old man?' she scoffed. 'Alex, if you were boring, I wouldn't enjoy your company so much. You can't be much older than me, and I'm far from old. Scarred — I'll give you, but it doesn't detract from …' She took a deep breath before starting that statement again. 'Um, so I don't know what caused the scarring, and I don't want to be insensitive about it. I'm sure the story behind it is unpleasant at best. But from a purely aesthetic point of view, it just gives you a bit of a dark and mysterious edge. You're a very, very good-looking man, with or without it, I promise,' she finished emphatically. 'And if you don't believe me, ask that woman your brother picked up on Saturday night. If the looks she was shooting you were any indication, I'm fairly sure Noah was her second choice,' she added.

Alex laughed hard at this, surprising her as she hadn't thought it was all that funny. Before she had a chance to ask what was so hilarious, his phone rang. When he'd gotten control of himself, he answered via the Bluetooth, effectively ending their conversation for the rest of their trip.

Sam wondered that morning if she'd inadvertently made things worse. Alex still didn't have much time for her, but granted, he was having a busy day. She left her desk at 5pm and stuck her head into his office. He was on the phone but gave her a smile and a wave, reassuring her somewhat.

She redid her makeup in the tiny bathroom mirror, taking the initiative to call her parents while she had an excuse to keep the conversation to a time limit. She was glad she'd had the foresight to grab a lamp on her way. It was too dark in the bathroom without it. Even with its added illumination, her primping took longer than expected. Added to the difficulty of getting her mother to stop talking, she was running a bit late by the time she exited.

Alex was sitting in her desk chair waiting for her, looking like sex on a stick. He'd changed into a different suit, subtly more dressed up than earlier in the day. She was no good at identifying the nuances of men's suits so couldn't quite put her finger on the difference, but she covertly drank in the sight all the same.

'Sorry I took so long,' she apologised.

Alex smiled, his eyes flicking down to take in her whole look, before answering.

'Even a ruder man than I wouldn't complain when this is the result,' he assured her. 'You look stunning, Sam.'

Caught off guard after their uncomfortable week of near silence, Sam blushed. She'd packed two outfits this morning, one sensible, and one more daring. If their conversation hadn't gone well, she planned to wear the sensible one, but if all were right with the world again, it wouldn't hurt to show some skin.

She'd worn the daring one.

A black, skin-tight bodysuit of understated lace covered her top half. It was lined, of course, but at first glance it gave the impression of being see-through. The sweetheart neckline dipped generously at her cleavage, and she had paired it with a voluminous bronze-coloured wrap around skirt. When standing still, its full length hid her legs, but as she walked, it occasionally opened enough to show an expanse of skin from stiletto-clad foot to mid-thigh.

Attempting to cover her awkwardness, she thanked him and stowed all her extraneous baggage under the desk. He stood as she straightened, and she realised he was staring at her desk for some reason.

'Do you really believe in that stuff?' he said, gesturing towards it.

She frowned in confusion, and he clarified. 'The crystals,' he said. 'What are they for? Do you just like looking at them, or are they supposed to do something?'

'Oh,' she said. 'Um, to be honest, I'm not sure. The amethyst is supposed to block negative energies; the agate helps concentration and self-acceptance, and the sunstone is just supposed to make me happy. I don't know if they work, or if the fact that I *believe* they work is the point, but it's never really mattered to me either way.'

Alex nodded, looking thoughtful as they walked towards the building entrance.

'I've never heard it put that way before,' he admitted. 'I usually just put it in the same category as alien abductions and Illuminati conspiracies.'

He held the door open for her as she answered. 'You don't believe in aliens?' she asked incredulously. 'The whole big, bad universe up there, and you think we're it?'

He huffed as he locked the door. 'I don't believe one way or the other if there are other civilisations out there,' he clarified. 'But if there are, I doubt they're kidnapping hillbillies and probing them up the …'

Finally convinced they were back to normal, Sam stopped worrying. They continued their banter as they walked out into the night.

The party was boring. They'd been there a little over half an hour, and Sam had just begun her second wine, sipping too often because she had nothing else to do. She resolved to order something non-alcoholic next time so as not to repeat last week's circus.

They had been greeted by the CEO, a singularly unpleasant man she'd instantly disliked, almost as soon as they walked in the door. Even if Eva had never met Bernard (and Dimitri had Jeff Bezos level riches), she doubted the two would have ended up together. True, they'd grown up in the same town, and their families had apparently been close, but surely Eva had better taste than that. Dimitri's assistant, Isaac, was nicer. Too nice almost. While the CEO only stayed with them for as long as courtesy dictated, Isaac kept coming back, ensuring they had drinks and introducing them to people. Alex already knew many of them because a lot were his clients. Or had been. He became increasingly agitated to see so many of them there, although he hid it from everyone but Sam.

'How did you guys come to be in the same business?' she asked Alex as Isaac walked away again. 'Were you trying to annoy him?'

She didn't really care about the answer, but Alex obviously needed some distracting.

'No,' he muttered darkly. 'Dimitri's a sneaky prick. He always has to one-up my family somehow. About ten years ago — right when I announced I was going into business — he very conveniently confided that he'd been planning to branch out into dash cameras as well. He'd mostly concerned himself with GPS systems before then.' He'd been hunched defensively as he told the story, but he appeared to notice his stance as he finished and stood straight before he spoke again. 'We're pretty sure it's the only reason he hasn't retired. He wants to drive me out of business first.'

Sam realised she was frowning and smoothed her face. *Wouldn't want anyone to think we're intimidated.*

'Do you invite him to stuff?' she asked, more to divert herself from the rapidly emptying glass in her hand than out of any real interest. 'I mean, does he come to our product launch parties? Actually, do we even have product launch parties?'

Alex was clenching his glass so hard his knuckles were turning white. Only his eyes moved as he scanned the room. 'No,' he said distractedly. 'Dave keeps trying to talk me into it, but it feels stupid. Who's excited enough about dash cams to come to a party for them? Besides,' he continued, 'the real money is in the built-in versions for car manufacturers, and those are all customised, which kind of defeats the point of a product launch event. Dimitri is just showing off. Most of these people don't even have anything to do with the industry.' He gestured to the room of obviously wealthy people, all busy drinking, dancing, and schmoozing.

It wasn't hard to imagine that the majority of them were there just to be seen at a rich party. They all seemed to be competing with one another — an expensive watch here, a designer outfit there — and she had a sneaking suspicion most of them didn't even really like each other.

Alex's dark mood took a turn for the worse when he got a good look at the new product range. Sam admired his outward composure. If the things he said for her ears only were indicative of his real mood, he had a keen poker face.

The features and specs were almost identical to their new line, coming out in a few weeks.

Concerned that Alex might be considering doing something reckless, Sam began advocating for an early finish. 'We've been here an hour, and it's your competitor,' she said, hushed enough that no one could overhear. 'You wouldn't be expected to do anything beyond put in a polite appearance. I think you've covered your bases.'

It was obvious to Sam that Alex was quietly fuming. He shook his head just a little too emphatically. 'Not on your life. We came to get information,' he said.

'We came to see if we could link my wannabe cash benefactor to a suspected info leak,' Sam reminded him.

'And you haven't seen him, but we have veritable proof that information is being leaked,' Alex countered in an irritated undertone. 'I'm not leaving it at that. I want to know how he's getting it.' As he said this, he moved towards the lift.

There was a steady stream of people going up and down as the party was on two levels. The large building housed many different companies, and both the expansive foyer and function room one floor up had been commandeered for the party tonight.

They had to stop talking when they found themselves in the lift with several other people. Exiting on the second level, they hung back to continue their conversation as the doors closed on the people going down.

'Just what are you going to do, exactly?' asked Sam, hoping his idea wasn't too crazy.

'Dimitri's offices are on the top floor,' said Alex, confirming her worst fears. 'I'm going to see if I can find anything.' He pushed the call button to take the lift upwards, determinedly not meeting her worried look.

'Alex …' she began, trailing off when she couldn't think how to finish. She was honestly not sure how to talk him out of this. Not when he had that pig-headed expression.

Alex looked her full in the face, and she noticed his eyes had softened. Hope flared tentatively. Maybe it was a sign he might come to his senses?

His next words disabused her of that notion.

'Stay down here. I'll come find you when I'm done,' he said as the lift doors opened, and he resolutely entered.

No one was there to see him push a button for a higher floor, except Sam, who looked on helplessly. As the doors started to close, she made her decision and quickly joined him. Alex looked at her questioningly. 'You'll need a lookout,' was all she said.

Staring forlornly at their reflection as the mirrored doors closed, Sam decided this was a very bad idea. 'Candice is going to be so mad at me,' she mumbled.

Chapter 13 – Faking It

Sam stood just inside the door to Dimitri's office, leaving it ajar so she could see though the gap. She peered down the hallway so she could warn Alex if their unauthorised presence were pending discovery. Unable to relax, she repeatedly lamented her decision to accompany him. All that stopped her from abandoning her post and returning to the party was her fear she'd be caught on the way, thus making it more likely Alex would also be busted.

She'd uselessly checked the clock on her phone twice already. It made no difference, as Alex hadn't specified a time limit. He wasn't going to suddenly give up just because their breaking and entering had totalled ten whole minutes. But it gave her something to do, and she sorely needed a distraction to take the edge off her panic.

She periodically turned to watch Alex, hoping he would either find something soon or give up. He was going through Dimitri's desk, skimming papers, and meticulously putting them back in the same order. So far, nothing out of the ordinary had shown up.

She'd already voiced her opinion it was unlikely anything so important would be written down on paper, and Alex had admitted she was probably right. Short of hacking his desktop, this was almost certainly a futile exercise. He'd confided that he was holding out hope because Dimitri was somewhat 'old school'. There was potentially an interesting hardcopy stashed somewhere.

Finishing with the drawers, Alex started on the single tray of documents on top of the desk. Dimitri's workspace was unencumbered by the clutter littering Alex's. Being well past retirement age, Sam suspected he didn't have as much to do with the day to day running of his company as Alex did.

I wonder how much work it would take to make Alex's desk look like that, she thought. Probably more than she'd care to contemplate. Even if she managed it, the lack of visible tasks would only serve to make him anxious anyway. He was too used to having three people's work to do.

Her head whipped back to the door when she heard a bell ring in the distance. 'Someone's getting out of the lift,' she whispered urgently.

Alex looked up, startled. He was only about halfway through the tray, and she saw his eyes dart back to the pile, eager to keep looking. He spoke distractedly, more engrossed in his task than their conversation. 'I'll just finish looking at this and we'll …' A sick pallor washed over his face as he looked up at Sam again, who was frozen in shock.

They had both realised their predicament at the same time. Her self-appointed position as 'lookout' was completely useless. The only way out was the lift or the stairs beside the lift. If someone was coming this way, they were going to be caught red-handed.

Sam couldn't believe they had both been that stupid. Alex's eagerness combined with her discomfort had blinded them to the obvious. They'd trapped themselves. Their only hope was that whoever it was didn't plan on coming in this direction.

Watching the hall nervously, she saw shadows coming from around the distant corner, and her heart sank as she realised the voices were getting closer. There was no doubt about it, they were coming this way.

Swiftly closing the door, she confirmed this fact to Alex. He uselessly put the papers back into the tray. No one would ever know he'd been through them if they could just somehow not be caught.

Their mere presence made his intentions obvious though. Even without the physical evidence of disorder, what other reason could they have for being here?

Sam answered her own question as she watched Alex stride around the desk looking grim. He appeared to be mentally preparing himself to face the music, but maybe they didn't have to.

It's crazy, she thought. *Too crazy, but I can't think of anything else.*

It was a risk on a lot of levels. They'd still be 'busted' in a way, and she was sure Alex wasn't going to like it, but it was all she could come up with on short notice. 'Take off your jacket and undo your tie,' she whispered.

Alex's look of bleak determination turned to confusion. The request certainly didn't fit the situation, but she didn't have time to ease him into it gently.

'If we can't get out before they come in, we need a different reason to be here. Take off your jacket, and undo your tie and some buttons,' she whispered again, more urgently this time, beginning to untie her skirt.

Realisation dawned on his face as she unwound the material and artfully draped it over the couch. He made no move to comply with her instruction though, seemingly thunderstruck by her exposed skin. The bodysuit she wore still covered her mostly, but it hugged her curves and was cut high over her behind.

Sam could appreciate this was not a turn of events he'd expected, but she didn't really have time to be sympathetic as the voices and accompanying footsteps were getting steadily closer. Their uninvited guests seemed to be moving in and out of the other offices. They had a little time, but not enough to discuss the merits of her plan. It was this or get caught.

Moving towards Alex, she gently pushed the jacket from his shoulders. He allowed this and began mechanically loosening his tie, as instructed. Focused on getting him to a convincing state of undress, Sam didn't notice his face until his jacket lay discarded with her skirt, and his tie and three buttons were undone.

His expression of torment made her heart ache.

She didn't have time to comfort him properly, so contented herself with running a gentle hand down the side of his face. It settled on his chest as she brushed her other thumb softly over his hand. 'It will need to look convincing,' she said apologetically.

Alex nodded jerkily but made no move to similarly touch or embrace her.

It would be up to her, then.

She tilted her chin and moved her face towards him, lowering her lashes but not quite closing her eyelids. Staring into his eyes had seemed too confronting, but there was no way she could reach his lips if he didn't lower his face, so she still needed to see a little. Thankfully, she'd left her shoes on so the gap in their heights wasn't as pronounced, but this was still going to be impossible without his cooperation.

She relaxed as Alex bent his neck, only then realising she was as tense as him. Sam had imagined kissing him on many guilt-ridden occasions, but never had it been in a situation like this. In her mind, they'd always gradually capitulated to their mutual feelings, culminating in a slow, non-threatening and romance-filled first kiss. Instead, she was stressed out and half-naked in a strange office, forced to fake passion for the sake of a pending audience.

And somehow, she was still hopeful he wanted this. It was stupid, really. His reluctance was obvious. The only reason Alex participated was because he couldn't think of another way out. She shouldn't be entertaining these hopes that a necessary charade would finally win him over, that his lack of enthusiasm was caused by something other than his unwillingness.

Alex paused then, with their lips an inch away from one another. Sam reflexively opened her eyes and gazed into his for a long moment. Whatever he saw in hers, he seemed to calm slightly. She lowered her eyes to his mouth and slowly, gently, brushed her lips against his, hesitant to start with anything more demanding.

Pulling back, she looked up at him again.

He exhaled shakily and cautiously moved towards her. He kissed her this time, longer and more intensely than before. Sam closed her eyes and tried not to sink into the sweet bliss, but damn, he was good at it. His mouth grew less hesitant with each second, leading hers in a slow, practiced dance of seduction. It simultaneously left her feeling she could never get enough, but also couldn't take much more.

Finally, his hands moved, one to the small of her back, the other travelling up her arm to tangle in her hair. She shivered at his touch and adjusted herself, hoping it would disguise the involuntary movement.

Unsure if her movement had camouflaged her reaction, she stopped caring when she realised it'd pressed her body closer to his, and he'd reacted by pulling her tighter to him. Her breasts rested gently against him, tingling with the sensation. The kiss became more urgent, less careful. She felt his tongue brush against hers and completely forgot they were about to be interrupted, giving herself over to the moment.

Alex used his hand in her hair to tilt her head back, breaking the kiss. He grazed his lips against her jawline instead, making a slow path towards her ear. Pausing before he reached it, he nibbled gently against her jaw and made her gasp, before changing direction to move down her neck.

Desire had long since pooled in her lower abdomen, and it was lucky he held her so tightly now because she would have staggered if still holding her own weight. Her knees were useless, and her centre of gravity had completely disappeared.

Alex again used his teeth when he reached the join between her neck and shoulder. Her approval would have been embarrassingly audible if the office door hadn't opened, interrupting them.

She'd completely forgotten their audience was entering at any moment. The surprise and shock on her face as she turned to face the uninvited guests was laughably real.

Fighting to bring herself back to the situation at hand, she held onto Alex for reassurance. She dimly hoped her shock and confusion would at least make things look more authentic. She had deliberately positioned herself and Alex so that her semi-uncovered backside faced the door, hoping her state of undress would cause a bigger distraction, but she'd turned so quickly they probably didn't get much of an eyeful.

Isaac was holding a box of promotional materials, his mouth opening and closing like a fish, which explained why they'd been moving in and out of offices. They must have been gifts for their employees, celebrating the product launch.

Dimitri's face went from shock to lecherous enjoyment in a short space of time, and Alex quickly moved to position himself in front of her. Taking pity on her, Isaac put down the box and moved to the couch, picking up her skirt and handing it over as Dimitri began to speak.

'I am sorry for the interruption, Aleksander,' he drawled, his accent much less pleasant than Sam remembered Eva's being. 'I just came to collect my glasses. I did not realise you were back here. And I certainly did not know you were with him, my dear,' he directed at Sam, leaning to look around Alex as she fumbled with her skirt.

'We're very sorry for the imposition,' said Alex, finally finding his voice as he buttoned his shirt. He stuffed his tie into his pocket and took the jacket Isaac proffered.

'We'll leave you to your errand,' he finished, taking Sam by the hand to lead her around Dimitri.

With that, he left the office and closed the door behind him. Not making any eye contact, he hurried them down the hall, still with her hand in his. Sam hadn't yet recovered from her shock at his ardency, and so she paid less attention to their path and more to the warm hand gently cradling hers. They'd long since left their audience, but Alex showed no sign of letting go. This was just fine with her, and she tried to quash the doubt and elation warring for dominance inside her mind. This wasn't a moment for questions. It was a moment to be enjoyed.

Chapter 14 – A Surprise Encounter

As the lift doors closed, Sam struggled to bring her attention back to the present. Reluctantly removing her hand from Alex's, she caught a brief look of surprise and hurt on his face. It was quickly replaced with confusion as she reached into his pocket. A wary understanding blossomed when she pulled out his tie and draped it around his neck, wordlessly knotting it back into order.

Pausing briefly when Alex realised he hadn't pushed the button, she still managed to finish before the lift doors opened up to the foyer. She noticed him scrutinising her handiwork in the mirrored walls before they left and wondered if it was up to his standards.

It was her turn to be surprised, as instead of skirting the nearby knot of couples dancing in front of the band, he steered her among them. Taking her hand in his again, and placing his other one on her waist, he finally looked down at her and paused, hesitating.

Belatedly comprehending that her shock must have registered on her face, Sam placed her hand on his shoulder and tried to relax. A smile came tentatively to her face, but Alex's returned expression was more distracted than anything. They began swaying in time to the music as he finally spoke.

'Sorry if you didn't want to dance,' he apologised. 'I didn't want to talk to anyone else, and this seemed like a good way to keep people from interrupting.'

Sam shook her head. 'Don't apologise,' she reassured him. 'I like to dance. You just surprised me.'

Alex's answering smile was more convincing than his last attempt. She became aware of his closeness as they moved through the throng, her thoughts straying back to their kiss. Her lips, jawline and neck were cool and tingling, contrasting against the rest of her heated skin. She felt vulnerable, like the private sensation on her skin was visible to him in some way.

Was he thinking about their kiss too, or was he preoccupied with their failed mission? Surprisingly, he soon revealed he was thinking about neither.

'Where did you learn to tie such a perfect a Windsor knot?' he asked.

Sam's answering laugh was perhaps a tad giddy. She was relieved he hadn't picked up on her neediness. 'YouTube,' she said. 'My husband was terrible at it, so I had to learn how to do it for him. He claimed having little hands helped me, but really I think he just didn't have the patience.'

She'd mentioned Logan without thinking, and almost stepped on Alex's foot when her words caught up with her. She rarely spoke about her lost love, let alone so casually. The ease of her intimate admission overwhelmed her so much she almost missed Alex's surprise entirely. He'd gripped her hand a little tighter at the word 'husband', and she prayed he wouldn't focus on her slip. To her relief, he didn't mention it.

'You do have small hands,' he mused after a small pause. 'And long fingers, come to think of it. Do you play an instrument?'

Sam chose to fall back on humour to mask how off balance she still felt. 'That depends on your follow-up questions,' she said. 'Are you going to ask me to audition for your band, or are you just in the mood for a soulful rendition of "Three Blind Mice" on the recorder?'

Alex laughed out loud at this, attracting the attention of a few other couples around them. One woman seemed especially interested in their joke, forcing her dance partner to turn around so her back was no longer to Alex.

She was unpleasantly attractive, in the sort of way that was a little too well groomed. Her thin body was perfectly draped in an expensive silk dress, and her impeccably dyed and coifed hair was crowned by a fascinator Sam was sure at least one animal had died to contribute to.

The woman smiled predatorily at Alex, her talon-like nails gripping the shoulder of her dance partner a little tighter. Fine lines crossing her hands made a mockery of her too smooth face. She seemed decidedly more used to looking down her nose at people than smiling at them, however obnoxiously.

'Alex,' she said, nodding condescendingly.

Sam realised they knew each other, and she swiftly looked back at Alex.

He'd stopped dancing, his hand going limp and clammy in hers. His face was similarly slack with shock, and she suspected he wasn't breathing. Whoever this woman was, Alex wasn't pleased to see her.

The unpleasant woman's smile widened at his obvious discomfort, and she pointedly turned her gaze to Sam. She sneered a little while looking the younger woman up and down, evidently not impressed with what she saw. Feeling defensive, Sam reminded herself she preferred to dress according to her own tastes, and not to suit the demands of current fashion. This skirt was her favourite piece.

'Bit young for you, isn't she?' asked the woman, lazily. 'Better get her some Botox if you want her to stay that way.'

Still visibly shaken, Alex didn't respond.

The woman's dance partner had a chuckle though and turned to smirk at them. His gaze lowered to Sam's cleavage and lingered a moment, before looking back up at Alex. 'Not going to introduce us?' he asked, his face widening into a grin to rival the woman's.

They both laughed at this, and Alex flinched.

Frightened of his reaction and sick of being sneered at, Sam let her big mouth do what it did best. 'Excuse me,' she said sweetly to the woman, gesturing to her fur and feather headdress. 'Did you know your cat has caught a bird?'

The woman frowned in confusion.

Sam saw the exact moment she understood she'd been insulted

and decided to drive it home before her opponent had a chance to respond. 'You should really put a bell on its collar,' she said seriously, beginning to lead Alex away. 'It's kinder to the wildlife.'

The woman narrowed her eyes, clearly reassessing her initial impression of Sam as she walked away.

What I wouldn't give to have one of those 'resting bitch faces' everyone complains about, thought Sam. *It might keep people like that away from me.*

She led Alex directly to the bar and ordered him a scotch and herself a wine. He still hadn't said anything, and she was a lot more worried than she could express in such a public setting. Taking their drinks, she made a beeline for the door to the garden, bypassed the smokers, and led him a short way down a path.

They sat on a convenient ledge, the cold night air crisp around them. The noise from the party was muted this far away, and the lighting softer. Alex breathed raggedly, gazing into the shrubbery across from them.

Sam looked at him calculatedly, wondering how best to pull him out of this stupor. 'Jokes on her,' she tried. 'I already have Botox. Just not enough to compete with her "department store mannequin" look.'

It didn't work. His jaw clenched, but his expression didn't change, his eyes continuing to stare unseeing into the bushes. Sam got the feeling the small movement was the most he could manage for a reaction.

Noticing his drink was in danger of slipping out of his hand, she stood, taking it from him and placing it with hers on the ledge. She moved to stand in front of him, placing her hands on his shoulders. Alex finally moved when she brushed one hand gently over his beard, jerking to look up at her.

Frightened she'd overstepped the mark, Sam let go of him and made to step back. He stopped her by placing his hands on her hips, holding her tightly in place while he breathed shallowly.

Slowly lowering his head, he leaned his forehead against her torso. His breathing deepened, and for one moment Sam thought he was finally relaxing. Feeling his shoulders start to shake, she realised he was closer to hyperventilating. She put her arms around him and stroked his hair, murmuring reassurances.

Who was this woman, and what about her had caused such a dramatic reaction in Alex? The closest she'd seen him come to losing his equilibrium before this was the night in the hospital. The conversation about her with his brothers sounded like it'd thrown him. This was a whole other level, and she was frightened he'd lost control so completely.

Briefly, she considered their staged moment of passion might have something to do with it. She quickly dismissed it, as he seemed fine up until noticing the couple on the dancefloor, laughing easily, and showing no discomfort with their charlatanism. The problem was unquestionably caused by the mysterious woman.

Alex seemed to calm eventually, breathing more evenly and not gripping her hips so tightly. He eventually exhaled a long breath, relaxing his shoulders and looking up at her.

Sam was surprised to see tears. She gently wiped one from his cheek, again rubbing a hand along his beard. 'Do you want to talk about it?' she whispered.

Alex winced and sat back, letting go of her hips and pulling her by the hand to sit beside him. 'You've met my daughter,' he began heavily, 'but I don't think you've ever asked me about her mother.'

Understanding instantly dawned on Sam. She couldn't believe she'd been that dense. 'That was your ex-wife?' she asked incredulously.

Alex nodded tiredly, before looking down at Sam's hand, tightly held in his own. He began to trace the length of her fingers with his free hand, seemingly intent on not making eye contact.

'I'm guessing you haven't seen her in a while,' said Sam cautiously, not quite a question.

Alex grimaced, but didn't look up from his study of Sam's hand in his.

'I haven't seen her in eleven years,' he said, 'and I hoped I never would again.'

Surprised, Sam considered her next query carefully. Alex seemed highly fragile, and he technically hadn't invited her to question him. 'Stacey doesn't see her?' she asked tentatively.

Alex shook his head emphatically. 'No,' he confirmed. 'She hasn't seen her since then either. Victoria happily gave up visitation rights in exchange for a lot of cash and some pretty strict custody conditions.'

Sam couldn't imagine giving up the rights to see your own child. She'd only met Victoria briefly, but even considering her disagreeable personality, this seemed like a drastic move. She wondered just how much Alex had offered to get her to agree. She'd gleaned he was a rich guy even independent of his company, but still …

'I'm guessing her unpleasantness out there was just the tip of the iceberg if you felt it was necessary to keep them apart,' she offered carefully, unsure how this would be received. She didn't want to pry, but she did want him to know she was there if he needed to talk.

She also couldn't deny her curiosity was piqued. Sam was sure this was the name she overheard Alex mention to his brothers. This woman was the reason she was falling in love with a man that might not be able to love her back, and she wanted answers almost as much as she wanted to erase the pain in Alex's eyes.

Chapter 15 – Confessions from the Murky Past

Alex stared into the bushes with futility. The pain in his eyes looked old, so old he'd stored it carelessly at the back of his brain, never to be considered again. Sam ached to put it back there, covered in dust and cobwebs until the end of time, but she didn't think that would be possible under their current circumstances.

He was silent for so long, she decided he wasn't going to say any more about it. Shivering in the cool night air, she resolved to just be there for him — a kind face and a warm embrace to comfort him and keep him in the present.

When he finally began his story, she understood he hadn't been avoiding talking about it. It was just that hard to find the words.

'She wasn't bad to start with,' Alex said quietly. 'In the beginning, she was everything I thought I wanted in a woman. I'd known her for a little while already before she showed any interest in me. I didn't think I had a shot, to be honest. She always had so many men chasing her. I think that's why I was so dazzled. Out of all the men that wanted her, she picked me. I ignored all the early warning signs because I felt so lucky.

'Her demeanour changed relatively quickly though. She started to manipulate me, always getting her own way, and twisting everything I did and said to make it look like I was trying to hurt her,' he said, grimacing. 'We got into this routine where she'd pick a fight and then play the victim when I fought back. Then she'd cry and I'd have to grovel and commit some grand act of contrition — usually an expensive one — to prove my apology was genuine.' Parched, he picked up his scotch from the ledge and took a sip before continuing his story.

'Every year, my brothers and I go on a golf trip with our dad. It's just a weekend away, nothing crazy. We spend two nights drinking and two days pushing through our hangovers on the course the next day. I mentioned it was coming up about eight months after we started going out, and Victoria pitched a fit. She claimed I'd hidden it from her. She told me if I really loved her, I wouldn't want to spend a whole weekend away from her. She was afraid some other woman would steal me away; she felt like I always put my family before her; she didn't like my brothers and thought I spent too much time with them … blah, blah, blah,' he said bitterly.

Sam watched silently, wanting to comfort him, but afraid she would stop the flow of words if she spoke. He needed a chance to lance the poison.

'I ended up telling her I wouldn't go. This wasn't enough to appease her, because of course she knew I really wanted to. She sulked, and I walked on eggshells for about a week, unsure whether to go through with it or not, and then one day she changed. She told me she realised how much it meant to me, and she wanted me to go.'

Alex paused briefly to look up at Sam, a self-deprecating smile on his face. He must have noticed she was hunched against the chill, as he paused his story to insist she wear his jacket. He would be fine in his shirt.

'I can't tell you how relieved I was when she gave her blessing,' he continued, after Sam was protected from the spring night. 'The thought of telling my family I was going to miss it was stressing me to no end. I knew they already didn't like her, but I'd been careful to defend her around them. They didn't need any additional fodder. So, I went,' he confirmed. 'And the first night we were there, I called her, but she didn't answer. Twice. And then the next day she still didn't answer, didn't return my calls or texts. By the time we got home on Sunday, I didn't know what to think. I went to her house and she lost it. Crying, screaming that I shouldn't have gone, should have known she didn't really want me to go, and if I truly loved her, I wouldn't have wanted to go either. It'd been a test, and because I'd failed it, there was no way she'd ever believe I could love her "the way she needed me to",' he said.

Sam tentatively put her hand over his, giving it a reassuring squeeze.

'I cried, I begged, I pleaded … in hindsight, she had me right where she really wanted me. She had trained me to pander to her fake insecurities, and then manipulated me into doing something she could frame as unforgivable. She told me she needed to think things over, and I left with my tail between my legs. I thought long and hard, and then did the one thing I could think of to convince her I was really committed.' He sighed, his hand twitching in Sam's.

'I bought a ring, and I asked her to marry me,' he confessed, shaking his head at his younger self's naivety. He looked over at Sam again, hopeless acceptance in his face, and she squeezed his hand tighter. He looked down at his drink before starting to talk again.

'She said yes, of course. Many years and many therapy sessions later, I figured out this was exactly where she'd been leading me from day one. She wanted to lock me and my family's money down, and she wanted to lock it down quickly. Conditioning me to make bigger and bigger apology gestures each time, making a huge deal out of completely normal things … it was her way of keeping me too busy and confused to defend myself.

'Things got worse after the wedding. She refused to speak to any of my family because they'd pushed for a prenup. Eventually, she stopped me from talking to them as well,' he said, the shadow of remembered loneliness in his eyes.

Sam thought of his brothers, and of Eva and Bernard, and the effortless relationship they all shared. *She must be a pro, to pry them apart.*

'Once she had me estranged from all my family and friends, she started to be cruel. Subtle stuff at first. Disparaging comments, offhand insults. Demeaning me, but claiming I was overreacting when I protested. Then she stopped talking to me for days at a time. She'd disappear without a trace, sometimes for a night, sometimes for a whole weekend, and wouldn't tell me where she'd been. Belittled me for being "too insecure to deal with her having a life outside of me". She was gaslighting me, and my confidence was shot to hell.'

Sam noticed he'd gone pale, even in the semi-darkness. She was desperate for his story to finish before it got much worse, but she was painfully aware that Stacey hadn't been mentioned yet. There had to be more.

'She upped the ante after that,' he said, his voice breaking. 'Started throwing stuff at me on the rare occasions I had the nerve to question her. She told me she didn't trust my judgement, so I couldn't spend money without her permission. I wasn't allowed to go anywhere without her, except work.'

His eyes had glazed over, and Sam was sure he was right back there in that moment, remembering how it felt to be so alone and downtrodden. She couldn't sit quietly without doing anything anymore, so she stood again to put her arms around him. He held her as well, pressing his cheek to her abdomen.

The force of his need showed in the strength of his grip and his shaking voice as he continued. 'She would throw her food and drinks at me when she was bored, just because she could. She'd pinch me or smack me as she walked past, just to remind me she could do that too. She destroyed a lot of my stuff, photos and mementos mostly, killing all my links to the past.'

Sam's sorrow at his sadness had morphed into outrage that anyone could treat him so disparagingly. She struggled to contain her reaction and just be there for him. Alex was more entitled to his emotions than she was to hers at this point.

'Then one day, I got home from work and she wasn't there,' he said, the ghost of his apprehension in his voice. 'And again, the next day. I didn't think too much of it at first. She often disappeared for a few days, but after a week, I started to worry. So, I called her,' he said heavily, looking up at Sam. 'And she screamed at me. Really flipped her lid. She'd never gone off at me like that before. I was so scared, I actually considered leaving her, afraid of what she'd do when she came home. Honestly, if she'd stayed away a few more days, I might have worked up the nerve.' Still holding Sam's waist, he began to stroke her hips with his thumbs.

Sam watched him staring at his hands on her, wondering if it was time for her to speak up yet. He certainly hadn't finished the story though, and he began to talk again without prompting.

'She came home the next day. I was in the kitchen, too scared to move. She walked over to me with a smile on her face, and I thought it was a trick, that she was going to hurt me. I flinched when she lifted her arms, but she just put them around my neck and kissed me. It was the first affection she'd showed me in months. We hadn't had sex in a year at that point, but she took me into the bedroom and made love to me then and there, and pretty much every night after it for a couple of months.'

Sam stroked the hair at the nape of his neck, trying to ignore her sick suspicion of where the story was headed.

'I had no idea what was going on and I was too scared to ask,' Alex admitted. 'I found out later she'd been having an affair since right after our wedding. She'd been planning to leave me for the boyfriend, but she slipped up when I called. He got a front row seat to her real personality while she was screaming at me, and he broke it off. Victoria knew she'd have to lock me down a bit longer if she wanted to transition from one rich husband to another, so she came up with a plan.' He looked up at her, bitterness now the only expression on his face, and Sam's suspicion firmed.

'Stacey,' he explained. 'Stacey was her plan. We hadn't talked about having kids since we were engaged, but two months after she turned over her new leaf, she told me she was pregnant. She claimed she was as surprised as me, and I let her get away with it because I was too fragile to question her, but I knew it was on purpose.' He was quiet for a moment, evidentially lost in memory, but soon continued.

'It took a while, but eventually I started to delude myself the past wasn't as bad as I imagined it, and Stacey's impending birth had saved our marriage. You have to understand,' he said, looking at Sam earnestly, 'I'd become totally dependent on her. Anything I could use to rationalise staying was woven into my justification.'

Sam nodded, sickened Victoria was so skilful. She'd exploited Alex's basic human need to be safe and loved so thoroughly that he'd lived and died by her approval.

'You couldn't bring yourself to leave, so you convinced yourself you wanted to stay,' she said, doing her best to validate his feelings.

He nodded too, seeming relieved she understood. 'She snapped at me sometimes still, but I put it down to pregnancy hormones. For the most part, things were much better. She was mostly nice to me, and we even saw my family a couple of times.'

A smile twitched the corners of his mouth up so briefly that Sam wasn't sure she hadn't imagined it, before his expression turned bitter again.

'Things started to go downhill again after Stacey was born, but I told myself that was normal too. A new baby is a stressful addition to any relationship, so it was easy to justify as she got more and more distant.' He paused then, distracted by the sound of people walking down the path towards them. 'Do you want to go?' he asked. 'I can finish this in the car, and I really don't feel like talking to anyone else.'

Sam agreed and they continued down the path, which conveniently led around the side of the building to where he was parked. They both stayed silent until Alex pulled out onto the road. As they left the building behind them, he concluded his story.

'Things eventually ended up like the first time, except she was pretty open about her new affair. I'm not 100% sure when they began seeing each other, but I stayed with her for a whole year after she started taunting me with it,' he said tonelessly. 'That was him inside,' he said. 'I'm surprised they've lasted this long, but I guess if a sociopath is going to make it work with anyone, it'd be with another sociopath? He was married when they started seeing each other too.

His wife died about six months before Victoria and I finally imploded. I'm pretty sure the only reason she stayed that long was to figure out how to get as much cash as possible when she left.'

He didn't come out and say it, but Sam now finally understood why Alex was so gun-shy about women. She wasn't quite sure what to say. Ideally, she'd like to pour her heart out to him, tell him how much it hurt her that anyone could subject him to so much abuse, but the very nature of the problem prevented her from being so demonstrative.

Her quest to find the right words came to a screaming halt when he asked about the one subject guaranteed to throw her off track.

'So that's my horrible divorce story,' he concluded. 'I hope yours was less traumatic, but if you want a sympathetic ear, I'm here for you.

Chapter 16 – Honeytrap

Shocked, vulnerable and needy, Alex tried to concentrate as he drove down the quiet streets. He hadn't talked in depth about his marriage to anyone but his therapist before tonight.

His family (and now Sam) knew about Victoria's manipulation, her gaslighting, and some of the emotional abuse. But the really intense physical stuff? He kept that between himself and the therapist. And even the therapist didn't know about Victoria's coup de grâce. He hoped Sam didn't put two and two together. It didn't take a huge mental leap to realise 'severe emotional abuse' + 'big, ugly scar' = physical abuse.

After all these years, he was still ashamed. And he was angry at himself for feeling that way. Intellectually, he could validate his reasons for staying. She was a master of manipulation and had eroded his self-worth to a point where his consciousness still baulked at the idea of crossing her. He'd been conditioned to do whatever she wanted him to, to fear doing anything she didn't want him to, and to depend entirely on her for emotional fulfilment and validation.

He knew all this. But it didn't stop the little voice in his head that kept reminding him how easily he could've stopped it all.

He was significantly bigger and stronger than her and could have shut down her punches, kicks and slaps almost effortlessly. Sure, there had been occasions when he was physically powerless to stop her. She'd tripped him multiple times. He 'fell' down the stairs often, through a glass table twice, and on one particularly memorable occasion, into a large and sharp cactus.

But he still could've left. He had money and a supportive family, and if he'd reported the abuse and absentee parenting, he could have won custody of Stacey. His more serious injuries would be documented by the hospitals, and there were plenty of witnesses to Victoria's indifference to her daughter. No matter what 'happy family' front she tried to present, he would've had her.

But he hadn't left. He could list all the reasons why, all the mind games she'd played with him, but he couldn't stop blaming himself. His therapist had trained him to recognise when he used words like 'let', 'allow', and 'complicit' to describe his time with Victoria, and he was used to self-correcting when they crossed his train of thought.

Belief was a lot slower to come than the new words.

He noticed it had been quiet in the car for a long moment. Sam hadn't responded to his invitation to share her own pain, and he looked over at her, concerned. Her mouth was open, and he saw her try to frame words twice before interjecting. 'I'm sorry, Sam. I don't mean to pry. It's none of my business what went on in your marriage. I just meant I appreciate you hearing me out, and I wanted you to know I'm happy to listen too if you ever wanted to talk,' he finished. 'I'm sorry for dumping all that on you,' he added, 'I guess it was just the shock of seeing her again. I don't normally talk about it. Even my family don't know the full story.'

And neither do you, thought Alex. *But I've told you more than anyone but my therapist. Why do I trust you so much?*

Looking relieved, Sam met his eyes while they sat at the traffic lights and smiled. 'I'm flattered you confided in me,' she began, 'and I understand why you have such a hard time talking about it. My story isn't the same as yours, and I struggle to talk about it for a whole different category of reasons.' She paused, looking thoughtful. 'I'm not hiding anything exactly. It's just overwhelming. I struggle to put it into words. Limiting it withing the boundaries of language doesn't do it justice.'

Alex nodded emphatically. This was why therapy hadn't fixed him yet. 'You could say the words to me, but even in your head they don't convey enough meaning, let alone out loud,' he offered.

She nodded sorrowfully, and they drove in silence for a short while, both lost in their own pain.

Eventually, Sam spoke again. 'I'm sorry,' she said. 'For everything she did to you, I mean. I know it's inadequate, but if there's anything at all I can do to help you or comfort you, it's yours for the taking. Having said that, I understand why you're uneasy around women now. I really hope you know me well enough to look past my gender, but I appreciate you might still want to keep your distance,' she said.

Alex was quiet for a long moment, before reaching over and taking Sam's hand in his own again.

They didn't talk for the rest of the drive, both reeling in a cacophony of thoughts about the past, and the present.

Massively tempted to accept Sam's invitation to come in for a drink when he dropped her home, Alex decided it was probably best not to. He was a mess of raw nerves and didn't want to risk doing something stupid.

It had been a long day with many shocks to it. He'd been completely blindsided by Victoria's appearance, and he was also still recovering from his kiss with Sam. He could have cheerfully thrown a punch at Dimitri for interrupting, and he'd privately vowed to do something particularly nasty to the man for leering at his half-naked assistant.

Still, his belligerent thoughts were the height of stupidity. Dimitri had been meant to see her like that. Her mouth-watering body had been purposefully displayed in sacrifice to their cause. Sam's state of dress (or undress) had been orchestrated specifically to lend credibility to their charade, and it'd worked.

It wasn't for me, Alex reminded himself. *None of that was for me.*

He'd been terrified at first. The thought of simulating that kind of intimacy had taken him back to his time with Victoria. Her erosion of his confidence had a whole separate subcategory in the bedroom, and he hadn't been able to perform during their last couple of years together. Not only had this given her a tangible topic for derision, but it'd also stayed with him after they were over. Even in his imagination, he hadn't been able to deal with the touch of a woman until Sam. Masturbation had been mechanical for years, intended as stress relief only.

Sam was the first woman he'd been sexually attracted to since Victoria. No wonder he kept letting his guard down with her. He saw her in a whole different light to other women.

Or was it the other way around? Was his attraction a result of his comfortability with her?

Her hesitancy at kissing him first had helped. If she'd just planted it on him with no lead up, he probably would have shut it down. As much as he appreciated her assertiveness, it reminded him too forcefully of Victoria. Sam had been vulnerable too, and it had validated his own timidity. The hesitant touch of her lips had crumbled the already eroding wall he'd erected between himself and his sexuality.

And in that moment, he'd kissed her the way he truly wanted to. He hadn't faked that kiss, had in fact done his best to convince her he was worthy of her attention. He wanted to turn her on, to have her think about him the way he couldn't stop himself from thinking about her.

His secret enjoyment of their staged lust was one thing, but he was ashamed of how tempted he'd been to push the implied boundaries. It was all he could do to stay rational and keep his hands from straying below her waist. Dimitri hadn't been the only one to crave the feel of her ass under his hands.

He might not have dared to take it so far if it hadn't been for Sam's revelation that morning. Her matter-of-fact statement she thought him good-looking had been a serious ego boost. He kept trying to tell himself she hadn't really meant it, was just being nice. The genuine surprise she showed when refuting his claims of unattractiveness was burned into his brain though, as hotly as the feeling of her body pressed against his and the taste of her mouth on his tongue.

Shortly after he began drifting off to sleep that night, Alex was suddenly wide awake. A horrible thought had entered his head. He tried not to lend it any credibility, but once there, all the dots connected without his conscious volition.

Sam hadn't been working at the company long. Maybe about as long as the information had been leaking? He couldn't believe he hadn't considered this before. He'd been completely blinded by his growing attraction... and maybe that was by design. Sam was beautiful, adorably sweet and friendly, intelligent, dazzlingly strong-willed, and possessed a sense of humour just quirky enough to give her a unique charm. She politely ignored all the romantic attention she garnered, thus reinforcing the non-threatening impression she wouldn't be trying to attract him either.

As his assistant, Sam conceivably had prior knowledge of where he would be at any given moment. He didn't differentiate between his work and social schedule. Both categories were carelessly added to the same electronic calendar, and he'd run into her two weekends in a row 'accidentally'. And somehow, on both his recent drinking binges, he'd ended up in cosy situations with her, primed for romance.

The bar fight was too much. She could never have orchestrated that, could she? But maybe that hadn't been her plan. Maybe she was just supposed to run into him there, accidentally-on-purpose, to do a little flirting; perhaps tempt him into something inappropriate? Their intimate moment at the hospital could easily have been engendered spur of the moment. He'd been taken aback by her easy affection, after all. Maybe it wasn't as unconscious as he originally thought.

And then there was last weekend. What a coincidence Sam had exited the bar in need of rescuing, right when he was walking past. Two weekends in a row she was the damsel in distress, and he was the knight in shining armour.

But, he thought, *it was her that bought Dimitri to my attention in the first place.* Without that, it would've taken him so much longer to understand something fishy was going on. Had her divulgence been calculated? She'd revealed to him something he would have eventually figured out anyway. Was it her way of gaining his trust and leading him in a different direction?

And what a fluke that on the second night he'd 'saved' her from a mysterious attacker, she 'just happened' to be out with a friend, who 'just happened' to be a private investigator … who then proceeded to take the whole issue off his hands — while emphatically cautioning him to keep out of it.

And tonight.

Sam had been dead against him snooping for information, only joining him at the last second. She was trying to talk him out of it even while he was already doing it. Come to think of it, he was sure he'd seen her on her phone. Could she have been texting Dimitri? Had they been interrupted deliberately before he could find evidence linking her to the situation?

And how much had she used that interruption to her advantage? Her idea for an 'alternative reason for being there' now seemed suspiciously well thought out. A quick text to Dimitri, telling him to come to the top floor, but to delay his entry to his office, an innocent excuse to give him an eyeful of her very distracting body … and there was the kiss.

Had she been trying to entice him as much as he had been her? If so, she succeeded beyond measure. He was so wild for her he hadn't trusted himself to go inside her home. His body still cried plaintively for hers now, and his libido urged him to end this train of thought before he lost all trust for her.

Alex couldn't stop though. Had Sam done it all on purpose? Was she trying to gain his trust, and then exploit the knowledge she garnered? He wouldn't put this past Dimitri. The old man was cutthroat, and keen to get his revenge on Alex's mother. Driving Alex out of business by any desperate means would be well within his repertoire. But why would Sam do it?

Money, of course. Dimitri would pay liberally for the information and even better for her services as a 'distraction'. A less screwed up man would be balls deep inside her right now, lost in the feel of her, the smell of her, and the taste of her, and certainly not worrying about what Dimitri was up to.

And she would need to be well paid to welcome his embrace. Her compliment this morning was a part of the ruse. He knew what he looked like. His only attractive feature was his wallet.

It all made sense. Alex hadn't been inside her house, but even from the outside it didn't seem to fit within her budget. He knew what he paid her. Sam shouldn't be destitute, but a house that size in that neighbourhood was a bit of a stretch. She had to have an alternative income.

And then there was this mysterious husband she didn't want to talk about. Had her slip earlier in the night been exactly that: a slip? Was he not supposed to know about him? Did it not fit with the uncomplicated image she was to present? Horror of horrors, was she perhaps even still married to him?

And where did Victoria fit in all this? Alex hadn't seen her in so long it was ludicrous to think it had been a coincidence. For one panicked moment, his mind considered one of the more restrictive custody conditions. He dismissed it though. It didn't fit with Dimitri's plan, and Victoria had never wanted custody anyway. The clause had been added purely to mess with him for as long as possible, and besides, it was barely relevant now Stacey was sixteen.

Was she just another distraction? Was Sam the honey, and Victoria the stick? Two women, who when combined made it impossible for him to think clearly. Dimitri had known Victoria for years. The unpleasant man had been a reluctantly accepted 'friend of the family' since before Alex was born. Clearly, the two fiends had kept in touch since the divorce. Why else would Victoria be at his party?

His ex-wife's involvement in his current troubles was almost a given. While he was sickened at the thought that she could become a part of his life again, even so peripherally, he knew logically she couldn't do much beyond play mind games, and so she wasn't the main focus of his thoughts.

Sam, on the other hand …

He was in love with her. He'd admitted it to himself earlier tonight, finally understanding why he would trust her with the details of his abusive marriage. How had this happened? And so quickly? His lack of complicity in the process left him feeling helpless.

Even without the suspicions now eating away at him, he didn't want to feel like this. He'd spent so many years feeling absolutely nothing for every woman he met, and then suddenly in the space of a few weeks he was completely head over heels for one. And worse, she was as overbearing as Victoria. No wonder he'd been attracted to her. Even years of domestic abuse hadn't elicited a change in his 'type'.

Had Sam planned it that way? Or was she the unwanted blessing she seemed?

The next morning, Alex leaned against the benchtop in his kitchen, sipping a coffee he hoped would be an adequate substitute for the sleep he missed last night. He hadn't managed to get into the office the last two weekends in a row, and his work was starting to get to alarming proportions. He planned to spend the whole day there today.

Because of this, he was determined to not think about Sam, Victoria or Dimitri. There was too much to do, and useless worry would only serve to hinder his productivity. As would daydreaming.

A knock at the front door interrupted his thoughts, but before he could answer it, Stacey skipped past him announcing she would get it.

Upon opening the door, she greeted whoever was there and excitedly told them she just had to get her shoes and bag. 'Come in,' she told their mystery visitor. 'Dad's in the kitchen.' Stacey breezed past him again, an unexpected look of delight and anticipation on her face.

Alex stood up straighter, half-suspecting it was the dishwasher from the party last week. Stacey was seeing her admirer today, but he'd thought it was scheduled for tonight, not this morning.

His heart jumped and his mind blanked when Sam walked into view, a bright smile on her face. As his brain moved into motion again, his first action was to scan her expression for artifice. Upon noting nothing but genuine pleasure to see him, his dominant emotion swiftly changed from suspicion to guilt. She couldn't be playing him. Could she?

Sam warmly greeted him while he reminded himself the two ladies had arranged to go shopping today. His daughter uncharacteristically wanted to buy new clothes, and Sam had offered to help. The other events of last Saturday evening had made him forget his secret happiness that Stacey had finally found a role model.

After his sleepless night, he was of two minds about them spending the time together. On the one hand, it was a relief to see the tentative changes in Stacey's confidence and happiness. On the other, if his distrust turned out to be valid, their growing closeness could blow up in his face.

After they left, he sat over his empty mug for a bit longer and thought about Sam. The only tangible thing he could think to do was hire a completely different private investigator to do a background check on her. If he could find out more information on her mysterious ex-husband, why she seemed to have more cash than she should, and rule out any links to Dimitri, he might be willing to trust her again.

Grimacing, he realised his resolution to not be distracted from work today was already broken. Not that it could be helped when one distraction showed up in his kitchen.

He was putting his empty mug in the dishwasher when there was another knock at the door. Sam and Stacey had only been gone a few of minutes, and he wondered if Stacey had perhaps forgotten her keys.

Opening the door, his world imploded for a second time in less than twenty-four hours. Victoria stood on his front step.

Chapter 17 – Her New Demands

Alex's ex-wife strolled through the doorway before he could think clearly enough to stop her. She proceeded towards the dining room, sending a questioning look over her shoulder at Alex in the process. 'Are you coming?' she asked, making no effort to acknowledge the confusion she caused.

Alex stood, dumbstruck, still holding on to the open door.

Victoria disappeared around the corner, and he heard her sit down in a chair. 'I'm waiting,' she called, irritation evident in her voice.

He thought furiously. What was she doing here? And more importantly, how could he get rid of her? He contemplated the open door and empty street, feeling a little of his old fear bubble to the surface. Leaving it open, he slowly made his way to the dining room. He took a deep, calming breath and walked around the corner.

Victoria had positioned herself so she could face him directly as he walked in. Sitting back in her chair, tapping her nails on the table, she looked relaxed but ready to pounce. As Alex came into view, a languid smile crossed her face. He saw her eyes travel across his T-shirt — it was pulled tight across his broad shoulders and muscular chest — and then down to where his pyjama pants hung loosely from his hips. 'You've been working out, Alex,' Victoria said, a hint of lust colouring her tone.

He ignored her comment, crossing his arms and standing against a wall. From here, he could watch her as well as the open front door. 'You're not welcome here,' Alex said, pleased he sounded decisive and there was no tremor in his voice. 'Leave.'

Her smile widened as she pushed a chair out for him with her foot. 'I'll go as soon as I get my money,' she said, waving a hand at the displaced chair to encourage him to sit.

Alex ignored the invitation, standing his ground, but couldn't hide his confusion at her pronouncement. 'Money? You already got your money. You got a good chunk of mine too, if I recall correctly,' he said.

Still smirking, Victoria continued to rake her eyes over his body, making him self-conscious. He felt vulnerable, shifting uncomfortably as he did his best to hide his alarm.

'I think it's time I got some more,' she countered, evidently not fazed by his refusal to sit.

He raised his eyebrows at this bold statement, wondering what she had up her sleeve. There was a time in his life where he would've done whatever she requested without even thinking about it, and an even more recent time where he'd have thrown cash at her just to get her out of his house.

Both of those periods were ancient history, he reminded himself. Her presence still caused him no end of stress, but she didn't have him by the balls anymore. She couldn't possibly think it was going to be as easy as asking for it, could she?

'Your new assistant is a pretty girl,' she said, shocking him with the subject change. 'What's she like in bed?' She watched him carefully as she spoke, possibly looking for a reaction.

He could practically smell the danger now. 'Why, Victoria,' he said mockingly, hiding his growing fear, 'I didn't realise you inclined that way. No wonder we didn't go the distance.'

The horrible woman ignored his facetious response, pressing for the information she really wanted. 'You are sleeping with her though, yes?' she asked. 'Dimitri was very … illustrative … when he described your indiscretion in his office. Quite frankly, I was surprised by your daring. I'd never found you all that adventurous.'

A notion for concern started to grow in his mind. It might never have occurred to him; except he'd already considered and dismissed it when trying to connect Victoria to his predicament last night. He didn't want to look at it head on, so he again dodged her question.

'What do you WANT, Victoria?' he demanded. 'I haven't heard a peep from you in eleven years, and suddenly you're in my dining room, trying to milk me for cash, and curious about my sex life? Get to the point, and then get out.'

Still smiling unpleasantly, Victoria reached into her bag and pulled out a document. She slid it across the table to him, and sat back, waiting for him to pick it up.

He considered it for a moment. Flicking his eyes towards the front door again, he confirmed it was still open. This allowed loud noises or screams to escape into the street, but it also permitted unrestricted access for other unwanted visitors. He hadn't seen anyone else enter yet, but he'd have to leave the door unattended if he were to pick up the document.

Moving swiftly, he snatched it and resumed his sentinel position. The whole process had taken less than two seconds. Victoria flinched at his sudden movement, a circumstance he took a certain amount of pleasure in. He would never stoop to his ex-wife's level, so she was completely safe, but he felt more confident knowing she viewed him as a threat.

After checking the door again, he looked down at the document. It was their custody agreement, opened to a specific page, with the paragraph she wanted him to read marked by a small sticky note.

Panic. Sheer, blind panic.

He forgot to keep checking the door, working furiously to get his emotions under control as quickly as possible. He didn't want Victoria to know how much of an upper hand she had right now.

'We're not in a relationship,' he said through a clenched jaw, still not looking up from the papers in his hand.

Victoria laughed, cruel amusement in her voice as she answered. 'I have two witnesses that can attest to your physical relationship, and I myself saw our daughter leave with her mere minutes ago. The agreement clearly states you are not to expose out daughter to anyone you are involved in a sexual or romantic relationship with, or I will assume full custody.'

He tried to calm himself enough to think clearly. She was technically right, but he and Sam weren't in a relationship. Victoria didn't have a leg to stand on. As soon as this got in front of a judge and the true nature of last night's encounter came to light, there would be no cause for alarm.

But … there were two problems with this. Possibly three.

First, if he and Sam admitted to their ruse, they were tacitly confessing to having a different reason for trespassing in Dimitri's office. Dimitri would waste no time very publicly suing him, probably twisting it to look like Alex was the one thieving information, and his reputation would be tarnished beyond measure. The business might never recover. Compared with losing custody of his daughter, it was a no-brainer, but that didn't mean it was an easy way out. He could afford the loss of income without blinking an eyelid, but he had to think of his employees.

The second problem, he could only admit because of his heightened state of panic. Alex genuinely wanted to be with Sam. They weren't in a relationship now, but enforcement of this clause effectively prevented him from doing anything about that.

And the third one … well, he didn't really want to face that possibility, but it couldn't be safely ignored. If his fears proved true, and Sam was a part of the master plan to screw him over, she'd probably lie. It would be his word against hers. And then he'd lose custody of his daughter, leaving her to the mercies of a mother who had never cared for her.

He followed that train of thought, asking before he'd properly thought through the implications. 'Why do you care?' he asked quietly. 'You haven't seen Stacey in eleven years. She was five the last time you had anything to do with her. And we both know you had almost as little to do with her first five years as you've had in the last eleven.'

This was the true conundrum. Victoria wanted a daughter like she wanted a roundhouse kick to the face. Her threat made no sense.

'Alex,' she began gently, almost kindly, 'I truly don't care. This is just business, my "job", if you will. It's how I make money, and I'm very, very good at it. I married you for your money, and I took some more with me when we divorced. I married Paul for his money, and I've just about finished spending that. He won't really have much to give me when I leave him, so I've come to get more from you.'

Sickened by her logic, he continued listening as she laid out his options.

'I'm not in the slightest bit interested in enforcing our custody agreement. It's just a bargaining chip. You can completely avoid this whole circus by just paying me. Or,' she continued, clearly enjoying her power games, 'if you're going to be silly about it, we can go to court, and I'll take Stacey. Then you can pay me child support instead. I won't get as much money that way, so it's not my preference, but it's your choice,' she finished with a smirk.

Defeated, Alex decided it was time to sit before his legs gave out. It didn't sound like Victoria's husband would be joining them anyway, so his door vigil was unimportant. She didn't have anything to gain by Paul's presence.

He sat carefully, choosing the seat as far from her as possible. 'How much?' he asked colourlessly.

He listened without emotion as she eagerly threw the numbers at him. She'd almost been reasonable, probably to make it less likely he would fight her. There was to be a partial payment now, and then the rest in six months, giving him time to liquidate a significant number of assets. He wasn't surprised to hear the down payment was almost exactly what he'd saved for the building renovations and staff expansion.

The corporate mole strikes again, he thought.

He rallied enough to play his Hail Mary card.

'I could tell them what you did,' he said quietly, forcing himself to look into her eyes.

He thought he saw a flicker of fear before she laughed, but he couldn't be sure. The laughter didn't sound faked, but you could never quite tell with Victoria.

'And you think anyone will believe you?' she asked, echoing his long-hidden fear.

There were three reasons he never told anyone what she did, never went to the police. The shame, the leverage, and because he'd been frightened he wouldn't be believed.

'It's my word against yours,' she continued. 'You have no evidence I was even in the house that night. As far as the rest of the world is concerned, I was four hours away. And you can bet money on the fact that when I tell it, I'll have been hiding from my "abusive husband".'

Alex's hands convulsed reflexively around the useless custody agreement. She'd do it. No question about it.

Victoria's smile widened as she got into the rhythm of her fabricated story. 'What judge is going to believe a mother didn't want anything to do with her child? In my sob story, you threatened me. I was so scared, so downtrodden, you were able to intimidate me into giving you full custody, throwing a lot of money at me to keep quiet. You've spent the last eleven years brainwashing our daughter and lying about me to anyone that will listen. I've even spent the last couple of years building up some credible trauma history with a therapist. Why would anyone believe you now? If it were true, why didn't you go to the police immediately after it happened? Sounds an awful lot like a desperate lie you've fabricated to get your own way again,' Victoria finished with a predatory grin.

Alex's mind raced. She was right. It would sound completely made up. He had no witnesses, no evidence it had ever happened. If Stacey hadn't … well, best not to dwell on that.

No one had ever questioned the timing of their separation, had ever suspected there was more to it than met the eye. Not even his therapist. To suddenly come out with this story all these years later would completely ruin his credibility, and he'd probably lose custody by default.

Victoria had won. Again.

He briefly considered running. There was no evidence of their meeting today, and their current custody agreement still held. She hadn't put any wheels in motion yet, and if she couldn't find him, it wouldn't be a possibility. He and Stacey could spend the next couple of years in hiding, until she turned eighteen. She'd have to drop out of school though. And he'd have to abandon his family and his business. *And Sam*, he thought with regret.

Was all that worth it, just for some money? Their whole lives, in exchange for a dollar figure? Sure, it stopped Victoria from getting what she wanted, and it kept Stacey with him, but was the sacrifice equal to the benefits?

Alex looked up at the hateful woman again, swallowed hard, and nodded.

Having gained what she wanted, Victoria was suddenly all business. She threw a card on the table and sashayed out of the room. 'My bank details,' she explained over her shoulder. 'I'll expect the initial payment within the week.'

Alex stayed at the table, listening to her leave his home. He felt hollow. With one short conversation, Victoria had managed to destabilise the life he'd spent eleven years building. His daughter, or his money. There was no choice really, but that didn't make it any easier.

Chapter 18 – Building a Backbone

Alex hadn't been home when Sam dropped Stacey off on Saturday afternoon, and he also hadn't answered her phone call a bit later. She'd left him a voicemail though, checking how he was feeling after Friday night's fiasco. He'd sent her a text a little while later indicating he was fine, but had a busy weekend ahead catching up on work and would speak to her Monday.

This seemed kind of dismissive, but she'd resolved not to test him. She understood why he was so hesitant to let her into his life now, and she was trying to give him the appropriate space to acclimatise to her presence.

Something was wrong though.

It was obvious from the moment she walked into his office on Monday morning. She couldn't put her finger on what exactly. Maybe it was just that he wouldn't meet her eyes, or that his smile seemed forced.

Walking to her own desk, Sam wondered now if she should've pushed. It was what she did best, after all. Had she left him alone so long he'd completely turned his back on the progress they'd made? Or was it her fault for not opening up about Logan? Alex had really put his trust in her on Friday night. She baulked against the idea of 'owing' him similar honesty, but she really did want him to know. Telling him was just a struggle. Anything to do with Logan was a struggle.

She'd been reminded of this on Friday night, shortly after Alex dropped her off. He hadn't accepted her invitation to come inside, and for some reason this left her feeling as fragile as she suspected he was. Maybe that was why he hadn't come in. He needed to be alone, where he felt safe.

Being alone didn't make her feel any safer. It just made her more aware of her loneliness. She'd burst into tears almost as soon as she walked in the door, completely overwhelmed by everything that'd happened that night. Her heart ached for Alex, but it also yearned for Logan. Alex's assumption she was divorced had pushed her guilty conscience to the limit.

She rarely spoke about her late husband. People never knew what to say to a widow her age, and she too often found herself changing the subject or making a joke. Treating his death so flippantly didn't sit well with her, so it was easier to just stay quiet.

If she was honest, this wasn't the reason she hadn't corrected Alex though. That night was her first kiss since her bereavement, and the depth of the emotions she felt during it scared her. She didn't feel comfortable sharing details about her life with Logan while she was that vulnerable.

It'd all happened so fast. She hadn't been ready to develop feelings for someone. The word 'love' kept vying for her attention, but she was diligently ignoring it. Alex had completely blindsided her. And it hadn't been until Friday night that she'd realised just how much.

On her hands and knees where she'd collapsed just inside the door, Sam had given into her self-pity and wept. Sobbing loudly and unselfconsciously, she'd stayed there until she was forced to run for the sink. Vomiting with the strength of her convulsions, she'd registered this was the first time she'd cried at all in weeks. A deep sense of shame had washed through her when she realised it was because she'd thought about Alex more than Logan.

Long since having emptied her stomach of its contents, she'd finally got herself under control enough to stop heaving. She was still crying, but not alarmingly so. After rinsing out her mouth, she'd stood up straight, taken a deep breath and closed her eyes.

She had stood like that for a long time, just being, drifting — the still night and her abiding sadness washing through her.

She'd floated for so long she eventually found her way back to Logan, willing him back to life there in her mind. His presence was so solid that she could feel him standing just behind her. He was poised to embrace her, to hold all her pieces together so she could break down safely within his protection.

Sam had rested in that moment, convinced he was a mere second away from touching her, until she could no longer kid herself. No amount of imagination, no matter how vivid, could bring back the dead.

A hollow, numb feeling had visited her periodically throughout the rest of the weekend. She'd avoided her father's call on Saturday morning (ostensibly to see how her night had gone, but more likely just an excuse to check up on her again) instinctively knowing she didn't have the energy to convince him she was okay. Because she was definitely not okay.

Her time with Stacey had been a brief, shining moment in the darkness. Whenever she was alone, she felt more alone than ever. She'd looked forward to work on Monday for more reasons than Alex's presence. Any company was welcome.

Well, except perhaps Tristan's.

Her annoying suitor spent an inordinate amount of time at her desk Monday morning, enthusiastically telling her about a party he'd attended on Saturday night. He kept hinting about a girl he'd picked up, no doubt waiting for Sam to show an interest so he could brag about his one-night stand. She knew he was trying to make her jealous, and the juvenile nature of the move irritated her.

She was nearing the end of her patience when Alex came to her rescue, asking her to come into his office.

Thank God, she thought, putting down the amethyst she'd been toying with. *This crystal is not blocking the negative energy hard enough.*

Relieved to be rid of her admirer and for the opportunity to check on Alex, Sam mustered an apologetic smile for Tristan and followed

Alex into his office. To her surprise, he shut the door. Her mind immediately pulled one of her favourite fantasies out of storage, but as he didn't turn to press her against the wall and kiss her passionately, she figured Monday morning sex on his desk probably wasn't on the agenda.

Ah well, Sam thought flippantly. *A girl can dream.*

Settling into the seat across from him, she consciously banished lustful thoughts for the remainder of this conversation. Alex had a look on his face she could only describe as 'crumpled'. Her concerns weren't unfounded. Something wasn't right.

'Alex, what's wrong? Is this about Friday night?' she inquired, voicing her concern before he could start talking.

Alex shook his head tiredly and waved his hand to dismiss the question. It didn't seem that it was meant to convey 'no', but rather to shelve her query so he could ask a question of his own. 'Sam, how much of the renovations are we locked into? If we stop now, how much money will we have spent?' he asked.

Taken aback, she took a moment to respond. 'Um, I'm not sure exactly on the amount. I'd need to check the contracts and have a better look at how far they've come,' she said, scrambling to get on board his train of thought. 'I think there are more materials getting delivered today, and there's not much point leaving them to collect dust, so it wouldn't be an ideal stopping point.'

Alex sat back in his chair, chewing his bottom lip. He seemed almost as agitated as he had on Friday night, and she was seriously concerned the question didn't seem hypothetical.

'Alex,' Sam said hesitantly, 'you're not really putting a halt to it, are you? It's already happening. The staff know about it. I mean, technically you could stop it, I guess, but why? I thought you were looking forward to it as much as everyone else.'

Alex hadn't looked at her during that speech, but at the end he sat forward to lean on his desk, staring right into her eyes. Whatever he saw there, he didn't want to keep looking, as he almost immediately sat back again, this time looking up at the ceiling. When he spoke, he did so with a strain in his voice. 'Something has happened,' he whispered. 'I need the money.'

Sam waited him out when he stopped talking, sure he was just trying to find the words to explain. When nothing was forthcoming, she spoke up. 'What's happened?' she asked, as gently as she could muster.

She was trying to not take his sudden change of heart personally. It was difficult though. It had been her idea in the first place, and she had put quite a lot of work into it. Still holding out hope he could be talked around, she waited impatiently for him to explain.

Realisation hit her like a punch in the face when he finally looked at her again and she saw the unshed tears in his eyes. 'Victoria,' she whispered, and Alex nodded, looking down at his hands. 'What did she do?' asked Sam. He didn't respond, and she tried to reign in her temper. Her anger wasn't meant for Alex, but if she misspoke, he might get the wrong idea. 'Alex, please,' she said, not able to keep the strain from her voice. 'After everything you told me about her, I'm not surprised she was able to pull something. I respect your right to make the decision, and I understand it's not what you would choose if you had a viable alternative, but I need to know why.' Sam realised she was leaning forward, her shoulders hunched against her disappointment, and deliberately sat back and untensed her muscles. 'I know it's none of my business,' she finished lamely, 'but I worked so hard on this, and I'm going to get questions from the other staff. I just want to understand.'

Alex met her eyes again and she saw the struggle on his face. When he answered, it was to explain his hesitation at telling her. 'I don't think knowing will make it any better,' he explained. 'It might make it worse.'

She looked at him steadily, her heart softening at the knowledge he was trying to protect her, but she was still determined to make him talk. 'I'm a big girl, Alex,' she said. 'Try me.'

He exhaled, defeated, and began to explain. 'Victoria came to see me on Saturday,' he said tiredly. 'She reminded me about a clause in our custody agreement that prevents me from being in a relationship while Stacey is still a minor. Under the agreement, if I enter into a sexual or romantic liaison with Stacey's knowledge or allow the other party to be involved in her life, Victoria automatically gets custody.'

Confused, Sam spoke up. 'But you're not in a relationship? Why would that be an issue?'

This was the question he'd really been avoiding. She could tell.

'She is under the impression that you and I are involved. Dimitri wasn't quiet about our ... well, about when he caught us in his office on Friday night. You and Stacey have been getting to know each other quite well lately, so ...' He shrugged.

Horrified, Sam sat rigid in her seat for a moment before responding. 'It's my fault,' she whispered.

'No!' said Alex forcefully. 'Absolutely not. You had no idea it would be an issue. We had a problem and you solved it, end of story. I should have thought it through. It's my fault, not yours.'

Only listening peripherally, Sam's mind raced as she tried to work through the repercussions. She voiced her confusion, unsure why Alex hadn't already refuted the evidence. 'But we're not involved. You and I can both attest to that. There is a plausible explanation for what Dimitri saw Friday night,' she protested.

'At which point, Dimitri will immediately sue,' said Alex tiredly, 'dragging my name and the company name through the mud. We'll lose money to him, and we'll lose even more business than we've already lost. I wouldn't be surprised if we went under.'

Sam thought furiously, trying to come up with a way out of this. Now she knew the problem, she was in her element. Playing devil's advocate came naturally to her, and if she poked enough holes, she could usually start a leak.

'Wait,' she said, frowning. 'How does the money come into this? I mean,' she said, abashed at her insensitivity, 'I don't want to lose sight of the more serious problem, but I don't get where that fits in?'

Alex had been nodding along. He had been lost on that part until Victoria explained it to him too. 'I have three options,' he explained.

'Well, two that Victoria knows about. She genuinely thinks there's something going on between us, so she doesn't know we have the option of disproving her claims. As far as she's concerned, either I give her that money and a whole lot more in six months, or she can take my daughter and get a decent chunk via child support.'

Sam finally understood Alex's position, but she wasn't as accepting as he seemed to be. 'Hang on, isn't Victoria married? Why don't these funky custody rules apply to her?' she asked.

'It's called a "morality clause",' explained Alex. 'It doesn't apply to married couples. And she's planning to leave him, anyway.'

That information presented an interesting solution to their predicament, but she didn't think Alex would go for it. The fleeting image of him waiting for her at the end of an aisle made Sam feel a little queasy too. Much too soon for that kind of serious.

She looked at Alex properly for the first time since the start of their conversation and realised he'd already accepted defeat. This was what that woman had done to him. Even with this much time and space from her, he couldn't see past the cages she created for him.

Not on her watch.

'Okay,' Sam began insistently, 'it's time to snap out of it.'

Alex's head whipped up, confused.

'Victoria has presented you with two options. You've already realised she doesn't get to limit you like that by coming up with a third. I'll admit it — that one is also pretty crappy. But you're on the right track. If she's only built two doors, let's open some windows,' she said decisively.

Alex looked intrigued, but not quite convinced.

Old habits die hard, thought Sam.

'I think you should call your lawyer,' she suggested. 'Actually, maybe you should call a different lawyer. One that doesn't let ridiculous clauses get signed into custody agreements.'

Alex actually smiled a little at this, and she took it as a good sign.

'I already have a different lawyer. The one I had during the divorce retired years ago. The firm assigned me a new one after he left,' he said absentmindedly. He looked to be seriously considering what Sam was suggesting.

Her offhand comment about his previous lawyer had given her a more tangible glimmer of hope though. 'Alex,' she said excitedly, 'how set in stone is a custody agreement from that long ago? Stacey is much older now. Isn't it time it was revised? If you can get a new one, you can have that condition removed.'

Alex looked thoughtful at this suggestion, frowning as he chewed his lip. 'It's got some merit,' he admitted, 'but if we're revising the custody agreement, Victoria can try for alterations of her own.'

Sam shrugged. 'Then you're no worse off than you are now. If it's looking like she'll get custody, we've got time to think of something else. And worst-case scenario, you just pay her the money and she'll go away, right? At least you'll have tried. And possibly dragged it out long enough that Stacey will almost be an adult,' she pointed out.

Alex stood up and began pacing while he considered her suggestion. Even merely considering defying his horrible ex-wife had put some life into him, and she was excited to see it. Sam stood too, leaning against his desk, waiting for him to make a decision.

After a few laps he stopped, facing her and grinning. 'She might actually have given me some info we can use to our advantage,' he said. 'The reason she's trying to leverage me for cash is because Paul's money is starting to dry up. If Victoria realises there's going to be a fight involved, she might start to baulk at the lawyer bill.'

Relieved he had stopped thinking so negatively, Sam reached out and hugged him without thinking. Alex hugged her back tightly. The feel of their bodies pressing together evoked strong memories of their kiss Friday night. She felt herself respond to his presence, a tingling of electricity on her skin. Alex loosened his hold slightly, smoothing one hand down her hair and making her shiver.

Sam pulled back a little and looked up at him. He was looking at her too, his lips parted slightly, his eyes locked into hers. She breathed slowly, in no hurry to end the spell of the moment with a sudden movement. Alex's gaze moved down to her mouth, and she thought she saw him tilt his head down, just a fraction.

A knock at the door was all it took for him to let her go and smoothly step away.

Chapter 19 – Legal Advice

Alex sat in the waiting room of his lawyer's office, his heart full to the brim with hope. He had Sam to thank for his optimism. Without her suggestion, he never would have considered changing the custody agreement. It was funny how he'd come so close to this idea during his conversation with Victoria, but not quite made the connection. Yes, she could still tell her lies about him, but she didn't have any way of backing that up any more than he did. If anything, his therapist history went back way further than her fabricated one. And he had plenty of witnesses to her more public failings.

He was seriously considering using what she'd done to him against her. Being on the receiving end of her manipulations again had finally convinced him of what his therapist had been telling him all these years: it wasn't his fault. None of this was his fault. The fact that he fell in love with her, that he fell prey to her schemes to lock him down and isolate him, that he hadn't stopped her from hurting and humiliating him, that he hadn't left … none of it was his fault. He hadn't deserved it. It wasn't a punishment for being gullible. It was evidence of his own human nature.

His ability to love and trust weren't personality failings he needed to be ashamed of. He couldn't believe it had taken him so long to truly accept that. He'd known for years what Victoria had done to him was wrong. He just hadn't appreciated how it had warped his thinking. It wasn't just that she'd abused his love and trust. She'd instilled in him an unconscious belief that these were weak traits, meant to be exploited by whomever he was crazy enough to bestow his faith in.

This revelation had come to him while he paced in his office, Sam watching as he thought furiously. He'd felt the last walls around his heart start to crumble as she hugged him, stroking her hair without thinking, delighted when she shivered in response. If Dave hadn't knocked on the door, he would've kissed her then and there.

As it stood, he was glad he hadn't. His newfound emotional health was precarious at best, and he wasn't sure he could handle rejection. Hopefully, her tactile response was evidence she enjoyed his touch, but he couldn't be sure.

There was still the matter of the information leak, after all.

He'd convinced himself that Sam was guilty until she'd persuaded him to put up a fight. He was less inclined to think she was involved now; however, he still held back from total absolution. There was no way to know for sure that Dimitri and Victoria were in on the same plan. Their simultaneous attacks could be coincidence, so Sam's steadfast opposition of Victoria's plan didn't rule her out as Dimitri's accomplice.

He had high hopes though.

He was eventually shown to an office to meet with his lawyer, a likeable man named Michael, who had a reputation for exploiting every loophole. He was exactly what Alex needed when dealing with Victoria.

'So, what can I do for you today, Alex?' Michael asked, after the obligatory pleasantries were out of the way.

Alex had thought long and hard about how much to tell this man, ultimately deciding to trust him to do his job. He was going to tell him everything. Even the thing he hadn't told his therapist. If Michael thought it was usable and that meant Alex had to go public, so be it. Stacey was worth it.

He started simply, telling Michael about the conditions in the custody agreement he wanted to change.

'A morality clause,' mused Michael. 'Not unheard of, but unusual.

Have you spoken to your ex-wife about removing it? Even if she objects, we've got a decent shot at getting it eliminated. Your daughter is older now, and custody agreements usually have provision to be changed as the needs of the child change.'

Alex took a deep breath before responding. This was where it was going to get tricky. 'Actually, no, I haven't spoken to her about it ... not exactly, anyway. But she is indisputably going to object. And this is probably going to be a lot more complicated than you're expecting. It's a long story,' he finished.

Looking intrigued, Michael motioned for him to continue.

Alex launched into the tale before he could chicken out. 'My divorce and custody agreements were made when I was in a state of total desperation. My ex-wife was abusive. Not to Stacey,' he hastened to add, 'to me. I agreed to pretty much whatever Victoria suggested, just to get her out of my life.

'As a result, she was paid a lot of money, and she was able to add this clause and a lot of other stupid ones. There's stuff about how Stacey was to be raised, educated, and disciplined, restrictions to her time spent with my family ... you name it. If she could hinder my life in any way, she did it. I didn't care. She gave up custody and visitation rights, and that meant we were free of her.'

Having admitted to the abuse, and to the dog's breakfast of a custody agreement, Alex found himself gaining steam. He continued his story without prompting from Michael, who was busy taking notes. 'I've honestly ignored a lot of the conditions. Victoria never checked up on us, and even if she had, she's never wanted custody because she didn't want a child in the first place. She might have taken me to court if she felt like making a scene, but it would be to enforce compliance, not to sue for custody.

'The morality clause has been a complete non-issue. After my train wreck of a marriage, I never wanted to get involved with anyone. I wasn't avoiding it because of the clause, it was just an unnecessary restriction.' He hadn't finished talking, but Michael interjected anyway.

'If it's not necessary to remove it, are you sure you want to go to this kind of trouble? Your daughter will be an adult in a couple of short years. It won't be long before it's all in the past anyway,' he pointed out.

'Victoria has made it necessary,' he said, before telling Michael what had transpired since Friday night, including the lies Victoria planned to tell, and the story of his staged romantic encounter with Sam. 'So now, Victoria's trying to blackmail me. I suspect Dimitri is in her pocket, so even if I prove there's nothing going on between Sam and I, I open myself up to his attack.

'To be honest, I was all set to pay until Sam suggested I challenge the custody condition. And I'm still not even sure I want to do it. Once we open it up for discussion, there's a possibility she will be able to carry out her threat to take Stacey anyway,' he finished, a desperate note in his voice.

'All right,' began Michael, making another note. 'I can see why you'd have concerns, but we've definitely got something to work with here. Let's build you a hypothetical case. We want the non-visitation to continue, but the restrictive clauses in your custody agreement to be terminated. I don't foresee a lot of problems with that, as it's an odd combination in the first place. Voluntarily giving up custody and visitation is done so the estranged parent doesn't have to pay child support. It makes no sense she'd be allowed to direct Stacey's life. Why would she be involved in decision-making while having nothing to do with her? We could aim for the non-visitation to continue, with the more traditional "compensation" of her not paying child support.'

Alex nodded slowly. It was a good idea in theory, but there were some glaring holes to shore up.

'The problem is,' Michael continued, 'Victoria won't just be aiming to enforce the current conditions. She'll be out for custody. Visitation doesn't get her any money — in fact, it'll probably end up costing her in child support payments. That'd be her worst nightmare.' He tilted his head thoughtfully. 'Under normal circumstances, I'd say it would be unlikely a judge would award custody to her after having nothing to do with Stacey for so long. Visitation, maybe, but custody? They need to put the best interests of the child first. Taking her out of a loving and supportive home because of the whims of an estranged parent doesn't speak to that.'

Alex was feeling more positive as he listened to Michael extrapolate. The breadth of his experience was evident in his understanding of the stakes, and he had adapted to Victoria's less than humane motives with ease. He also hadn't batted an eyelid when Alex had mentioned the abuse, which had been a real relief. If the lawyer had displayed any doubt, derision, or pity, they probably wouldn't have come this far.

Michael summarised their difficulties succinctly. 'The problem is, she'll do her best to convince the judge that: a) her parental rights were violated via intimidation when the initial custody agreement was made, and b) Stacey is not in a loving and supportive home. She is in the home of a manipulative liar who abused her and has brainwashed her daughter.'

In full agreement with this summary, Alex nodded.

'So, we have two jobs. We have to convince the judge that you're a fit parent, and your ex-wife is a liar. A lot of this hinges on if we can prove the abuse. I know it won't be an easy subject to talk about, but do you mind if I ask a few questions?' Michael requested.

Alex nodded again, bracing himself. He had expected this, but he hadn't been looking forward to it.

'Can you please specify for me exactly what the abuse entailed?' asked Michael.

Alex began to speak while Michael wrote, detailing the mind games first. After listing all the habitual emotional cruelty, he moved onto the physical. He talked about the smaller things first: the slaps, pinches and kicks, the small objects thrown at him to indicate her derision. Working his way up to the bigger things, he noticed he was staring at the carpet instead of meeting Michael's eyes. With effort, he looked up. 'She threw knives at me sometimes. I got a few cuts, nothing serious enough for medical attention, mostly just because she happened to be holding one when she was angry. She punched me a few times too, but not often. I think it hurt her hand to do it hard enough to harm me meaningfully.' Alex took a deep breath, steeling himself against the memories that threatened to overwhelm him.

'The worst was when she would hit me with things or trip me up. The fireplace poker was her weapon of choice until she did it one day while it was still hot. I had a really hard time trying to lie about the burns to the emergency room doctor. I think it scared her away from using it again. Tripping and pushing me was also on the agenda. In front of the staircase especially. I lost count of how many times I fell down those stairs. I still grit my teeth now when people are walking behind me on a staircase.' Alex hesitated now, on the verge of telling the story he'd never told anyone else. He trusted Michael's strict adherence to client confidentiality, or he wouldn't even be considering it. It would still be up to himself if this information were used, but at least he'd have some solid advice before he did it.

He opened his mouth to confess, but Michael got there first. 'Is any of the abuse documented?' he asked. 'Did you go to the police, a counsellor, or tell the doctors anything?'

The moment was lost, and he chickened out. 'No,' he answered, 'I didn't tell anyone. She's half the size of me. I didn't think anyone would believe me. And I ... was afraid of her,' he finished with difficulty. 'I don't even tell anyone now,' he added, wanting to be sure Michael understood the precarious nature of this confession. 'Other than my therapist, you're the first person I've told about the physical abuse. I told Sam on Friday about the emotional stuff, and my family witnessed bits and pieces, but I mostly keep it to myself.'

Michael nodded and reassured him. 'I can appreciate that. Abuse comes in all shapes and sizes, and it can be difficult even for the physically *less* intimidating partner to be heard. It's unfortunate, but not uncommon for a man in your situation to feel his credibility is threatened. Now, while I understand you didn't tell anyone specifically what was happening, can I confirm if there was more than the one trip you mentioned to the emergency room?'

Alex confirmed that yes, there were many trips.

'Okay, so that means there are medical records we can access that will lend credibility to your story. If we're lucky, an observant doctor might even have recorded something suspicious. You also mentioned a therapist? At what point did you begin therapy?' Michael asked.

'Right around the time we broke up,' said Alex, getting nervous again now he was approaching his biggest secret. 'I was hospitalised after an attempted suicide, and my family insisted.'

Michael nodded, writing furiously for a moment.

Alex firmly closed his mouth, unsure how to do that subject justice.

'Were your mental health issues a direct result of your wife's abuse?' Michael asked.

'Yes,' agreed Alex, not commenting further.

'And Stacey? Does she also see a therapist?' said Michael.

'Yes,' he answered. 'She's been seeing a therapist for as long as I have. I wasn't sure how much she'd remember, as she only just turned five when it ended, but I wanted to mitigate the abandonment she might feel. Growing up without a mother was tough, even without the memories of Victoria ignoring her.'

Michael looked interested at this information, pausing his furious scribbling. 'Victoria ignored her? You mentioned there was no child abuse, but it's important to note that withholding love and support does fall in that category. Incidentally, so does allowing the child to witness the emotional or physical abuse of another. Was she ever present when Victoria was abusing you?' he asked.

Alex was floored. He'd always had a very frank dialogue with Stacey's therapist. He had been quite open when the sessions started (if a little vague on the specifics), about what Stacey might have witnessed, but the words 'child abuse' had never been mentioned by either him or the therapist.

Michael was looking at him questioningly and Alex realised he had been silent in his shock for a little longer than was polite.

'Sorry,' Alex apologised, 'I hadn't considered it constituted child abuse. Yes, she was around for a lot of this. I don't think she remembers any of it though. She was very young.'

Michael shook his head and explained. 'You'd be surprised what a five-year-old is capable of remembering. Some people can remember incidents as young as three. It also doesn't matter what age she was, anyway. Children are always learning. Even if they don't remember the specifics of an incident, they will learn something from it — consequences, behaviours, etc.' He paused to scribble on his notepad again. 'As distasteful as it is to say, that might be a big help in our case. I wouldn't normally suggest this, as I believe it's important for parents to work together to raise a child, but your circumstances constitute a different approach. Victoria doesn't have Stacey's best interests at heart. I think we should file to have her parental rights terminated,' Michael said seriously.

Alex listened as his lawyer voiced some realistic predictions about what he would be in for if he went ahead. The motion would need to be filed before Victoria could go ahead with her threats, which meant they needed to submit it to the court before her one-week payment deadline was up. He didn't have long to consider his choices, but he was still pleased to be doing something other than blindly following the instructions of his hated ex-wife.

Chapter 20 – Some Hard Truths

Sam sat at Alex's dining table, a bit nervous if truth be told, waiting for him to start the real conversation. He'd invited her over for dinner so she could be present for moral support when he talked to Stacey about their dilemma. Alex hadn't specified who's support, but Sam privately hoped her presence would be helpful to them both.

Earlier that day, they'd debated the merits of keeping Stacey in the dark, ultimately concluding there were more reasons for enlightening her than not. He was still apprehensive about upsetting her though. Sam suspected he was procrastinating.

Alex had relayed his lawyer's suggestions, and she was excited things were taking shape. He wasn't quite ready to give his lawyer the 'go ahead' just yet though. With any luck, Stacey's reaction would tip the balance in favour of action.

They technically had nothing to lose. There were three possible outcomes:

1. They could get exactly what they wanted.
2. Victoria could be awarded visitation rights (which she would never exercise, as it had no benefit for her and would likely cost her money).
3. Victoria could win, in which case he could pay the money and be done with it anyway.

They both agreed that option three wasn't particularly appealing, but it was better than doing it without having tried to beat her first.

Alex still seemed apprehensive though. Convinced it was a carryover from the abuse he'd endured, Sam tried to be understanding.

She'd been flattered when he asked her to be here tonight. She and Stacey had become quite close in the short space of time since they met. The young girl was excessively grateful for Sam's loaned clothing, and they had quickly bonded over a mutual respect for each other's different fashion tastes. They didn't agree on much, but Stacey seemed delighted to have her support and encouragement all the same. Sam got the impression she'd needed to be quite defensive about her preference for 'alternative' fashion prior to this.

They had spent most of Saturday together, shopping and going for a late lunch. Stacey had shared her nervousness about her date that night, and Sam had been understanding and reassuring. Stacey's follow-up call had been the highlight of her otherwise deeply depressing Sunday. Her excitement as she told Sam about how he'd kissed her had momentarily brought back the butterflies Sam felt when kissing Alex.

As they finished their dinner, Alex evidently decided it was time. He cleared his throat and began to speak, Sam smiling at him encouragingly. 'Stacey,' he began, 'something has happened that you need to know about.'

Stacey shot Sam a curiously hopeful look before turning her attention back to her father.

He took her hand and stroked it as he spoke. 'On Friday night I ran into your mother,' he said gently.

Stacey didn't respond, other than a shocked widening of her eyes. Sam was unsure if Alex had expected her to, as he kept talking without much of a pause.

'We only spoke briefly at that point,' he continued. 'I wouldn't have mentioned it if I didn't need to, but on Saturday after you left to go shopping, she showed up here.'

He briefly outlined what she wanted and what she was willing to do to get it, omitting any reference to the morality clause in their custody agreement or to his and Sam's related incident Friday night. 'So basically,' he finished, 'she's blackmailing me.'

The look of fear on Stacey's face had gradually magnified as the story went on, so Sam put her arm around her and spoke reassuringly. 'Your dad won't let her take you,' she said.

'You don't need to worry about that,' Alex hastened to add. 'If it comes to it, I'll give her every cent I have to keep you with me.'

Stacey nodded, seeming somewhat comforted. Sam was pleased at the evidence of her spirit when she finally spoke up.

'But then she wins. Isn't blackmail illegal?' she asked. 'Can't we get her in trouble for that?'

Alex waved an indecisive hand in the air, failing to hide the look of hopelessness that crossed his face. 'If we had any evidence of it, I'd go straight to the police. She's not stupid though, so I doubt she'll make that kind of slip,' he confirmed.

Sam looked at Alex over Stacey's head and nodded encouragingly, giving him a pointed look. Stacey had already showed she was keen to fight her estranged mother. It was time to bring her into the fold.

'I'm also not keen on just giving into her,' he admitted.

Stacey looked up with an expression of hope, and this seemingly encouraged him to keep talking.

'I went to see my lawyer this morning,' he said. 'He thinks we have grounds to petition for changes to the custody agreement. Specifically, he thinks we should file to terminate your mother's parental rights.'

Stacey perked up considerably at this news. 'Would that mean that "technically" she's not even my mother?' she asked. 'Where do I sign?'

Sam almost giggled at Stacey's cheek, only holding herself in check for Alex's sake.

'I honestly have no idea,' he was saying, 'but it would mean she wouldn't have any right to see you or make decisions about your life.'

'Sounds like a great plan to me,' said Stacey enthusiastically. 'Let's do it that way.'

Even Alex smiled at this. 'It's not quite that simple,' he began. He outlined the lies Victoria planned to tell, and how this could sway the judge if she was convincing. 'But if it gets to that, I'll just pay her the money,' he hastened to add. 'I still won't let her take you.'

Stacey glanced at Sam before looking back at Alex. 'Dad …' She hesitated, flicking another nervous look at Sam. 'I know you don't really talk about how … I mean … what she was like to you, but can't we tell the judge about it? If she's going to say you did those things when really, she was the one who … I mean, couldn't we just tell the truth?'

Astonishment flooded Alex's face. Sam started to think she was comforting the wrong person. Victoria had made no effort to hide her cruelty from Stacey, but Alex had been adamant she was too young to remember.

'Stacey,' he said with difficulty, 'how much do you remember about life with your mother?'

Stacey again looked nervously at Sam before turning her eyes back to her dad. Sam realised that Stacey was trying to protect Alex. She felt a rush of love for this kind-hearted young girl, and a flood of bitterness towards Victoria. That woman was responsible for the pain of two people she cared for fiercely. She hoped the bitch would pay dearly for it.

Alex must have also realised Stacey's predicament, as he hastened to reassure her that she could speak freely, looking troubled as he did so.

Stacey began to cry in earnest, held by Sam on one side and her father on the other, as she recounted what she knew. 'I remember all the shouting,' she said. 'She was always shouting at us. And the stairs. I remember you falling down the stairs lots. And … I remember calling the ambulance.' Stacey's crying intensified at this.

It was too much for Sam to bear, especially when she noticed Alex was also crying. Tears formed in her eyes too and began to fall. She admonished herself for the indulgence. She was here for moral support, not to pander to her own emotions.

Spying a box of tissues in the adjacent kitchen, she briefly pressed a kiss to Stacey's head before collecting them and depositing them on the table. The practical move had calmed her. She took one before smoothing Stacey's hair, rubbing Alex's hand, and encouraging them both to avail themselves too.

Alex took matters a step further. He encouraged his daughter away from the table and pulled her into his lap on the couch, where she promptly buried her face in his neck. She was almost too tall to fit, and Sam was pathetically glad that Stacey hadn't inherited her father's height.

Sam followed with the tissues, ignoring the proprieties of personal space as she held one of Stacey's hands and sat close by, her leg pressed against Alex's.

He had stopped crying and was occupied with rocking Stacey while he murmured encouragements to her. 'It's all right, my baby girl,' he whispered, 'it's all right. You did so well. I'm okay, and she can't hurt me anymore. I was so proud, you did exactly what I taught you. You were so brave.'

Sam had suspected Alex omitted something from his abuse story. She hadn't questioned when she listened originally, but she'd later reflected that from what he described, it was only a small step to more serious injuries. She wondered what had happened that necessitated an ambulance, her eyes lingering on Alex's scar.

Stacey eventually cried herself out and slid off Alex's lap. Sam moved over so Stacey could sit between them.

'I'm sorry,' said Alex hopelessly. 'I'm so sorry. I didn't know you remembered so much, or I wouldn't have brought it up. I should have just paid the money and left you in peace.'

Stacey frowned at this, but it was Sam who answered him. 'I think it's good you're both talking about it, actually,' she said, smoothing Stacey's disarrayed hair. 'It's cathartic, after keeping it inside for all these years.'

Stacey nodded emphatically as she wiped her eyes and blew her nose. 'You had to tell me, Dad,' she said. 'We can't give in to her, and I can't tell the court what it was like living with her if you hadn't told me that you were fighting her again.'

Alex's eyes bugged at this. 'Stacey, you're not testifying,' he said worriedly. 'That's not why I told you what's going on. I just don't think I can go to court and keep it from you.'

Stacey rounded on him, angry, and opened her mouth — no doubt to protest.

Alex frowned and forestalled her. 'It was never an option,' he said sternly. 'I won't discuss it with you tonight while you're still upset, but we can argue about it another night if it means so much to you.'

Clearly not mollified, but momentarily forestalled, Stacey sat back on the seat, an indecipherable expression on her face. Alex just looked tired — not like he needed to sleep, more like he needed to lock himself in a room for a hundred years, shut off from the world.

'I didn't know there was a custody agreement,' said Stacey abruptly. 'Can I read it?'

Alex seemed surprised, but he agreed and went to retrieve it. Sam looked over at Stacey and realised how delicate the young girl was still feeling. She held out her arms and Stacey just about threw herself into them. Sam closed her eyes and laid her cheek on Stacey's hair, holding her to her chest and rubbing her back. It was moments like these that really made her yearn for a child of her own. Or better yet, that she was the mother of this fragile, abandoned little girl.

When she opened her eyes, Alex was poised in the doorway, watching them with an unreadable expression. Stacey and Sam broke their embrace as he joined them on the couch again, handing over the document to his daughter. After reassuring them both she was fine alone for the moment (and making Sam promise to see her before she left), Stacey went upstairs to read in privacy.

Sam took Alex's hand as Stacey left the room and voiced her concern. 'Are you all right?' she asked him quietly.

Alex looked over at her for a long moment before resettling his position on the couch so they both faced inwards, their knees touching. Propping his head in his free hand, he proceeded to ignore her question. 'You would make an excellent mother,' he said, catching her completely off guard.

Because it'd already been such an emotional night, because she hadn't been expecting it, and because she'd just been wishing for that very circumstance, Sam reacted before she had a chance to put the walls up again. Tears rolled down her face unchecked, and she sobbed as quietly as she could so as not to disturb Stacey.

Alarm painting his face, Alex reached for her …

… and it wasn't so bad. She still ached for the life she'd missed out on and the husband she'd thought to share it with, but Alex's presence helped. The crushing loneliness that had her convulsing and vomiting the other night was mitigated by the warm chest her tears spilled onto, and the solid arms around her. When she felt strong enough to loosen her grip, she readjusted herself so she could continue to shelter in Alex's arms without having to lean so far forward.

As she wiped her eyes with another tissue, she apologised. 'I'm so sorry,' she said. 'It's not the night to be indulging my own issues.'

Alex took her hand and raised it to his mouth. He kissed it and then turned it over to kiss inside her palm. Touched by the unfeigned tenderness of the gesture, Sam smiled for him.

'Tell me,' he invited simply.

And she did.

'I can't have children,' she explained. 'My husband and I tried for ages, but it wasn't meant to be.' She paused, before accepting that it was time. 'He died three years ago,' she said. 'I know it's probably better a child didn't have to go through that, but there's this part of me that wishes …' she trailed off, knowing the sentence didn't really need to be finished anyway.

'I'm so sorry,' whispered Alex.

They sat like that for hours, hands entwined and heads together, talking about their pasts. Her happy marriage and tragic childlessness, and his disastrous marriage and love for Stacey.

She told him about life with Logan. The trips together, the laughter-filled house they built (which his life insurance had allowed her to keep), the quiet nights enjoying the summer breeze in their yard, how he proposed and their wedding day, her joy at greeting him every night after work, his goofy sense of humour ... anything she could think of.

And she told him about the bad times too. Their rare arguments, the time he lost his job and they were broke, their sorrow at not being able to conceive, and the accident that had taken him from her. She cried again at that, and Alex comforted her.

He told her about his happy memories too. Stacey's ability to make him smile even on his darkest days, the support of his family, starting his business, and his sheer and utter relief when Victoria was no longer a part of his life.

They also talked about his darker memories. The incidents where he had ended up in hospital, the fear and distrust of women that kept him from finding love again, and his sorrow that Victoria was still able to cause so much pain.

'There's more,' he said cautiously. 'To the story of what happened with Victoria, I mean. Stacey started to talk about it, but I don't think I'm ready to face it all just yet. I'd really like to tell you someday though,' he added.

Sam nodded. 'Whenever you're ready,' she told him.

She got up to leave shortly after that, first keeping her promise to Stacey. The young girl had fallen asleep still clothed, lying across the covers. Sam woke her up and put her to bed properly, kissing her forehead goodnight.

She hadn't once thought about kissing Alex tonight, but felt closer to him for having shared so much. Hopefully, it was only a matter of time before they came together. Tonight had confirmed she'd been right to not rush that. She was at peace now, having brought Logan into her present, but somehow also having left him in her past.

She slept better that night than she had in years.

Chapter 21 – An Unexpected Betrayal

Sam smiled politely as Tristan hinted again that she should visit him in the new wing when he was working late tonight. His team had become insufferably smug since they moved, especially since it had been confirmed that the rest of the renovations were being put on hold. The staff were curious about the turn of events but had been surprisingly accepting for most part. Clarice had tried to dig for the reason why, of course, but Sam had been firm in her rebuff.

While they were disappointed, there was many a muttered comment that at least they didn't have to put up with the PD team underfoot anymore. Alex had agreed it didn't make any sense to waste the materials that were already ordered and paid for. Subsequently, the new wing had been completed after all.

This (and the other works already completed) alleviated many of their problems. They now had heating, cooling, carparking and bathrooms adequate to their needs, as well as room to spread out and hire some desperately needed new staff. The new salesperson and receptionist in particular had been welcomed with pathetic enthusiasm.

Tristan still visited the main office with maddening regularity. He greeted a few people but spent most of his time at Sam's desk, and at Rebecca's to a lesser extent. Clarice had spoken to Rebecca about him again, but the younger woman seemed inclined to ignore her advice.

Rumour had it they were hooking up now. Evidently, Tristan was trying to keep it casual. His amorous attempts at Sam also seemed to be getting bolder. He appeared to be under the impression she didn't realise he was flirting. It'd obviously not occurred to him that she just wasn't interested.

What I wouldn't give to have the confidence of a good-looking, well-hung idiot, thought Sam, as he prattled on.

Alex interrupted them so often that Sam suspected it was on purpose. She appreciated his concern, but Tristan had also picked up on it. Annoyingly, he mostly came over now when Alex was out of the office or otherwise occupied. This seriously reduced her own list of reasons to cut their chats short. She'd even found herself *relieved* when a phone call from her mother had chased him off once.

Her admirer needed to be shut down soon, and it was going to be so much harder now she'd let him go on for so long. Perhaps she should mention his tryst with Rebecca. If she said it right, she could send him packing and mollify her single-minded co-worker at the same time.

Rebecca had taken to ignoring her 'rival', reportedly making snide comments about Sam to anyone that would listen. She also kept shooting evil-eyed glances across the room whenever Tristan came to visit.

It bothered Sam that she bore the brunt of Rebecca's frustration with Tristan. This was exactly the kind of childish behaviour that made her wonder if people ever really left high school behind. She wanted to shout at the silly girl to just kick him to the curb and move on. The idea that Sam was her only obstacle to gaining his commitment was laughable.

'I'll see you in an hour or so then? I'll be here till six at least, all alone in the new wing. You can come see me on your way out, and I'll give you a private tour of my office,' finished Tristan with a cocky smirk, just as Rebecca walked by.

Sam hid her amused tolerance (and her knowledge of what he really wanted her to privately tour) while answering. 'I won't be leaving anytime soon either. Alex and I have lots to do, what with the product launch next week,' she said, not entirely dishonestly.

Mercifully, the phone rang before he could clarify the ambiguity of her statement. She turned her back to answer it, effectively ending their conversation. Out of the corner of her eye, she saw Alex turn around in his office and head back to his desk. She was right. He'd been coming to interrupt Tristan, aborting his mission now the phone had done it for him.

Stifling her laughter, Sam turned her attention to the phone call.

Later that night, she sat in Alex's office silently taking notes while he frowned his way through an international conference call. Recent times had been stressful on Alex for more reasons than the obvious concerns about his personal life. Dimitri's antics had necessitated some serious damage control.

In addition to giving their large clients some personalised attention (not to mention some enticing offers), Alex had given Lauren permission to increase their IT security. He privately admitted she'd been pushing for this for years. Watching Lauren struggle to keep her 'I told you so' internalised had been almost comical when Alex had confidentially explained to her why he was caving.

They hoped that compartmentalising staff information access would narrow down their suspect list, if not cut the guilty party off altogether. Lauren had promised to report anyone asking fishy questions straight away.

The call finally finished, and Alex breathed a sigh of relief. It had been successful, although they wouldn't see the financial benefits for several months to come. Sam watched in silence as he closed his eyes and rubbed the bridge of his nose. Sitting back in his chair, he folded his hands behind his head, looking at her with a relieved smile.

'How are you doing?' she asked, her answering smile tinged with concern.

He made a noise of derision, leaning forward and putting his elbows on the desk before answering. 'My company is under attack, my ex-wife is trying to blackmail me, and I'm still at the office at nine pm for the third night in a row,' he answered. 'But at least I have you,' he finished playfully.

These comments had become more frequent since the night he'd told Stacey about the pending custody battle. Alex had relaxed. Around her, anyway. His life was obviously more stressful than it'd been in a long, long time, but their newfound closeness somehow mitigated that. Sometimes she almost thought he was flirting with her, making her resolution to be patient with him difficult to stick to.

Alex left her alone in the office shortly after the call finished, to use the bathroom before his next call, and to find some information he thought was on the PD manager's desk. He'd indicated he might be a little while, as the exact document was hidden in a pile of many similar ones, so Sam was surprised when the office door opened again a mere minute after he exited.

Rebecca entered and closed the door behind her, a determined look on her face.

'Hey,' said Sam, surprised to see her. 'I didn't know anyone else was still here. You're working late.'

Moving forward, the younger woman stopped a few paces short of the chair Sam occupied before she answered. 'I stayed to talk to you about Tristan,' she said, no expression on her face.

So, thought Sam, fighting the urge to roll her eyes, *it's going to be like that.*

'I heard that you were seeing him,' said Sam noncommittally. She noticed the office door had started to open slowly. Rebecca hadn't latched it properly in her haste.

'And I know you're trying to steal him from me,' countered Rebecca, an ugly look on her face.

Sam smiled gently and set her straight. 'I'm not in the slightest bit interested in him, actually,' she said. 'He just comes to chat to me sometimes, and he's a bit of a flirt. If it weren't me, it'd be someone else. I don't think he's looking to commit.'

'Sure,' scoffed Rebecca, her voice thick with sarcasm. 'You're not *encouraging* him at all. You can't just settle for finding a man of your own. You have to creep on someone else's too.'

Her patience wearing thin, Sam couldn't keep the exasperation from her tone. 'Rebecca, I'm telling you, I'm not interested in him. I'm not keeping him from you. I don't think he's the "commitment" type. Just leave it be,' she said.

Rebecca took a menacing step forward, obviously having noticed Sam wasn't taking her seriously. 'We both know that's a load of crap,' she said, her voice dripping with venom. 'Why would you set Clarice on me if you didn't want him for yourself? You can't handle the competition. You walk around like a stuck-up bitch, acting like you're better than everyone, kissing up to the boss, but you just can't deal when you're not the centre of attention.'

Sam recoiled like she'd been slapped. She'd known Rebecca was too close to the problem to see clearly, but she hadn't realised just how much her jealousy had poisoned her.

Noticing the girl had taken another step forward, Sam began to feel vulnerable. She wanted to stand and give herself some manoeuvrability but was frightened it would be perceived as threatening. Rebecca didn't need any encouragement.

Instead, Sam deliberately relaxed her shoulders and kept her voice even as she answered. 'Clarice is trying to look out for you, the same as I am. I didn't put her up to anything. She just knows what Tristan is like and doesn't want you getting hurt. I promise you, I'd prefer a lot less attention from him,' she said, swallowing her anger. A sweet, reasonable tone and comforting words certainly weren't what she wanted to use, but desperate times called for desperate measures.

'Oh, don't give me that bullshit,' Rebecca said scathingly. *We just want what's best for you,*' she mocked. 'You've managed to do the impossible and get Alex to screw you. I'm actually a little impressed. I heard he hadn't touched a woman in years. But you can't just leave it at that, can you? You need to play with Tristan too, keep him on the hook. Do you like giving him blue balls or something?'

Confusion spiked through Sam's fear. 'Alex?' she asked. 'There's nothing going on between Alex and me.'

Why would she think that?

'And I keep telling you, I'm not interested in Tristan.'

Rebecca got even closer, a maniacal grin taking over her usually pretty face.

'I know what happened at Dimitri's party,' she said menacingly. 'Don't play coy with me. Are you the reason Alex didn't pay off the ex-wife? Didn't want Victoria getting her hands on the money you worked so hard for?'

The realisation hit Sam so fast that she forgot her deliberately non-threatening stance and jumped out of her chair, knocking it over. How else would Rebecca know about the incident at Dimitri's party and Victoria's blackmail attempt, unless …?

'You're leaking the info,' she said, astonished.

Rebecca's mistake registered on her face for an instant, before rage took over and she flew at Sam. They both fell to the floor. Rebecca did her best to impart some visible damage, but she didn't stand a chance. Sam's would-be attacker hadn't seen the inside of a gym since high school. If the look on her face was any indication, she'd known she wasn't going to win almost as soon as they hit the carpet. Even if Alex hadn't pulled her off mere seconds after they went down — at best, Rebecca was finishing humiliated.

'FRIGID WHORE!' Rebecca shouted, struggling uselessly, and mostly for effect, Sam suspected.

'Rebecca,' said Alex calmly. 'You're fired.' He lifted her and walked out of the office as tears began to trickle down Rebecca's disarrayed face. She didn't fight him until they were through the door, wriggling her way out of his grip and shooting Sam a resentful glance. She walked the rest of the way to the front door with Alex dogging her steps, not even pausing at her desk. She grabbed her bag while still walking, and soon disappeared from Sam's line of sight.

Sam sat on the ground for a long moment, overwhelmed by what had just taken place. She'd thought long and hard about who could be leaking the info and had quietly assumed it was someone from sales, fed up with the workload. It would be a savvy (albeit disgustingly immoral) way to source a position with their competitor.

Eventually standing up, she straightened her outfit and hair. She was just righting her chair when Alex re-entered the office. He gave her a swift, assessing look, confirming for himself she wasn't hurt.

When he spoke, Sam suspected his nonchalance was on purpose, to diffuse the tension. 'How exactly does one become a "frigid whore"?' he asked. 'I would have thought the two terms were mutually exclusive.'

Smiling briefly, Sam played along, even though her heart wasn't really in it.

'I guess the "moron" part of "oxymoron" was especially prominent in her,' she answered.

Alex smiled too, belying his confident exterior with his next question. 'Are you all right?' he asked.

Sam nodded. 'I'm okay,' she confirmed. 'Just a little overwhelmed by the turn of events. I can't believe it was her all along.'

'Me too,' agreed Alex. 'She's worked here for years now. I'd assumed it was someone newer. I wonder why she waited so long?'

Sam shrugged, not convinced the timing was all that relevant. 'Dimitri probably didn't approach her until recently,' she answered.

They stayed late that night, speculating about the repercussions of their findings. They didn't get any more work done, but Sam was glad to be with him regardless. She had never enjoyed working late more.

Chapter 22 – Sex and Drugs

Watching Sam hold Stacey the night he'd decided to fight Victoria, Alex had finally decided to trust her. The truth would come out eventually, but he couldn't live his life like that anymore.

This hadn't negated his relief when the real perpetrator exposed herself. He knew he should feel saddened. He trusted all his employees and had been incredibly disappointed by the turn of events, but Sam's exoneration left him feeling as if a huge weight had been lifted.

That weight had slowly been replaced by an even more oppressive one as the custody hearing loomed. It was useless to worry, but he did it anyway.

Michael had pulled out all the stops. His witness list included Alex's therapist, Stacey's therapist, family members present during Alex and Victoria's fiasco of a marriage, and a doctor who had coincidentally treated Alex on three separate visits to the emergency room. The poor woman was riddled with guilt for not making the connection, and she'd insisted on helping.

Not on the witness list was Stacey. She wasn't even going to be present at the court proceedings. Alex had put his foot down, and Victoria hadn't protested, probably so she could twist the fact of their daughter's absence in her favour.

Sam had been requested as a witness for Victoria, which surprised exactly no one. It seemed like she was really going to try and have that morality clause enforced.

Michael was much less concerned about the possibility they would incriminate themselves in a breaking and entering charge than they had anticipated. 'Just tell the truth.' He shrugged. 'The relevant parts anyway. You were invited into the building, snuck off where you weren't supposed to be for shits and giggles, and then panicked. It explains the position you were caught in, and if they press for more information I can object to the relevance. All that matters is you were faking it, not why.'

The day of the case dawned hot and bright. Alex took a moment to appreciate the short, sleeveless dress Sam wore. Summer had arrived all at once about a week ago. The new air conditioning at the office worked like a dream. Maybe a little too well if this was the first he'd seen of this dress.

'Did you bring me a magic rock?' he asked, to distract himself from her legs.

Sam arched an eyebrow. 'I thought you didn't believe in that stuff,' she said, entering the courthouse with him.

'I don't,' he admitted. 'But I'll take all the help I can get today. I'd let you nail a horseshoe to my forehead if I thought it'd bring me good luck.'

She smiled as they stopped to look around. They were quite a bit earlier than necessary. Alex had reasoned he would be calmer, given the opportunity to familiarise himself with the surroundings.

Surprisingly, Michael was already there, busy speaking to a man Alex vaguely recognised as having worked under his previous lawyer. The familiar man glanced their way, his face blanching for no apparent reason, before hurrying off in the opposite direction without greeting them.

Ignoring this impoliteness, Alex greeted Michael, belatedly noticing Sam was watching with a frown as the rude man left.

Michael followed the direction of their gazes and explained. 'My colleague, Adam Tannis,' he said. 'You might remember him, Alex. He was a junior lawyer during your divorce and worked on your custody agreement. He's been extremely helpful while I've been preparing for today, but he has a meeting at our office shortly so had to run.'

Rather than be reassured by this explanation for his abrupt departure, Sam seemed more troubled. 'Adam, did you say?' she asked. 'He introduced himself to me as Richard Holland.'

She gave Alex a significant look, and he clicked that this was the man he saw harassing Sam the night of his parents' anniversary party. No wonder he'd looked familiar.

Now feeling as concerned as Sam looked, Alex listened as she explained to Michael how they met.

Michael looked bewildered. 'It's potentially just coincidence,' he speculated. 'He has clients of his own, after all. But the fake name bothers me. I can't see any reason for giving an alias if the offer was above board.' He frowned. 'I'd be curious to see the NDA. Your lawyer was right to advise you not to sign it.'

'Could it be linked to the custody hearing?' asked Sam, concern evident in her voice. 'He seemed in an awful hurry to leave without me getting a good look at him. What if he's passing information to the other side?'

Michael didn't seem to be as worried about this possibility as Sam and Alex. 'The repercussions of that kind of meddling would be massive,' he explained. 'Confidentiality is astronomically important in our industry. There are very few people without something to hide, even if it's just that they'd rather keep their financial assets private. People wouldn't hire lawyers if they were gossiping their private information all over town. I just can't see him compromising his reputation to help your ex-wife win a custody agreement.'

Alex knew Victoria. She'd stop at nothing. 'What if Victoria offered him enough money?' he asked. 'We've already established the fake name is evidence he's probably involved in something shady. Could he be susceptible to bribery?'

Michael had begun shaking his head before Alex even finished talking. 'Look, he's a snake, no question,' he admitted. 'If it's legal, he'll do it for the win, even if it's immoral. And I'm not even saying he's immune to a little corruption. But we're talking about legal malpractice. If he were caught, he'd lose his licence, his considerable income, and potentially need to stand trial. Victoria would have to be offering every cent she stands to gain for it to be worth the risk, if not more.'

Alex and Sam both looked at him for a long moment, unconvinced.

'But I guess that's no guarantee there isn't another reason,' Michael acknowledged begrudgingly. The lawyer chewed his lip for a moment, indecision marring his face. 'We don't have a lot of time,' he said, looking at the clock on the wall. 'I could try to have my firm investigate his cases, but they're probably not going to do that based on the speculation of a witness that isn't even under oath. At best, they'd probably ask him for a plausible explanation, and he's not an idiot. He'll have a story worked out.'

'Candice?' suggested Sam, giving Alex some hope.

Her friend had been neck-deep in the investigation of the company 'leak' before Rebecca incriminated herself. Alex had shelved the idea of using the information and confession to go after Dimitri for now, but Candice had been looking for a firm link between Rebecca and Dimitri in case he decided to pursue it after the custody battle was over.

He explained all this to Michael, who looked increasingly interested.

'Establishing a link between Victoria and Adam might be a good start. Assuming there is one, I can use that evidence to leverage an internal investigation,' he said.

They called Candice, who promised to get right on it, before turning to more pressing matters.

Making their way into the courtroom, Alex's gaze immediately homed in on Victoria. Even though the judge hadn't entered the courtroom yet, she was already playing the part of the desperate mother. He couldn't fault her acting skills. If he hadn't known the pleading looks and fearful glances at him were fake, he'd probably believe her too. It was going to be a long day.

Michael structured their petition perfectly. Alex's therapist had been called to the stand first, establishing Alex's long history as a domestic violence survivor. An objection by Victoria's lawyer as to its relevance was quickly overruled. Michael was right, Victoria had made a big mistake not sheltering Stacey from her mistreatment of him.

Alex had volunteered to speak about his experiences himself, but after Victoria had subpoenaed him, Michael decided to use his testimony strategically. Rather than opening the hearing with his experiences, they were waiting until the cross-examination gave them the opportunity to remind the judge of the severity of her abuse later in the trial.

After the therapist, the doctor took the stand. She spoke to the injuries she'd treated Alex for, also providing expert testimony on his other documented injuries. Forced to admit she suspected nothing at the time, she'd been quick to add that if she'd known of his other visits she would have investigated further. Victoria's insistence he divide his visits between multiple hospitals had been a smart move. As Christian succinctly pointed out when he testified: no one was that clumsy.

Alex had been surprised to learn his family already knew about the abuse. All their expressions of support and offers to help had new meaning when he considered it in this light. They had truly tried to show him every escape route, but he'd been too scared to look. Unconditional love was hard to accept when he was still fighting to convince himself of his worthiness for any kind of love. Victoria had a lot to answer for. His family had all jumped at the chance to testify on his behalf, so much so that Michael had needed to interview them all and choose a few to represent the many volunteers.

Having set the stage with so much testimony as to the abuse of Alex and neglect of Stacey, Michael called Stacey's therapist to the stand. Alex had been hesitant about this, concerned about violating his daughter's privacy. Stacey had thrown a spectacular tantrum though, and he'd relented. He was afraid that if her point of view wasn't sufficiently represented, she would show up to the court uninvited.

True to her word, Victoria was countersuing for full custody. Her petition included accusations of spousal abuse and child neglect, intimidation during their divorce and custody settlement, and curiously, the unsuitability of his current lifestyle to raising a child. As suspected, she framed Stacey's absence from the hearing as another attempt to keep her from her 'beloved daughter'.

Her lawyer, a young but well-respected woman named Laura Myrtle, had a killer reputation. She helped Victoria weave an intricate web of lies about Alex's supposed abuse. Victoria explained the lack of medical records with a tearful proclamation that he wouldn't allow her to seek treatment. She alleged he threw himself down the stairs each time she tried to leave, to ruin her credibility, so he could tell the exact 'lies' his side had told today. Her larger share of the divorce settlement was framed in the same way.

All in all, the combination of skilful questions and outright lies had done a magnificent job of discrediting the testimony Michael had so carefully built.

Distracted by the knowledge he would soon be called up, Alex tried to listen attentively as Victoria's therapist gave her testimony. He wouldn't have put it past his ex to bribe the woman, but she was very convincing. She might even believe what she was saying.

He was incredibly nervous by the time he took the stand, but he was determined to not let it rattle him. Victoria wasn't the only one with a verbal picture to paint, and his testimony had the benefit of being true.

He realised quite early that her lawyer was searching for inconsistencies in his answers to exploit. Michael objected so often, the judge had to remind Laura three times that she was there to ask questions, not speculate on the truth of his answers.

The real fireworks didn't start until they arrived at her last line of questioning. Victoria's allegations that he lived a lifestyle 'unsuitable for raising a child' had left Alex perplexed. What was going on in his life that she could possibly exploit?

'Mr Whitaker,' Laura began, 'what can you tell me about the drugs you regularly supply for selected employees?'

Completely caught off guard, Alex took a moment to respond. 'I have never provided drugs for any of my employees,' he said cautiously. 'Selected or otherwise.'

The lawyer looked at him with polite disbelief before asking another question.

'So, you're telling the court you have never hosted a party or social gathering in which you made drugs and alcohol available to someone employed by you?' she clarified.

Still confused as to how Victoria had any chance of making this stick, Alex answered again, this time trying to inject some confidence into his voice. 'I have hosted the odd party, occasionally invited employees, and I have provided alcohol, but never drugs,' he answered.

'Okay,' said Laura. 'Maybe not a party, as such. Maybe just a smaller gathering. You and a handful of people, maybe just one other person. You've provided drugs on these occasions, yes? Perhaps not actually handing it out, but was it there for the taking? On a table, out in the open, or similar?'

'No,' said Alex, remembering how Michael had cautioned him to be brief when a long answer was unnecessary.

'You claim to have never given cocaine or extasy to an employee?' she asked.

'Objection,' called Michael, a bored tone in his voice that Alex suspected was there on purpose. 'Asked and answered.'

'Sustained,' said the judge.

Taking this in her stride, Laura moved on to her next sensationalised topic.

'And prostitutes? How often would you say you hire them?' she asked innocuously.

There was a murmur from the gallery at this, distracting Alex from his incredulity. 'I have never hired a prostitute,' he said, struggling to keep his tone even. He flashed a glance at Sam, hoping she wasn't taking any of these ludicrous questions seriously.

Not yet finished, Laura began rapid-firing insane questions at him, only giving him an opportunity to present a 'yes' or 'no' answer.

'Have you ever offered a woman money, or something else of value in exchange for sex?'

'Have you ever offered a woman something of value in exchange for having sex with someone else, or several other people?'

'Have you ever hosted an orgy or a party that involved public sex while your daughter was in the house?'

'Has your daughter ever witnessed yourself or any of your guests having sex?'

'Has your daughter ever witnessed yourself or any of your guests taking drugs?'

'Have you ever been involved in a sexual relationship with an employee?'

'Have you ever terminated someone's employment because they wouldn't comply with a sexual request?'

'Do you take drugs?'

Alex looked over at Michael, wondering why he wasn't objecting. The questions that didn't involve Stacey were irrelevant, surely? His lawyer was sitting back in his chair, a troubled look on his face, but he motioned for Alex to continue answering.

'How many hours a week do you work?' asked Laura, switching tactics.

Perplexed at the change of topic, Alex indicated it was rarely less than fifty, and occasionally it topped out at seventy. He'd hoped Sam's plans would help to decrease this (and had presented the same information to Stacey), but the attack on his profits had negated any positive effects so far. This wasn't relevant to the question though, so he didn't bother mentioning it.

'And you don't take any sort of stimulant to keep you going through this?' Laura asked, bringing it back on brand.

'Not unless you count coffee,' said Alex. He was getting tired of this charade. He'd denied all the questions, but he worried the fact they were asked was enough to cast doubt on his answers. Bracing himself for more of the same, he heaved a small sigh of relief when she indicated she had no more questions.

He relaxed a little as he and Michael went through his rehearsed testimony. His answers had been coached to augment the facts that had already been presented by his other witnesses, painting a vivid picture of the life Stacey had witnessed him leading with Victoria. Michael had warned him Victoria's testimony might require a deviation from their script, so he was expecting more questions about his non-existent sex life and drug habit. He was perplexed when nothing of the sort was forthcoming.

As he resumed his seat, the judge called a recess for lunch. Surprised four hours had already passed, Alex belatedly realised how hungry he was. All that nervous anticipation really worked up an appetite.

Chapter 23 – More Sex and Drugs

Sam tried to quash her trepidation as she walked back to the courtroom after lunch. She was technically a witness against Alex, albeit an unwilling one, and she was dreading saying something that could be used against him.

Michael had indicated the line of questioning directed at Alex was likely to have some bearing on the questions asked to her. Alex had been angry at this, but she was comforted with the knowledge that Victoria still thought there was a romantic link between the two of them. Any queries about their supposed sex together should prove as much of a dead end with her as it had with Alex.

Michael had apologised for not interrupting Victoria's lawyer when she questioned Alex, explaining that his decision to let it play out was strategic. His constant interruption would have lent credibility to speculation that Alex really was leading a sordid life of drug fuelled sex parties. The decision to pay no attention to it when he questioned Alex himself was for the same reason.

'Be prepared,' he cautioned Sam as they took their seats. 'They're probably going to ask some invasive questions about your intimate life.'

'Lucky I don't have one,' she said under her breath.

Sam was immediately called to the witness stand when court was reconvened, relaxing as the opening questions proved to be easy ones. She confirmed she was an employee of Alex's, how long she had known him, the nature of her relationship with Stacey, and that she was currently single.

'So, you're saying yourself and Mr Whitaker aren't involved in a romantic or sexual relationship?' Laura clarified.

Sam had secretly been looking forward to this question. She knew they believed the answer was a reluctant 'yes' and assumed the planned follow-up questions relied on this. It was going to be great to trip her up. 'Correct,' she answered smugly.

To Sam's surprise, Laura didn't show any shock, not missing a beat as she continued to question her. 'In that case, could you please explain to the court why you and he were caught semi undressed in a passionate embrace by Dimitri Ivanov?' she asked.

Without breaking her stride, Sam nodded and proceeded to explain. '... we ended up in Dimitri's office. I was standing at the door, thinking we should leave, when I heard the lift door open down the corridor. We panicked when we realised it was Dimitri, and I came up with a fake reason for being there. The whole thing was staged to distract him,' she finished.

Sam had deliberately not gone into detail about their kiss, afraid her emotions would shine through and cast doubt on her insistence it was faked.

Also faked was the smile on Laura's face. 'And could you please tell the court what Mr Whitaker offered you in exchange for denying your involvement with him?' she asked.

Sam had been prepared for follow-up questions, but the casual implication she was lying caught her off guard. Incensed, she answered without thinking. 'Nothing!' she said, insult evident in her tone.

'You did it out of love for him then?' pressed the lawyer. 'You are in love with him, yes?'

A hopeless sense of dread filled Sam at the question. Yes, she was absolutely in love with him. But so far, she'd told the truth. She had omitted their real reason for being in Dimitri's office, but it wasn't relevant to today's proceedings anyway, so she didn't feel particularly guilty about that.

But she didn't want to admit that she loved him to anyone, let alone a whole courtroom, and Alex most of all. Even discounting her vulnerability, it would lend credibility to the suggestion she was lying to protect him.

'Objection!' called Michael, sparking some hope. 'Leading question, speculation, even badgering the witness. Your honour, she has answered the question and there has been no evidence presented that contradicts this.'

'Sustained. Keep on track, Ms Myrtle,' admonished the judge, to Sam's relief.

Having sown her seed of doubt, Laura reinforced her bribery suggestion by coming at Sam with a different question. 'Ms Faulkner, how long have you worked for Mr Whitaker?' she asked.

'Around five or six months,' Sam answered, curious where this was going.

'And did you recently receive a significant pay rise?' Laura asked.

'I was promoted,' answered Sam.

'A circumstance which involved a pay rise?' pushed Laura.

'Yes, I was promoted to a more senior position, and it came with a pay rise, for obvious reasons,' answered Sam, trying to keep her impatience from her voice.

'Obvious reasons? After having worked there for less than six months? Do you mean because Mr Whittaker is so happy with your performance in this unusually short space of time, he decided to reward you, or because the two of you have developed a … close … relationship?' she asked suggestively.

Sam was prepared for the insinuation this time and kept her tone even as she answered. 'You would have to ask Alex for the exact reason why he promoted me, but I like to think it was because he thought I was more valuable to the company as its office manager than as his assistant. Not because he has any nepotistic tendencies.'

'Have you ever participated in an orgy?' the lawyer asked suddenly, to the general shock of the room.

Michael objected again, noting Sam had already answered

questions about the nature of her relationship with Alex, but this time Laura protested.

'Your honour, my client has become aware of sexual proceedings taking place at Mr Whitaker's home involving multiple men and women. While Ms Faulkner might not consider herself to be in a *relationship* per se, that doesn't mean she is not involved.'

Looking irritated with all the byplay, the judge questioned Sam himself. 'Ms Faulkner, have you ever had sex with Mr Whitaker or other guests under the same roof as his daughter?'

Cutting through the crap, Sam answered his question, and then some. 'Your honour, the last person I had sex with was my late husband, and he has been deceased for over three years. In case it comes up, I also haven't done any drugs since the time I ate a pot brownie in Amsterdam when I was twenty-two. Nor have I been offered any by Alex or anyone associated with him. To the best of my knowledge, the earlier testimony presented by Alex himself and backed up by his therapist is true. He hasn't had sex since he was married to the awful woman sitting in the front row, contemplating how many puppies to skin for her new coat.'

A short bout of quiet laughter erupted, mostly from Alex's side of the courtroom, and Victoria raised a sardonic eyebrow. The judge's mouth became a thin line, the frown on his forehead deepening.

Oops, she thought, blushing. *Me and my big mouth.*

'The editorial is unnecessary, Ms Faulkner,' the judge said sternly. 'Your witness, Ms Myrtle.'

Laura gave Sam a considering look before indicating she had no further questions, and Michael also elected not to question her.

She hoped that was a good sign, and that her facetiousness hadn't done any damage. *I really need to learn to control that.*

Alex started visibly as the next witness was called. The young woman shot him a triumphant look before making her way to the witness stand.

'Who is that?' whispered Sam, noticing Michael was also looking at Alex questioningly.

'My previous assistant,' he answered shortly.

Even though Alex hadn't talked about her in detail before, Sam had heard plenty from Clarice. Tiffany was young, pretty … and that was about it. She wasn't particularly nice or interesting, and she had next to no sense of humour. Her predecessor was also lazy, and if she were any less intelligent, she'd have to be watered twice a week. Predictably, she was the type to only smile for men. Tiffany didn't ignore women exactly, just made no effort to interact with them.

Sam wondered what she was doing as a witness for Victoria. This couldn't be a good sign.

Victoria's lawyer dived right in and validated Sam's fears as quickly as she could. 'Ms York,' she began. 'How do you know Mr Whitaker?'

'I was his assistant,' she said. 'Up until about six months ago, when he fired me.'

'And on what grounds was your employment terminated?' asked Laura.

Tiffany launched straight into a well-rehearsed tale of debauchery. Alex had seduced her, she claimed. He told her everything she wanted to hear, bought her presents and drugs, and slowly introduced her to his perverted sex life.

They had started with small indiscretions. Blow jobs under his desk while he talked on the phone, sex in his office in the middle of a busy workday, his hand in her panties in the office kitchen.

As time went by, his requests became more ambitious. When she started to baulk at his more outrageous suggestions, he bought her expensive gifts to placate her, or just straight up gave her cash. He hired prostitutes so they could have cocaine-fuelled threesomes. He introduced her to heavy bondage. Against her better judgement, she'd allowed him to lend her to a few of his friends one night when she was high. All this supposedly happened in Alex's bedroom while Stacey slept down the hall.

And the pièce de résistance? He'd invited her to a party where everyone was openly doing all kinds of drugs, in various stages of undress. Stacey had been in her room upstairs, and Tiffany had been worried that she would come down unexpectedly. The party had grown louder and wilder as the night wore on, culminating in an orgy in and around the swimming pool, which Stacey's bedroom window overlooked.

'Alex's brothers were there too, and they didn't seem to care if she saw either,' said Tiffany, sorrowfully. 'I was really intimidated and ended up having sex with Alex in the kitchen instead of outside where everyone else was doing it. He tried to convince me to let his brothers do it with me too. I said no because I didn't want to, and some of them are married. He offered me money and then got angry and hit me when I still said no.' A poignant tear leaked down her face as she sniffed, the very image of corrupted innocence. 'He told me I was fired after that, and then left me alone,' she said. 'I was really shocked, so it took me a couple of minutes to follow him outside. He was having sex with someone else in the pool by then, so I left,' she finished forlornly, ending her incredible story.

Alex was white and shaking with anger. Sam was worried he was going to lash out in front of the court, and evidently, so was Michael.

'Keep it calm, old boy,' murmured his lawyer. 'We can fix this. I'll ask the judge to call a recess at the end of this, and we'll talk it through before I question her.'

Having done her damage, Laura didn't ask many further questions of Tiffany. Michael was granted his recess, and they exited the courtroom so they could speak freely.

Alex requested his family leave them be as they began filing out, earning a hard look from his mother. Their presence would be more hinderance than help, with too many voices vying to be heard in the short space of time.

Surprisingly, Candice practically bowled them over as they left the courtroom. Michael ushered her out the door with Sam and Alex, to a quiet spot in front of the courthouse. Sam fleetingly longed for the cooler air inside, but privacy was more important, and they'd see anyone approaching well before they could be overheard.

'So did Tiffany and Rebecca testify yet?' asked Candice, to the general shock of the rest of the group. Alex was the first to find his voice.

'Tiffany just did,' he said grimly. 'Rebecca hasn't. Rebecca Donaldson?' he asked.

Candice nodded, confirming Sam's fears. She wondered what lies Rebecca was planning to tell in retaliation for losing her job and her 'boyfriend' in one fell swoop.

'Hey, party people,' Candice said cheerfully. 'Don't look so glum. I'm coming with good news, not bad.'

'Wait,' said Michael, holding up a hand to her and gesturing to Alex. 'Who are these women, how do you know them, and why don't I know about them?'

Continuing to look troubled even after Candice's optimism, Alex haltingly explained. 'You've already heard the Rebecca story. She leaked the information to Dimitri. I fired her about a month ago,' he began. 'Tiffany goes back further. She was my assistant up until shortly before Sam started. She flirted ridiculously for a while, and then took it too far one night.'

'How far exactly?' asked Michael, not settling for this evasive description.

Alex cleared his throat, obviously uncomfortable. 'I was working late. I went to the bathroom, and when I got back, she was sitting on my desk, wearing … well, wearing not much of anything, really. She took my shocked paralysis as confusion and said something about having a gift for me while she opened her legs.' He looked faintly sick. 'I was livid,' he continued. 'I fired her immediately, escorted her out of the building to make sure she was truly gone, and left her in the cold, still wearing her lingerie.'

Candice had been nodding along like she was expecting something of the sort. Michael motioned for her to start talking and she spilled the results of her morning efforts with glee. 'I found a link between Victoria and Adam,' she said. 'In the form of an email conversation Victoria had with Dimitri. She's blackmailing him.'

'Blackmailing Adam, or Dimitri?' interjected Michael.

'Adam,' she clarified. 'Dimitri is a willing participant. It turns out Victoria bribed Adam during the divorce all those years ago, when he was younger and poorer. And stupider, I assume. He provided her with information about assets she thought Alex was hiding, but it didn't help her uncover anything new. She's been bitter about not getting her money's worth ever since.'

Candice had really worked herself into a frenzy by now. She was speaking quite fast. Sam suspected this was why she loved her job. Uncovering the juicy information people tried to hide was almost euphoric.

Her audience listened with devoted attention as she continued describing the intricate web of espionage and deceit Victoria had woven.

'So, she put him to work! Adam approached Rebecca with an NDA, hoping to get some useful information, and she signed it. I have no idea how he knew to target her. Probably just staked out the office and got lucky.' She was practically bouncing on her heels now, so caught up in her tale. 'He had her spy on you to gather material Victoria could use to blackmail you. Unfortunately for them, she didn't find anything. Victoria considered having her seduce you to exploit the morality clause in your custody agreement, but Rebecca was adamant she wouldn't have a shot. It was her that suggested Tiffany instead, claiming a 'finder's fee' if she managed it. I get the feeling Rebecca didn't want to risk losing her job and its potentially lucrative surveillance opportunities. Adam of course had Tiff sign an NDA too — is this sounding familiar?' she asked Sam pointedly, before continuing without letting her respond. 'Tiffany shot her shot and failed, as we know, leaving Rebecca with no cash bonus, Victoria with no information, and Adam with no end to his evil messenger boy predicament in sight. Victoria was getting desperate for dollars by this time, so she started paying Rebecca for information about the company instead, which she promptly sold to Dimitri for a modest mark-up. She'd given up on blackmailing Alex, until Rebecca suggested they try the honeytrap again.' She turned pointedly towards Sam. 'With you.'

Sam nodded slowly, her mind racing to keep up with the complicated story.

'You'd already established a much better rapport with Alex than our friend Tiffany ever had. He obviously trusted you. The plan was basically the same as was presented to Tiffany, but with a better chance of success. Rebecca tips Adam off to go to the gym with a new NDA, he convinces you to seduce Alex, then Victoria gets the money she wants. And hopefully Dimitri's antics would provide a distraction in the meantime, leaving Alex more vulnerable. You threw a spanner in the works though,' she said to Sam, grinning, 'because you refused to sign.'

'Hang on,' interrupted Michael. 'Back up a bit. Why is Victoria selling information to Dimitri? If he hurt's Alex's business, he'll have less money to throw at Victoria.'

Alex smiled tiredly, a self-mocking glint in his eye. 'The business is only a small part of my assets,' he clarified. 'Victoria's trying to take pretty much everything else. Properties, shares, other investments … and of course, the money I have set aside for the renovations.' He shrugged. 'There's no point in her going after the company,' he reflected. 'She wouldn't know how to run it, and I'd never be willing to work for her. It'd go under in months with her at the helm, and she knows it. Giving the information to Dimitri costs her nothing, and possibly gains her an edge by splitting my focus.'

Candice nodded impatiently, her obvious excitement making her less sympathetic than she should be. 'So anyway,' she continued, 'the first email I read listed all the stuff Victoria tried that hadn't worked. She forwarded Adam's email about Sam's refusal to Dimitri, furious about the setback. It detailed her frustration at all the work she'd put in for no payday.' She shifted her weight from one foot to the other and back again, clearly too fired up to stand still. 'I can only imagine her glee when Dimitri later told her you'd given her all the leverage she needed without having to pay you a cent,' she speculated. 'She was pretty pissed off when Adam told her it was faked, and even angrier when Alex beat her to litigation, but she'd shown her hand by then. She had to expand her plans. It looks like she's in direct contact with Rebecca and Tiffany now. They've both been promised money if she's successful in getting it from you, so they have more incentive than revenge to be convincing on the stand.' She frowned. 'There's one catch though.'

'Wait,' said Michael. 'You said Adam told her the incident in Dimitri's office was faked. Why is he volunteering information? He's only on their side reluctantly, right?'

Candice waved her hand in the air indecisively as she explained. 'Victoria's threatening to reveal what Adam did during your divorce if he doesn't do anything and everything to help. His main job at this point is to report on your strategy. If they'd showed up to court without that knowledge, he'd be a goner,' she explained. 'And speaking of showing up with or without dangerous information,' she said, 'that catch I mentioned — I didn't get this information legally, and having my face splashed over the papers is bad for business, so you're going to have to come up with a way to get it out of someone.'

'How did you get it?' asked Michael curiously. 'Did you hack Victoria's email or something?'

'Nope,' she said cheerfully, 'Dimitri's. I've been slowly getting his staff used to seeing me for months. They all think I work there and don't question when I pop up randomly. Dimitri always has a meeting late morning, so I knew he wouldn't be in his office. I stood around the corner and snuck in right after he walked out. He hadn't locked his computer, so I just started reading.'

'This is all very interesting,' said Alex, concern still evident in his voice, 'but how does it help us if we can't use it?'

'I think I can turn it to our advantage,' assured Michael. 'I don't have time to explain though. We have to get back.' With that, he walked decisively back to the courtroom, the rest of them following like a trio of ducklings. He paused to make a phone call before going back inside, shooing the rest of them ahead of him.

Sam wondered what he had up his sleeve.

Chapter 24 – Lies and Mistakes

'Ms York,' began Michael, 'how long were you employed by Mr Whitaker?'

Tiffany looked distinctly more nervous now that she was being questioned by Michael. Considering her reputation as a slow thinker, Sam hoped they wouldn't have much trouble tripping her up.

'Almost three years,' she said, seeming faintly pleased at the ease of the question.

'And at what point in this period do you allege Mr Whitaker first propositioned you?' he asked.

She was more cautious answering this, evidently wondering where the line of questioning was heading. 'He came onto me about two and a half years in, maybe just after that,' she answered warily.

'So, around a year ago then,' clarified Michael.

'Yes, almost a year ago,' she said, responding to Michael's casual tone with a slight relaxing of her shoulders. She was starting to get into the rhythm of things.

'And your employment was terminated around six months ago then, if my mathematics is correct?' Michael said, with a self-deprecating smile.

Tiffany giggled, back on familiar turf. A man was giving her something to laugh at, and her reactions seemed almost rehearsed.

Michael's gentle, almost flirtatious behaviour didn't fool Sam. He was giving the silly girl a false sense of security, lowering her defences before he went in for the kill. She could almost smell the predator about him.

'Yes, that's right,' Tiffany said, tilting her head to the side and smiling cutely. This woman was about as sharp as a bowling ball, and twice as dense.

'Ms York — may I call you Tiffany?' Michael interrupted himself, waiting for her smile and nod before continuing. 'Tiffany, you have a lovely tan. Have you been enjoying the beautiful weather this week?'

'Objection!' called Laura. 'Relevance.'

'Sustained,' said the judge. 'Get to the point, Mr Davis.'

Unfazed, Michael nodded, smiling apologetically at Tiffany. He turned slightly so he was addressing the whole courtroom instead of just his victim. 'My point, ladies and gentlemen, is that six months ago it was winter,' he asserted, a vicious look blooming on his face. He turned back to face Tiffany. 'I'd imagine the guests frolicking in Mr Whitaker's swimming pool were a bit chilly,' he said to her.

The colour drained from her face. She opened her mouth, and then closed it again. On her second attempt, she even managed to make some noise: a kind of choking sound. A sheen of sweat now graced Tiffany's face, and she looked suspiciously like she was going to vomit. On her third attempt to speak, she managed to utter some faint words. 'I ... it wasn't that cold, really ... I mean ...' she trailed off, tears forming in her eyes. 'EVERYONE WAS HIGH!' she practically shouted, relief now painting her face. 'They didn't feel the cold.'

Had she come up with this semi-plausible excuse immediately, there might have been a chance the judge bought it. A small one. As things stood, she had done nothing but perhaps save herself from a perjury charge.

Michael chose not to press any further, allowing her to take her seat in the gallery. Further questions were unnecessary at this point.

Before he sat, Michael beckoned to his assistant, who had arrived during the questioning. They conferred briefly in a whisper, the assistant eventually nodding and exiting the courtroom again.

Curious at the turn of events, but accepting Michael was disinclined to enlighten them, Sam looked over at Victoria. She was also busy whispering, to her lawyer, her expression unreadable. Laura made a placating gesture, before calling Rebecca to the stand. The other woman had magically appeared after the recess, and everyone in Alex's camp had studiously ignored her until now.

Rebecca was going to be a more significant opponent. While she may be silly about men, she wasn't stupid as a rule. She'd be much better prepared, and much more likely to maintain a convincing testimony under Michael's questioning.

She told a similar story, albeit a shorter one, and from a different viewpoint. She'd always suspected Alex of degeneracy, avoided being alone with him, was uncomfortable with the looks he gave her, blah, blah, blah …

'Can you tell us about how you came to lose your employment, Ms Donaldson?' asked Victoria's lawyer sympathetically.

Nodding, Rebecca shot Alex and Sam a convincing look of distaste before starting the damning part of her story. 'I was working back one night about a month ago and needed to speak to Alex. His office door was closed, and I thought that was a little odd for so late at night. There was only me, Sam and Alex in the office, and Sam was nowhere to be seen, so why would he need privacy?' Her lips tightened briefly, her face almost (but not quite) betraying a smirk. 'I knocked, and he told me to come in,' she said. 'I was completely paralysed by what I saw inside. He and Sam were having sex. Alex gestured to some cash on his desk and invited me to join them.'

Eva shifted beside Sam, reminding her she wasn't alone, and she choked off the naughty swear word she'd been about to whisper.

'I was gobsmacked,' Rebecca continued, her face convincingly stricken. 'I didn't know what to do. I didn't want to lose my job, but I certainly wasn't interested. I tried to decline politely, but he insisted.' She took a sip of water, whetting her throat, presumably to lubricate the lies she was spewing. 'He told me if the cash there wasn't enough, there was plenty more for me if I came to a "party" he hosted most weekends. There would be ample drugs available to help me loosen up if I was nervous, and his friends would love showing me how much fun it was to let go of my inhibitions,' she said disgustedly. 'I tried to leave at that point, but he said that if I left, I was fired. He told me he didn't employ prudes. I cried and begged. I didn't want to lose my job.'

The muscles in Alex's neck were tensed, and Sam suppressed her desire to rub his back. It was difficult enough for her to hold her tongue amid all the lies being told about her. She could only imagine how much more difficult it was for him. He had a lot more riding on today than she did.

'I tried appealing to the father in him. I'm not that much older than his daughter, so I thought he might have a soft spot I could turn to my advantage. He laughed and told me if I wanted my "daddy" to protect me, I should have him send me upstairs like he did with his daughter when the grown-ups were playing,' she said.

Rebecca had welled up telling this story, and Sam was impressed. She was in the wrong career. 'Soap Opera Actress' would have been much more lucrative. She finished her crying spell, giving a brave little smile before finishing her tale.

'There's not much more to tell. I couldn't do it. I grabbed my things from my desk and left,' she concluded, sniffing.

'Thank you for telling us your story,' said Laura kindly. 'No further questions, your honour.'

Michael stood to begin questioning, shooting an inquiring glance at his assistant, who had just entered the room again. The man held up his hand, open palm with fingers spread, and mouthed 'five minutes' to him. Nodding, Michael moved to the front of the courtroom while his assistant exited again.

'Ms Donaldson,' he began, 'how convenient you should pick exactly the right thing to say to Mr Whittaker so he would reveal such useful information about his daughter.' Michael finished this statement with raised eyebrows and a disbelieving smirk.

'Objection,' called Laura. 'You honour, he's not even asking a question, just inferring my witness is lying.'

The judge agreed, and Michael moved on. He asked a few

questions, all vaguely related to the court case, but not really helping or hindering their cause. It finally occurred to Sam that he might be buying time. No sooner had she entertained these suspicions when Michael potentially hit on something relevant.

'How did you come to meet Victoria Fraser?' he asked.

Rebecca froze, shooting an imploring look at Laura, so fleeting that Sam almost thought she'd imagined it. Alex tensed as well though. It appeared Michael had stumbled upon something interesting.

'Objection,' called Laura. 'Relevance.'

'I would think it's highly relevant,' said Michael. 'Your client and mine haven't been in contact for eleven years, and Mr Whitaker is the only known link between your client and your witness. We already know that she hasn't pressed charges related to her alleged treatment, so how would you know to approach the exact two people who could provide you with such damning information.'

'Your honour,' answered Laura, 'as a part of my investigation, I had to look for people who might be willing to tell the truth about Mr Whittaker. Former staff, especially those that left unwillingly, were top of my list.'

'You admit you specifically went looking for people with a vendetta?' said Michael, directly to his peer this time. 'Not exactly impartial witnesses.'

'Who do you suggest I question, his current employees?' Laura exclaimed, offended. 'People who are all too frightened of losing their jobs, or who he hasn't targeted yet? It took him years to approach both my witnesses with his propositions.'

The judge interrupted them both sternly, reminding them this wasn't how it was done. 'You are not here to argue directly with each other. I will decide the outcome based on the evidence, not by who wins a shouting match,' he announced firmly. 'Mr Davis, next question.'

Michael nodded, giving no indication he was put out by this request. He began to ask what was probably another inane question;

however, he was interrupted by a small commotion at the entrance to the courtroom. His assistant had burst through the door, half-dragging a confused and none too pleased Adam by the arm.

'Could you please tell the court how you came to know that man?' asked Michael, pointing at Adam. A deadpan look settled on his face as he turned back to face Rebecca.

This time her distress was unmistakable. She looked imploringly at Laura again, who looked back confused. That was interesting. It appeared Victoria hadn't included her lawyer in the charade.

When no help was forthcoming, Rebecca sat, her jaw clenched, and her arms crossed, with only her darting eyes giving any indication she was more than a statue. The seconds grew longer, and with each passing moment it became increasingly obvious this was an important question.

It was at this point, Adam clearly realised he was in trouble. Reflecting on it later, Sam was never sure if he knew what was about to happen or if his fight or flight response just activated. He made to move urgently towards the door, trying to shake off the restraining hand.

'Never mind,' said Michael quickly. 'No further questions. Your honour, I'd like to call Adam Tannis to the stand.'

Chapter 25 – Revelations

It was Adam's turn to freeze. He appeared to age about ten years in three seconds. Alex saw a small glimmer of hope appear in his eyes when Laura began protesting.

'Your honour, the petitioner has had their time to call witnesses. If this man was so important to their case, he should have been subpoenaed well ahead of time,' she pointed out.

'Your honour,' began Michael imploringly, 'this man's importance to the proceedings was only revealed today. I didn't have time for a subpoena, so I sent my assistant to give him a less formal invitation to join us. I accept it is not appropriate for me to interrupt the respondent's presentation of evidence, but I humbly ask you to ensure he remains in the courtroom until such time as he can be called upon to answer my questions.'

The judge nodded. 'Take a seat, Mr Tannis,' he acquiesced.

Alex noticed the judge seemed almost pleased by the turn of events and saw Michael unsuccessfully try to hide a knowing grin.

Through all this, Rebecca was still seated in the witness stand, and Michael now motioned impatiently for her to leave. She came back to reality with a start, leaving with an almost indecent haste. Alex watched her hesitate in the aisle, shooting a desperate look to the door before seating herself slightly apart from the rest of Victoria's entourage.

Michael also returned to the gallery, ignoring everyone but his assistant — they held another whispered conversation. Alex overhead the phrase 'phone calls' as some documents were passed to Michael, who nodded and began riffling through them.

Adam had seated himself even more reluctantly than Rebecca. He hadn't seemed to know which side to pick but had in the end placed himself on the same side as Alex's party, much further back. He wasn't confident, apparently, but still had some hope.

Laura looked furious. She was also holding a whispered conversation, with Victoria, twitching angrily and shooting covert looks at Adam. Alex got the distinct impression that Victoria had kept her in the dark. He understood Laura's helplessness. Victoria had a way of fooling even the best-trained professionals.

All in all, things were looking much more positive than they had an hour ago. Alex was quietly pleased, but he tried not to feel too smug about it. Victoria didn't have the countenance of someone who'd been beaten. Not that she'd show it even if she felt it, but still … today had been a rollercoaster of confidence and doubt, and it wasn't over yet. *Don't count your chickens before they hatch.*

'Ms Myrtle,' called the judge, 'your next witness?'

Victoria's whispers grew more insistent, and her lawyer angrily shushed her as she turned to the judge. 'Your honour, will you allow me a moment to confer with my client?' she asked worriedly.

'I will allow you two more minutes,' he said.

They went back to their heated conversation, Victoria's husband Paul joining in. He looked nervous, and Alex couldn't tell whose side he was on.

Laura broke away from the group. Paul looked relieved, and Victoria as if she'd smelled something unpleasant. The uncharacteristic crack in her composure was swiftly replaced with a look of haughty disdain when she noticed Alex looking.

Laura motioned to Michael as she moved towards them, and the two lawyers met in the aisle. They conferred briefly, and Michael moved back to speak with Alex, veiled triumph in his eyes.

'They're scared,' he informed them with glee. 'They want to settle.'

He named their asking price, and Alex paused to consider it. It was still a hefty amount, life-altering even, although not anywhere near Victoria's original request.

'No one would blame you for taking the offer,' said Sam quietly, touching his arm for reassurance. 'She's plagued your life enough. If you can throw a manageable amount of money at the problem and make it go away, it's still a win.'

This was exactly what Alex was thinking, but at the same time he was reluctant to let Victoria get away with even this much. It was the first time he'd ever stood up to her, and he was worried he'd regret not stomping her into the dirt. He looked to Michael for some professional advice.

'Look,' began Michael, 'I can't make any guarantees, you understand. And if you want to take the offer, you've got my full support. But it'd be remiss of me to not remind you that we have her over a barrel right now. Her witnesses aren't as credible as yours, the unflappable Laura Myrtle is worried enough that they're trying to settle, this judge hates Adam with a passion, and his testimony should be the final nail in the coffin.'

Alex's eyes widened as Michael went on to explain the evidence his assistant had collected. Even if Adam lied through his teeth, there should be enough there to damn Victoria. Unless her lawyer could put some spin on it that Michael couldn't foresee.

Alex glanced up at the judge and uncomfortably realised the black-robed man was staring straight at him. He wondered what advice this man, with all his experience, would give him if he could. Shaking himself from his reverie, he turned to Michael.

'Let's see it through,' he said, an uncomfortable weight settling in his stomach.

Michael turned and shook his head at his opposing counsel, his excitement poorly hidden.

Looking disappointed, Laura again conferred with Victoria, who was agitated enough to raise her voice. Alex made out the phrase 'not a cent less', and his excitement piqued. Michael was right. She was scared.

Victoria.

Scared.

And desperate.

His inner monologue pronounced the words distinctly, almost lovingly. He fought to keep the corners of his mouth from turning upwards, a kernel of fear still pulsating in the pit of his stomach, but it was difficult.

Laura shrugged her shoulders and gave her client a look that clearly said, 'it's your funeral', before turning back to the judge. 'No further witnesses, your honour,' she said shortly.

The judge turned expectantly towards Michael, who promptly called Adam to the stand again. Alex did his best to quash his excitement and focus. This was perhaps going to be the most important thing said all day.

Adam appeared to have regained some composure sitting at the back of the courtroom while all the action was happening. No doubt he'd prayed for Alex to take the settlement so he wouldn't have to testify. *Tough luck,* Alex thought smugly, ignoring the niggling worry that events might still turn against him.

'Mr Tannis,' began Michael, no hint of the unease he must be feeling at questioning a colleague. 'Could you please explain to the court how you came to know Mr Whitaker?'

Showing as little emotion as Michael, Adam answered with a level voice. 'I was a junior lawyer during his divorce settlement, assisting Mr Whitaker's previous lawyer,' he answered shortly.

'So, you were involved with the particulars of the divorce settlement and original custody agreement between Mr Whitaker and Mrs Fraser?' clarified Michael.

Adam concurred, and Michael moved on to more recent events. 'Your honour,' said Michael directly to the judge, 'knowing of his previous history in this case, and also of his outstanding reputation in the field of family law, I happily accepted the help Mr Tannis offered in the lead-up to this custody hearing.'

Adam again concurred with this statement after Michael's

prompting. As he moved an arm to scratch his face, Alex noticed a damp patch under his arm. In sharp contrast to his tranquil appearance, Adam was sweating.

Michael strolled back to his desk and nonchalantly collected the papers his assistant had handed him. He leafed through them as he walked back towards Adam, whose jaw had tightened when the paperwork came into play. 'Mr Tannis,' said Michael, laying most of the papers in front of Adam, 'could you please explain why this phone record shows so many calls from your phone to Mrs Fraser's number?'

Even the judge had trouble hiding his reaction to this news. His eyes widened and he leaned forward.

Adam cleared his throat, before attempting to rebuff the question with false bravado. 'I called her in relation to the situation we are discussing today,' he said.

Alex admired his resourcefulness. Technically, that was true. He just hadn't specified to what end.

'Really?' asked Michael with deceptively polite interest. 'You were speaking to Mrs Fraser about this hearing, which was scheduled mere months ago, as far back as a year and a half ago?'

Adam didn't answer, perhaps hoping this was going to be treated as rhetorical so he could avoid perjuring himself. As the silence grew, it became clear his wish wasn't going to be granted. Michael was waiting for an answer.

Not bothering to hide his distaste, either at Adam's corruption or his lack of courage, Alex wasn't sure which, Michael appealed to the judge. 'Your honour, the witness seems disinclined to answer my questions. Would you be willing to compel him?' he asked respectfully.

The judge nodded. 'Answer the question, Mr Tannis,' he said, his dislike also evident in his clipped speech.

Adam looked to Laura, who shook her head, also frowning at the despicable behaviour of her peer. She had no grounds to object, and Adam knew it. Rather than answer, he instead appealed to the judge.

'Your honour, I would like to refuse the question on the grounds of self-incrimination,' he said.

This wasn't exactly the full confession Alex had hoped for, but it was a promising start. The rest of the courtroom agreed, assuming the noise level was an indication. Alex stole a glance at Victoria while the judge called for order. Her expression was composed, but there was a vein pulsating in the side of her face. He could feel the tension palpitating from her side of the room.

'Very well. Could you instead explain how these non-disclosure agreements, signed by Rebecca Donaldson and Tiffany York and dated well before this custody motion was filed, were found saved to your document file?' asked Michael, placing more papers in front of Adam.

Stony-faced, but now visibly sweating with tensed muscles and flared nostrils, Adam refused this question on the same grounds.

'No? Perhaps we'll call them back to the stand and see if they will tell us,' Michael continued, 'or are the specifics of your involvement a part of the information to not be disclosed?'

Adam just gritted his teeth, staring straight ahead. He appeared to be regretting his decision to come back to the court this afternoon. Alex assumed Michael's assistant had orchestrated that and mentally reminded himself to be generous in his thanks to both the men when this was over.

'What about the unsigned one with Ms Faulkner's name on it? What can you tell us about that?' enquired Michael, now gesturing to Sam.

She had been a pillar of support today, even more so than in the preceding weeks. Alex had been aching to reach over and take hold of her hand all day, reluctantly resisting. They had both testified to the fact of their platonic relationship, and he couldn't afford to draw suspicion.

There was still no response from Adam, a reaction more damning than if he'd said something.

Michael seemed inclined to accept it — it did help his case, after all — but the judge had other ideas.

'Mr Tannis, you have not responded to two questions in a row. You will need to record answers to them both. Either give Mr Davis the information he seeks, or give grounds for your refusal to answer,' he said sternly. He seemed to have grown even more steely as the seriousness of Adam's transgressions became clearer.

Victoria had forgotten herself by this time. Her neutral mask had slipped, a scowl marring her features while she whispered to Laura.

Adam appeared to have lost his voice. He had shrivelled in his chair at the judge's reprimand, swallowing twice before finally answering. 'I would like to refuse the questions on the grounds of self-incrimination,' he finally managed to whisper, so quickly and quietly Alex almost missed it.

It was enough for the judge though, who motioned for Michael to continue.

'I have no further questions, your honour,' he said. 'Your witness,' he added to Laura.

She had been sitting quietly, ignoring Victoria during Adam's questioning. Victoria's whispered demands that she 'do something' had travelled across the aisle, but Alex's limited experience of the law led him to suspect she had already done all she could. All Michael's questions to Adam had been relevant, polite, and for the most part, prompted via very incriminating evidence. The poor woman had been given an impossible mess to clean.

'We have no questions, your honour,' Laura said levelly.

'WE MOST CERTAINLY DO HAVE QUESTIONS!' called Victoria, making Alex jump. She turned back to her lawyer, face flushed and gritting her teeth. 'Do something!' she hissed again.

Both standing now, the angrily simmering lawyer turned to look her maddened client full in the face.

'What would you have me do?' Laura asked through clenched teeth.

Victoria almost choked, her eyeballs attempting to pop out of her face. She certainly wasn't used to people standing up to her (especially not people she was paying), and the necessity of restraining herself in front of the judge was obviously quite a chore. 'Your job!' she managed to force out, in a strangled whisper.

Alex didn't know why she bothered to keep her voice down. It was obvious she was upset just looking at her, and besides, he could hear her loud and clear. The judge wasn't so far away that he'd have trouble picking up most of it too. It was so quiet you could hear a pin drop.

'You have made it impossible for me to do my job,' answered Laura, her resentment obvious. 'I advised you to settle when it became apparent you had kept information from me, and you have chosen to see this out.'

'Either you question him, or you're fired!' hissed Victoria, an ugly expression blooming on her face.

'By all means, fire me,' goaded Laura, 'then you can question him yourself. What do you plan to ask him?'

Victoria spluttered for a few more seconds, but the fire eventually went out of her. She was beaten, and she knew it. She slumped back into her chair, carefully avoiding eye contact with Alex and his supporters.

This was a Victoria he'd never seen before. *I could get used to this.*

Laura turned back to face the judge, her back straight and her eyes meeting his.

'No questions,' she repeated loudly.

Adam, looking pathetically relieved, went to leave the witness stand but was stopped by the judge.

'A moment, Mr Tannis,' he said.

Adam paused, still hovered over the seat, his fearful expression returning in full force.

'If we were to search your phone records from eleven years ago, would we find a similar record of relevant calls?'

Adam swallowed, and then surprised Alex by answering the question. 'Yes,' he whispered quickly, still poised to leave.

'Thank you,' said the judge. 'You may be seated. In the gallery,' he added, probably in case Adam had any thoughts about escaping the courtroom.

Adam walked quickly and miserably back to his original seat, avoiding eye contact with both sides. The judge called for closing statements, which were mercifully quick. Everything important had already been said, after all. Laura gave an impassioned speech on Victoria's behalf, which Alex attributed to her professionalism. It certainly wasn't out of desire to do something good for the client who had left her in such an impossible situation.

The excitement on Alex's side of the aisle was palpable by the time they finished, but the judge surprised everyone by calling for a short recess, ensuring all the relevant parties understood they were expected back after it. The black-robed man looked troubled, and a little of Alex's old fear crept back in. Victoria always got her own way. Why would today be any different?

Alex stood at the bathroom mirror, staring at his reflection and trying to calm his racing heartbeat. He looked at the scar on his face properly for the first time in years, tracing the line over his cheek and down his neck, where it was too faint to see in most light. His hand continued over his shirt, following a path down his chest and abdomen, all the way to his thigh.

He was tired. He'd trained himself not to think about his life with Victoria, not to see his scar, but was only realising now how much effort it cost him. For so many years it had been something only to be acknowledged in his therapist's office and his nightmares. Even those few times with Sam where he'd broken down hadn't truly healed him. He understood now it would take something bigger. A confession, an acknowledgement maybe?

He shied away from the truth, shaking himself and turning to leave the bathroom. First, he had to get through today, then he could work on the next step.

Chapter 26 – The Verdict

Alex returned from the bathroom looking pale but determined. Sam wasn't fooled. He was worried. She did her best to reassure him, but privately she worried too. Why was the recess necessary? Victoria's lies were obvious. Even her lawyer didn't appear to be on her side anymore.

As the judge re-entered, Sam noticed he looked almost as troubled as Alex. He sat and got straight to business.

'This has been one of the most disquieting custody hearings I have ever presided over,' he began. 'The nature of the allegations made by both parties are extreme, to say the least, and the witness testimony has been a cacophony of outrageous tales. If it hadn't been for the last-minute attendance of Mr Tannis, I would have been hard pressed to ascertain the truth of these matters.

'As it stands, I am ordering Mr Tannis be investigated for professional misconduct. Mr Tannis, it seems to me as if you have abused your position and engaged in conduct that is prejudicial to the administration of justice. This is disgraceful. I intend that you be made to stand accountable for your actions.

'Ms Donaldson and Ms York, I am ordering both of you to attend a preliminary hearing, where it will be decided if the state will press charges for perjury. It is my intention to get to the bottom of these non-disclosure agreements, to ascertain exactly what they prevent you from disclosing.

'Mrs Fraser,' he continued, disgust evident in his voice, 'I suspect you to be behind the web of lies told in my courtroom today. I am disappointed there is currently no proof of this. My dismay extends to the lack of strong evidence that your own testimony is false. Because of this, and only this, you will not share Ms Donaldson and Ms York's fate.' He seemed to steel himself before continuing. 'As to the matter we have come to settle today,' he said, his tone filled with heavy regret. 'I have reluctantly had to dismiss both petitioners' requests.'

A confused hum of talk ran through the crowd on both sides of the aisle.

Dismiss the requests? Both of them?

The judge cleared his throat, and the room rapidly quietened. No one wanted to miss this.

'Both petitions were presented as amendments to the original custody agreement. Following the testimony of Mr Tannis, it has become clear the original agreement should no longer be valid. His involvement has given an unfair advantage to Mrs Fraser, and this injustice cannot remain.

'Mr Whittaker,' he said, genuine sympathy in his expression, 'I am truly sorry, but the same goes for your divorce settlement. I am ruling it is no longer legitimate. You will need to renegotiate a new one. For the time being, temporary custody is appointed to Mr Whittaker and no visitation rights are awarded to Mrs Fraser. If the decision were up to me right now, this would be a permanent measure. This is the best I can manage under the circumstances.' He looked apologetically at Alex. 'Mr Whittaker, I would like to apologise again and express my sympathy for your situation. It's not my intention to inconvenience or punish you, but to right an injustice. You should be allowed the opportunity for a fair settlement.'

On that shocking note, he closed the case.

Later that evening, Sam returned downstairs after seeing an exhausted Stacey to bed. She had been quiet this evening, with a sense of fragility about her. They'd hung all their hopes on a favourable outcome today, and the judge's ruling would affect her most of all. Following the lack of longed-for closure, she had retreated within herself. Her therapist had stopped Alex on the way out of the courtroom and scheduled an emergency session for tomorrow, but Sam had tried to give Stacey some special attention in the interim.

As she made her way back down the stairs, Sam reflected there wasn't a lot she could do. She'd tried to engage Stacey in conversation, without success. This last attempt before she went to sleep hadn't worked either, but she seemed to appreciate it when Sam stroked her hair for a little while and eventually kissed her forehead goodnight.

Alex wasn't doing much better. Sam paused and made eye contact with him as she approached the foot of the stairs. He sat in his lounge room, on a chair liberated from the dining table, surrounded by his chattering family. She hoped it was nerves, and not defeat, causing his introversion.

His family had obviously noticed his silence; however, they were avoiding confronting him about it. Sam wasn't sure this was the best course of action, but a whispered conversation with Rose indicated they'd never been successful in getting Alex to open up to them. Being present and forcefully on his side was the best they could manage.

The topic of conversation hadn't changed since she had gone upstairs with Stacey: unabated, unabashed and unapologetic Victoria bashing.

In hindsight, no one was surprised at the stunt she'd pulled. Her ability to convince two otherwise law-abiding citizens to commit perjury and espionage for her was impressive, but then, so were a lot of truly horrible things. They were worried about how she would push today's result to her advantage.

Victoria hadn't been pleased with the outcome either, obviously. Not only was she missing out on her second payday, but her first one might be retracted. Considering she'd already admitted to having money issues, the idea she might lose what she already had wouldn't be a pleasant one.

The indignant woman had swept out of the courtroom after they were dismissed, not bothering to speak to her lawyer or her witnesses. She had completely ignored Alex's side of the aisle, making no eye contact, and headed to the door with a purpose that suggested she'd walk through it if it didn't open. Paul had given a series of nasty looks to the lawyers, the judge and Alex as he followed in her wake.

Paul's presence had been a surprise. Everyone had assumed Victoria would instigate her divorce plans before the trial, so he wouldn't get any of the money she hoped to manipulate from Alex. Discussions since had concluded she'd been unsure about her ability to win. They'd all taken a moment to relish her doubt, the realisation vindicating their own stressful preparations.

Sam stood at the foot of the stairs, silently communicating with Alex. It was late, and he looked exhausted. She made a small head movement, inviting him to join her in a more private setting.

She had meant for them to convene in the smaller living room at the front of the house, but he instead turned in the opposite direction, leading her into his bedroom. Closing the door behind them, Alex turned and reached for her.

She chased her immediate thought down and locked it in a dark box, where it wouldn't disturb them. Now wasn't the time for amorous fantasies. Tense emotional situations that immediately led to desperate sex were the stuff of Hollywood. Alex needed comforting, not further complications.

They stood with their arms around one another, her head laying against his chest, and their bodies comfortably cuddled together. She could feel his cheek resting on her head, and his exhale ruffled her hair in time with the rise and fall of his chest. As his breathing gradually slowed and his muscles relaxed, she listened to his heartbeat thudding. With her eyes closed, she wrapped herself in his smell and the sense of his solidity, like he was her own personal eye in the storm. Hopefully, he was drawing the same strength from their embrace.

A quiet noise from outside the bedroom disturbed the sense of seclusion. His family were leaving, and obviously trying to be unobtrusive about it. Sam hoped they didn't think there were more private activities happening in this room than a long overdue hug. The fact they weren't making the effort to say 'goodbye' worried her. *Oh well.* Alex could set them straight in the morning.

When the last set of shuffling footsteps had ended with the sound of the door softly closing, Alex loosened his embrace, but didn't let go entirely. They still held one another as Sam looked up into his face. She could smell his breath as he exhaled, scented with scotch and an intoxicating warmth. His eyes unreadable, he lifted one hand and pushed her hair behind her shoulder, eventually bringing it back to cup her face. His other hand moved up to mirror it, thumbs slowly tracing her cheekbones.

An errant thought escaped from Sam's locked box of impropriety, and it gave birth to a tirade. Was this it? Would he kiss her? Would he regret it if he did? Would *she* regret it if he did? Should she break the embrace now, for the sake of their friendship? Could she bring herself to refuse him? Should she kiss him instead? Was she wearing decent underwear?

He moved. To Sam's intense disappointment, he didn't move towards her waiting lips. She felt him kiss her forehead, a gentle pleasure at the intimate contact flooding her body. He moved down the side of her face, so close she could feel his breath tickling her temple. His hand moved slightly, making room for his lips, which he pressed gently to her cheek. Having completed his errand on that side, he slowly travelled to the other side of her face, his lips lowering in line with hers, so their noses softly rubbed as he went past. He repeated his homage on her other cheek, and then moved back to the centre, his lips a mere inch from hers.

Alex paused here, his breathing slow and shallow. Their eyes were open, and Sam stared into his, barely daring to exhale in case it scared him away. The cacophony of questions bubbled back to the surface again. With a momentous effort, she pushed them aside and just enjoyed the intimacy of the moment. Even without a deeper affection, she was exactly where she wanted to be.

He inhaled deeply ... and exhaled. His kiss was gentle and lightning fast, so fast it took her body a half-second to catch on. When it did, blood rushed to her lips, her nerve endings primed to feel every movement, but too late. It ended as soon as it began, a mirroring of his contact with her forehead and cheeks.

He leaned back, still cupping her face in his hands. 'Will you stay?' he asked, naked vulnerability evident in his expression and his voice. 'I don't mean ...' he said, trailing off as his eyes darted towards the bed. He uttered his next sentence so quietly, she didn't pick up some of the words. '... don't want ... alone tonight,' she heard.

She nodded, wondering what the night would bring.

A short while later, Sam lay in Alex's bed with him, their bodies comfortably entwined. He'd loaned her a T-shirt, long enough to cover her decently, and he slept wearing one as well. They hadn't talked since she joined him in the bed, just laid there quietly, occasionally stroking one another's back or hair.

She felt as if she was balanced on the edge of a knife. It would be so easy, feel so natural, to make love to him now. All it would take was one small movement and it would all fall smoothly into place, like a row of dominos that just needed the first tile pushed.

But would that push inadvertently tumble them in the opposite direction? Would it invalidate the faith he'd placed in her? She'd come to understand just how precious his trust was as they'd grown closer. His willingness to be this vulnerable with her was a small miracle. As much as she wanted to take that next step, and as determined as she was to show him how love should really be, she couldn't do it tonight. Not after the day he'd had.

She listened as his breathing slowed and deepened, feeling him drift into slumber. Only after he was blessedly unconscious did her own exhaustion catch up with her.

She was asleep within minutes of him.

Chapter 27 – Should I, Shouldn't I?

Alex closed the door behind Sam as she left the next morning, a curious mixture of regret and relief preoccupying him. He wanted her to stay forever, but he couldn't be comfortable with his yearning.

Turning, he almost jumped out of his skin when he noticed his daughter sitting at the foot of the stairs. 'Stacey!' he exclaimed, his heart racing. What had she seen? 'I was just seeing Sam out.' He paused, but she didn't respond. 'I'm sorry you didn't get to say goodbye. We didn't want to wake you,' he added uncomfortably.

Stacey had an indecipherable expression on her face. Alex wondered what she was thinking and if he should clarify further, but she spoke before he could compose the right sentence.

'Sam stayed the night? In your room?' she asked.

Her expression was still a mystery, and he hastened to reassure her as he sat next to her. 'Yes, she stayed. In my room. But not … like that,' he clarified awkwardly. 'We just slept. I was very tired but couldn't choose between sleep or company so …' He paused, wondering if he should keep talking. He didn't want to protest too voraciously, or she'd think he had something to hide. Well, technically he did have something to hide. Not that anything had happened. Not really, anyway. But in that situation on any other night …

'Dad?' asked Stacey. 'Is there something … I mean, are you guys … has anything happened between you? Like … is she your girlfriend or something?'

Alex shook his head, perhaps a little too forcefully. 'No, no, nothing like that,' he said. 'I mean there was a situation once, but it didn't mean anything …' he trailed off again, cursing himself. He'd said too much not to continue.

He begrudgingly told Stacey the story of what had happened in Dimitri's office, leaving out how he'd burned for Sam from the moment their lips touched, and how he had wanted to throw Dimitri out the window for interrupting them.

Stacey was silent afterwards, and he regretted telling it more with each passing second. He searched franticly for the words that would put her at ease, but she beat him to it again.

'Dad,' said Stacey hesitantly, 'did you … like it? When you kissed Sam, I mean?'

Taken aback, he considered the question. He wasn't sure he wanted to answer it and chose to dodge it as best he could. 'Why do you ask?' he countered, his calm voice belying the chaos inside of him. His pulse was racing at the mere thought of their moment of staged passion.

Stacey opened and closed her mouth, squirming a little where she sat next to him on the stair, before finally answering. 'I like Sam,' she whispered. Alex was shocked when tears welled in her eyes. A veritable fountain of words spilled from her mouth as the tears began to trickle down her face. 'I love Sam,' she corrected. 'I know I haven't known her for long, but she's so nice to me. I'm so happy when she's here, and she's always there when I want to talk about something or ask something. Or even when I don't want to talk really, but I just want her to be there with me. And when I talk to her and we do things together … it's like …' She seemed to be about to confess to sins her innocent mind wasn't capable of conceiving. 'It's like having a mum,' she whispered guiltily.

Alex didn't have a chance to respond before his daughter began an unnecessary tirade of damage control.

'I don't need one or anything,' she added, crying harder. 'It's not that you haven't been the best dad ever. You're better than two regular parents, and I know why you never wanted a girlfriend after you and Victoria broke up. It's just that sometimes I wonder what it would be like, and since you and Sam are such good friends, I thought maybe …' They both appeared to be having real trouble finishing their sentences today. Stacey didn't specify exactly what she was hoping for, but the message was clear, made even more so by the way she was looking anxiously at Alex through her tears.

He had put his arm around her automatically during this speech, but his emotions were having trouble catching up with what he'd heard.

'I'm sorry, Dad,' she said, the shame in her tone breaking his heart. 'I didn't mean you weren't enough or anything, just —,' she broke off as he shushed her.

'Stacey,' he said soothingly, finally finding the right words, 'you don't have to feel guilty for wanting two parents. The universe did you a disservice when it gave you to Victoria. You've always deserved more than just me. I'm just sorry I was never able to give it to you.'

Stacey calmed somewhat, seemingly reassured she hadn't hurt her father with her neediness. She looked at him hopefully and spoke up again. 'What about Sam, though?' she asked. 'I love her, and she makes you really happy. Maybe you can be together? Do you like her that way?'

He was holding a live grenade. He'd stopped denying to himself how he felt, but he wasn't about to admit it to his besotted teenage daughter. That would be setting her up for a fall. 'Darling,' he said, dodging the question for all he was worth, 'Sam is a wonderful person. And yes, she's beautiful. I don't think many men would say no to her. But even if I were interested in her, there's no guarantee she'd feel the same. That doesn't have to change your relationship with her though,' he hastened to add. 'I know she loves you too, and she wouldn't have to be in a relationship with your father for you to look up to her like a mother. Do you want me to talk to her for you?'

Stacey had stopped crying by now. She was looking at him a little too cunningly for his comfort. 'You would ask her that for me?' she repeated, waiting for his nod before she continued. 'Would you ask her something else for me instead?'

'Of course,' he said. 'Whatever you need. What do you want me to say to her?'

Stacey grinned triumphantly, and his apprehension doubled. 'I want you to ask her to go on a date with you,' she said precociously.

Well. He'd walked right into that one. Shooting his clever daughter a dirty look, Alex prepared to start backpedalling for all he was worth. A knock at the door interrupted him before he could start. 'Hold that thought,' he said sternly as he got up to answer it. 'Or better yet, forget it altogether,' he mumbled.

On the doorstep were all four of his brothers, grinning at him like idiots.

'Morning,' said Noah, a wicked gleam in his eye.

'How was your night?' asked James, winking cheekily.

Alex groaned inwardly, remembering how they'd snuck away after he and Sam retired to his bedroom. This was the last thing he needed with Stacey still sitting on the stairs behind him, her agenda so closely aligned with theirs. 'Nothing of interest happened,' he said, a hint of force in his voice.

They pushed past him into the house, no hint of disappointment on anyone's face.

'In that case,' said Christian, giving Stacey a wink as he walked past the stairs. 'This is an intervention.'

Alex focused on Erik as they walked towards his kitchen. 'You're carrying a bottle of scotch,' he noted ironically.

'It's not about your drinking,' said Erik, making a beeline for the cupboard with the appropriate glasses.

'It's nine-thirty in the morning,' said Alex, trailing behind them. How was he ever going to gain control of this conversation?

'Where's your sense of adventure?' asked James rakishly.

'Stacey, honey, how about you go upstairs so we can have a chat to your dad in private?' asked Christian.

Stacey rolled her eyes and stood up. She ambled into the kitchen and grabbed a banana as she spoke. 'Fine, but I bet twenty dollars they're talking to you about the same thing I was talking to you about,' she directed at her father.

She scampered up the stairs as Alex privately conceded he'd be an idiot to take that bet. After she was safely ensconced in her bedroom, he reluctantly joined his brothers at the table. There was only one glass poured. 'Why am I the only one with a drink?' he asked, delaying the inevitable.

'Because you're more talkative when you've had a few,' answered Noah.

'And it's only nine-thirty in the morning,' said James, mock disapproval in his voice.

'Bottoms up,' said Noah with a wicked expression.

Alex sat unenthusiastically. He was too worn out for this conversation to go the way he wanted it to.

'What was Stacey talking to you about?' asked Erik curiously.

Alex waved his hand dismissively. He wasn't going to start the conversation that way. They didn't need the leverage.

'So,' said Christian, 'did nothing really happen, or did you just say that because Stacey was listening?'

'Guys, I don't feel like talking about this,' he said. Maybe he could guilt them into leaving him be. 'I had a big day yesterday and a late night. Can we do it another time?'

'Sure,' said James cheerfully, 'we can leave. But when Mama doesn't get an update, she's going to come over here and drag it out of you herself.'

'We almost had to tie her to a chair to keep her from coming in the first place,' added Noah.

Alex resigned himself to the inevitable. They'd make him talk eventually. He contemplated the table for a moment as he planned what he wanted to say. James pointedly pushed the glass of scotch closer, interrupting his train of thought. He pushed it away too forcefully, sloshing the amber liquid over his table. 'You don't need to give me that,' Alex said irritably. 'I'll tell you what you want to know. She stayed the night. In my bed, but we didn't "sleep" together. We just slept, in the literal sense,' he clarified.

His brothers nodded, no one looking surprised.

'And before that?' asked Christian intently. 'Did anything happen?'

'No,' said Alex, cursing himself for the uncertain note in his voice. 'Well, I kissed her, but it was more of a "thank you" kiss than anything. Last night I just needed her there, and she was. Like she always is.'

'Like she always is,' echoed Noah.

The emphasis opened a floodgate in Alex, and everything spilled out before he could close it. 'Yes, like she always is. If I need someone to listen to me. If Stacey needs something. If I need my mood lifted. If I need someone to bounce an idea off. If I need someone to talk some sense into me, to light a fire under me, to keep me on track. If I need ...' He paused, embarrassed to admit this to his brothers. 'I haven't had a lot of "emotional needs" since Victoria and I were over,' he prefaced. 'For most part, I've just been too pathetically grateful she was gone. Anything else has been a walk in the park by comparison. But lately ... lately I've needed someone to lean on. And she has been it. She talks to me about her past too,' he added. 'Her life hasn't exactly been without tragedy either. We've become close. Really close. She knows me better than my therapist ... And I'm scared,' he admitted.

His brothers were quiet, perhaps too afraid of destroying his momentum to interrupt. They sat in silence as Alex confessed, not even daring to move.

'No, I *want* to be scared,' he corrected himself. 'I've known this woman mere months, and she means more to me than I can put into words. I shouldn't feel this way, but the idea of not having her in my life is too distressing to contemplate. I keep trying to tell myself it's only the timing, it's only that she's a good person who happens to be here when I need just such a person in my life, but it's a lie. I was on track to fall for her even before Victoria showed up for an encore. You guys were right that night in the bar, and again in the hospital.

'I've had so many near misses with her. So many moments when something almost happened, but then didn't. Usually because I was too caught up in my own head to take the chance. And every time I miss an opportunity, I regret it, but I tell myself it's for the best. I remind myself I've spent so long avoiding this kind of situation that it's pointless to gamble now. I convince myself I didn't chicken out; I made a rational decision.' He got up from the table and began to pace, a caged animal yearning to escape the prison he'd created in his own mind. Out of the corner of his eye, he saw Noah open his mouth. Christian shot him a look, and he closed it again.

'But then it happens again. And again, I take the safe path,' he continued. 'One of these days, it's going to be my last shot. It's not like I don't have any competition. Even the idiots that don't appreciate her for the godsend she is aren't blind to her looks. She's stunning. I have to remind myself to breathe whenever she enters a room.'

It was Erik's turn to try and speak, but Christian quelled him too, and Alex was grateful. He couldn't stop now he'd started, and interruptions would just frustrate him.

'I keep telling myself it doesn't matter what I want, that I could never be that lucky anyway. Why would she want me? She could have pretty much anyone. I'm an emotionally damaged, ugly old man, and she knows it. She's seen me at rock bottom. Not the rock bottom I had when I was still with Victoria, but my current low points, my most vulnerable … it's all been with her.' Alex's hands were linked behind his neck now, and he stared at the ceiling while he walked back and forth. His tensed muscles stood out, gratuitously illustrating his emotionally charged state. 'And even knowing all that … sometimes I think maybe she's interested. Sam is never the one to end a moment, to break the spell. She says nice things to me; she instigates most of our affection, and she doesn't shy away when I do it instead. That night in Dimitri's office, I could almost swear she was turned on.' He sat down again, deflated after saying so many of the things he'd been holding inside for so long.

His brothers still didn't speak, allowing him to talk himself out.

'I don't know what to do,' Alex said helplessly. 'I love her. But I don't know if I *want* to love her. I've never felt like this before, and honestly if she rejects me, I don't know how I'll get over it. And even if she doesn't reject me, I don't know how to be with her. The only long-term relationship I've ever had was practically a horror movie. What if I screw it up?' He finally looked up, making eye contact with each of his brothers. He half-expected them to be laughing at him, but they all had varying degrees of excitement and relief on their faces. He looked at Christian last, knowing it was his advice he needed the most.

'Is she worth the risk?' Christian asked seriously. 'That's not rhetorical. I mean it. Really think about it. We all love her, and I honestly think you guys would be great together. I already think of her the same way I do Valentina, but that's not my call to make.' He leaned forward, gesturing earnestly. 'If it helps,' he continued, 'I doubt you have to worry about her rejecting you. She's smitten. I know it's hard for you to see, but trust me, she's all in. And even if she wasn't, when has that ever been an issue? You're just as capable of enticing a woman as the rest of the family. You do it now without even trying. You've got a reputation as an impossible target, but every woman Mama nudges your way still gives it a try. And plenty of others, without any encouragement. They're not wasting all that effort for some schmuck who doesn't know how to handle himself.'

Alex shrugged uncomfortably, not wanting to consider the women who'd made a play for him in the past.

'The only risk you really have to consider is if the pay-out is worth the emotional gamble. I can't see her turning you down, but that doesn't mean you'll live happily ever after. But does the possibility it could fizzle outweigh the probability this could be the best thing to ever happen to you? Well, second best,' Christian amended, gesturing to the second floor where Stacey was. 'But still, I think she's worth it. And so does everyone else. You just need to figure it out for yourself.'

Chapter 28 – Clarity

Alex sat in Sam's living room later that day, the calm surroundings taking the edge off his nerves. He'd shown up on her doorstep almost an hour earlier, surprising her by declaring he wanted to take her to dinner.

'I want to say thank you properly,' he'd lied, 'for the last few months. I couldn't have done it without you.'

That last sentence wasn't untrue. Without Sam, he would've just paid Victoria when she'd demanded it. In fact, last night he'd been quite bitter he hadn't done exactly that. He'd mentioned this regret in passing as he talked with his brothers today, but they'd shouted him down. The judge was right, they'd argued. This was his chance to make sure he got a fair settlement.

Alex had grudgingly agreed. Deep down, he knew Victoria hadn't deserved what she'd won. He'd always vaguely placated himself with the knowledge that custody of Stacey was the better end of the deal, and cash was a small price to pay for her happiness. Ultimately though, he understood why the judge had decided as he had. The coming fight left him feeling tired before it had even started, but he was determined to look upon this as an opportunity to right the wrong done to him.

Strangely, it was Sam professing her guilty conscience this afternoon that convinced him. She had apologised profusely for pushing him to fight, admitting she'd underestimated Victoria. Alex had spoken so eloquently to persuade her otherwise that he'd talked himself into believing too. Standing up to Victoria had been the right thing to do.

Now she was busy getting ready, leaving him to amuse himself, and to ponder his course of action.

He'd talked to his brothers for hours, eventually concluding he needed to see Sam before deciding. Their dinner tonight was to be something like a date. Not exactly, of course. With his ulterior motive hidden, he hadn't been able to gain the requisite permission to call it that officially. Hopefully, the romantic restaurant he'd picked would either provide the push he needed, or otherwise make him so uncomfortable he would close the door on this insane idea forever.

To distract himself from this impossible choice, he'd taken to exploring Sam's living room while he waited. It was inexplicably comfortable, being here. It took him a while before he realised it was because the room was so reminiscent of Sam herself it was almost familiar. His own house had a 'lived in' feel, but Sam's was much more 'homey'.

A scented candle burned on the mantle, giving the whole house a clean and woodsy scent. Simple acoustic versions of songs he knew and loved played unobtrusively, so as not to distract from the book she'd been reading before his unscheduled visit. The dog-eared romance novel was open, face down on the coffee table next to an intricately painted teacup, empty of all but the dregs. A soft blanket was casually strewn across the back of the deep, cushy armchair she was most partial to, forgotten in the summer heat. Mismatched knickknacks were plentiful, but not cluttered, and somehow they all looked like they belonged together. He ran one finger over a milky-coloured crystal and smiled, wondering what this one was supposed to do.

Most touching were the photos. Little windows into her life were visible everywhere. Candids from her travels, commemorative snaps of her achievements, and a plethora of moments with loved ones; all were grouped haphazardly on walls and shelves.

He stared for a particularly long time at a wedding photo, his thoughts and emotions refusing to settle. In it, a younger Sam laughed joyously while the likeable-looking groom dipped her on a dance floor, a mischievous grin on his face. The same man appeared in multiple other photos, providing a window into the full and happy life they'd led together. Sam was used to being loved deeply.

Alex turned as he heard her enter the room behind him, feeling abashed at being caught examining these mementoes of her life. Even displayed out in public, the glimpse felt voyeuristic.

He quickly forgot to feel anything except awe as he took in her transformation. It wasn't that she hadn't been beautiful before. She'd been dressed casually in jogging shorts and a tank top, her hair in a messy ponytail, but she didn't need the accoutrements of femininity to be attractive.

She certainly knew how to bring it to a whole new level though. The lace overlay of her flared cocktail dress made the deep neckline more subtle, but enough of her skin was displayed that he itched to see more. Small diamonds at her throat and ears, just visible through her long waves of hair, sparkled in the late afternoon sunshine.

Alex had a small moment of panic, second guessing his ability to secure her interest for the umpteenth time. He sternly reminded himself he hadn't decided what he wanted yet, so it was no use getting anxious about it. He'd cross that bridge if, and when, he came to it.

Sam noticed him looking at her photos and smiled. 'I like my memories out where I can see them,' she explained. 'But I noticed you didn't have many photographs at your place.' She opened a drawer in a cabinet as she spoke, removing a gift-wrapped parcel. 'I was supposed to give this to you yesterday, as a celebratory present, but …'

Her shrug as she handed it to him conveyed a myriad of meaning. Yesterday hadn't elicited much cause for celebration.

Alex took the gift, touched by her thoughtfulness. He carefully unwrapped it to find a framed photograph of himself and Stacey. It had been taken a few of months earlier, at his parent's anniversary dinner. Neither of them looked at the camera, instead facing each other while they laughed. He hadn't noticed Sam taking it and felt his emotions rising to the surface at this indisputable evidence of the changes in both himself and his daughter.

Stacey looked confident, relaxed, happy, and positively unashamed to be herself. He'd been at a loss about what to do with her for so long. His daughter had struggled, not wanting to conform to the mould she believed was the only way she could be accepted, but something had clicked in her since meeting Sam. The validation she'd found in the unconditional love and attention from this woman had been transformative.

… And he looked confident too. And relaxed. And happy.

He realised he hadn't seen himself smile properly in years. A socially mandated, upward curve of his lips in posed photos on occasion, but not a natural smile. He eschewed social media, not seeing any value in it for someone who kept to himself as much as he did. Because of this, he wasn't accustomed to the candour of casual photography so prevalent in that medium. He looked like his brothers: comfortable, at peace with the world, and if he was being honest … attractive. Maybe Sam hadn't been lying when she avowed him good-looking. He had no idea a genuine smile could do so much.

Delaying looking up at Sam, he attempted to dispel the lump in his throat before he had to speak to her. She had done so much for him. Stacey wasn't the only one who'd benefitted from Sam's presence in their lives. The unfettered happiness in this photo was an emotion Alex associated with her. He certainly couldn't recall feeling that way before. She had revived his true personality as surely as she had unlocked Stacey's.

And as simply as that, he realised he couldn't let her go.

His vulnerability turning to determination, Alex carefully placed the photograph on the coffee table. He looked up at Sam, stepping forward to close the distance between them before he could chicken out. The surprise on her face barely had time to register before he cupped her cheek in one hand, placing the other at her waist, and softly kissed her.

For one desperate moment, he second-guessed his course of action. Kissing her without warning hadn't been a very gentlemanly thing to do. The purity of his intentions wouldn't account for much in a sexual harassment lawsuit, and he had no wish to make her feel uncomfortable or violated besides.

A second course of action flashed before his eyes, in which he took the time to romance her, to charm her, to gain her consent before he took their casually affectionate friendship to the next level.

The imagined alternative disappeared from his mind's eye when he felt her hands rest against his chest, her lips beginning to move in response to his. She was kissing him back. His stomach dropped into the abyss as he conceded she did want him after all.

It was pure bliss.

The kiss deepened as they both lost their hesitancy, and he grew more confident as her hands roamed over his chest and back. Time lost all meaning as he revelled in the feel of her body, the taste of her mouth, and the faint smell of her perfume lingering around them.

Breaking the kiss as he had in Dimitri's office, he kissed his way down her neck, silently celebrating his certainty that no one would interrupt them this time. He gently sucked at her throat, right where it met her shoulder, and Sam cried out softly. Feeling himself harden in response to her obvious arousal, he decided to up the ante.

His hand skimmed down her thigh as their lips met again, reaching the bottom of her dress. Changing direction when he got to the short hemline, he angled up her leg underneath the fabric. He went slowly, giving her time to object, but she just kissed him more urgently, her hands behind his head, threaded into his hair.

Her rounded behind was bare to his hands in a G-string, and he kneaded it briefly before running down the back of her thigh and lifting her leg to his hip. Sam's whole body was pressed against his in this position, and there was no way she couldn't be aware of his excitement. He traversed his hand back to her ass again, making a guttural sound in his throat as he felt her grind against him.

She dropped her leg and broke their close contact suddenly,

alarming him enough that he felt some insecurity creep back in. Instead of admonishing him, she took him by the hand and led him out of the living room. She looked back at him as they walked, smiling, her face flushed and her pupils dilated, and he realised she must be taking him to her bedroom.

His fear intensified. He'd spent their embrace living very much in the present. As much as he wanted her, his mind had shied away from the obvious next step. Intense vulnerability threatened to dampen his desire as they arrived at their destination.

Sam turned to face him again, her face naked with her own emotion, her hesitancy now reflecting his. His panic receded as he remembered this was a big step for her too. She hadn't been with anyone since her late husband. Suddenly flattered, he understood they would never have come this far if he didn't mean as much to her as she meant to him.

'I love you,' he whispered, the only thing he could say to make the moment right. In fact, it was the only thing he could think to say at all.

Her face lit up and her eyes softened as she moved to wrap her arms around him again. 'I love you too,' she whispered back, leaning up to kiss him.

A while later, they lay relaxing in her bed, Sam's naked body half covering his. Alex slowly stroked her back, from shoulder down to buttocks, and then back to shoulder. She was doing the same to him, down his torso and thigh, and then to her starting position again.

Her hand traced the path of his scar, and he marvelled that he didn't feel self-conscious about it. He'd hidden the disfigurement from everyone for years. His family knew it was there, but he hadn't gone topless in front of anyone since he'd been smooth chested. He was even careful to hide it from Stacey.

Sam hadn't paid it any special attention while they were making love, but she also hadn't avoided it either. Her kisses and caresses had skimmed it the same as his whole and healthy skin, accepting it as a part of him. He didn't know what to make of her attention to it now, but he was glad it didn't seem to deter her. He was far too happy to worry about it overmuch.

He'd been frightened it would be awkward, or his recent inexperience would be all too obvious, but he needn't have been concerned. They'd taken it slowly, and her whispered encouragements and affirmations had given him the confidence to do her justice. He was left in no doubt as to her enjoyment, and he'd benefitted from the passion of her returned ardency. If Sam had any hang ups about her own performance, they were well hidden, and completely unfounded.

He'd forgotten it could be this way. *Was it ever?* He'd been with women prior to Victoria, but never with anyone he felt so connected to. He remembered enjoying sex, could even remember being carefree during it. There was a time in the misty past when he was motivated by the prospect of mutual satisfaction. More recent were memories of Victoria, where his diligence was motivated by a desire to avoid her disparagement. He quickly banished that memory, unwilling to let his despised ex-wife ruin this moment.

To distract himself from his morose musings, Alex spoke. 'I think we missed our dinner reservations,' he murmured, taking hold of Sam's hand to bring it to his lips.

She gave a low laugh, snuggling in closer. 'I'm not fussed, to be honest,' she admitted.

Her leg moved a little as she cuddled into him, covering his own, and Alex reached down and pulled her knee up across his hips. Her hand travelled over his face, combing through his beard as she smiled at him. Her face was only inches from his, so he kissed her again, marvelling at how naturally it came now.

He rolled her onto her back, keeping her leg wrapped around him. Running a hand up her leg, over her hip, and to her chest, he cupped her breast in his hand, gently squeezing it. Sam's hips moved, pressing into him briefly before moving back to make room for the hand she slipped between them.

Alex caught it before she managed to wrap it around him, moving both her hands above her head and trapping them there. 'You might not be fussed,' he said playfully, 'but I'm an old man. I'll need sustenance before I can do this a second time.'

She laughed as he let her go and jumped out of bed. Locating his pants, he pulled his phone from a pocket and settled back into bed with her. He quickly ordered them a pizza, before turning his full attention back to the lusciously naked woman in bed with him.

He caught her looking at the scar she'd been tracing, saw her connecting it with her eyes to the one on his face. It wasn't as deep on his face as it was on his body, and the inward curve of his neck had escaped with just a shallow gash. That part of the scar had long since healed, barely visible to the naked eye, but when viewed together it was clear they were part of the same mark.

Sam obviously realised he'd caught her looking, a guilty look flooding her face, before it changed to resignation. It was too late to pretend she wasn't curious. 'Was this her?' she asked. She looked as if she were about to speak again a moment later, perhaps to reassure him he didn't have to answer, but subsided when he spoke instead.

Alex already knew she wouldn't make him answer if he didn't want to. This knowledge was perhaps the main reason he decided to tell her. 'I told you awhile back there was more to the story,' he started. 'I guess it's time I gave you the rest of it.'

And so, he told her, bracing himself for her reaction. He could accept shock, horror at what had been done to him, but prayed she could still love him when she knew how damaged he was.

Sam didn't disappoint. She was stunned, yes, but there was no rejection in her response. Alex became overwhelmed as he relayed the series of events that led to his injuries, and she held him and cried with him, only letting go when a knock at the door announced their dinner.

When they were done eating, she seduced him again with whispered words of love and support. As they began to move together, Alex realised she was all in, for better or worse. Sam loved him. Unconditionally.

Chapter 29 – Some Welcome Assistance

'My last employer and I were *very* close,' said the woman, Minnie, leaning towards Alex. 'He used to call me his "busy little beaver". We were thick as thieves until I left.'

Sam hid her annoyance and asked another question. 'And why did you leave that job?' she asked.

As per usual, Minnie directed her answer to Alex, languidly crossing and uncrossing her legs as she did so. 'His wife considered me to be an unnecessary expense,' she explained, a faintly petulant look marring her features. 'She didn't have a lot to do with the day-to-day running of things, so her opinion shouldn't have mattered, but she was used to getting her own way. Roger quietly let me know that it might be best to start looking elsewhere before she really put her foot down.'

Sam privately wondered if Roger's wife had different motivations, jerking her eyes away from Minnie's cleavage for the umpteenth time. A display of that much bosom was distracting no matter what your sexual orientation. She eyed Alex again, hoping to catch him looking even once so she might have an outlet for her jealousy after the hussy left.

It's not his fault, she reminded herself. *He doesn't ask for women to throw themselves at him. They just do it.*

In Minnie's defence, she had no idea Alex and Sam were an item.

Not that it would probably have made much difference, assuming Sam's suspicions were correct. The ridiculous woman had probably been shown the door while her old boss was trying to frantically save his marriage, post-affair.

The interview wrapped up and they both walked her to the door, where Minnie turned and beamed at Alex again.

'Thank you for meeting with me, Alex,' she said, shaking his hand for a little longer than necessary. 'Nice to meet you, Sarah.'

Sam didn't bother to correct her, but she couldn't resist making a point. She moved closer to Alex and casually put an arm around his waist. 'We'll be in touch, Minnie,' she said.

A sense of smug satisfaction washed through her as Alex's hand settled on her back, and comprehension showed in the other woman's expression. Minnie's smile slipped a little, but she nodded and turned to leave without saying anything.

'Well, that went well,' said Alex. 'I think we've found my next assistant.'

Sam jerked her eyes away from Minnie's retreating figure to stare incredulously at him.

He only managed to hold his innocent look for half a second before doubling over with laughter. 'I've never seen you mark your territory before,' he teased when he could speak again. 'Maybe I should I get a badge made up for future interviews. "Property of Sam Faulkner" or something.'

Fighting the colour rising in her cheeks, Sam answered curtly. 'Maybe I'll just sit in your lap next time,' she said. Alex's face went carefully blank, and she hastened to soften the sting of her tone. 'Sorry, that was meant for her, not you,' she explained. 'I can't stand women like that.'

Alex had proven to be quite sensitive to her criticism since they'd capitulated to their feelings, and she grieved their easy banter. With any luck, they'd grind Victoria into the dirt next week. Maybe then he could heal.

He smiled for her though, nodding at her explanation and giving her a quick kiss. The new receptionist caught them and smiled too, winking at Sam as they made their way back to Alex's office.

Sam and Alex hadn't shown a lot of affection around the office yet, and it was nice to get the support. Both of them had been nervous about presenting the news, keeping it under wraps for two whole weeks while they figured out what to do.

They hadn't wanted to 'announce' it as such (the prospect of inferred narcissism didn't sit well with either of them) but neither had they wanted to go completely under the radar. The changes in their respective demeanours were sure to give birth to illicit rumours, and they didn't want the information so completely out of their control.

In the end, Sam had solved their problem with the simple expedient of just confiding in Clarice, who had been over the moon for them both. She'd also ensured everyone in the office knew the facts within half a day. Her friend wasn't known as the 'office gossip' for nothing.

As she followed Alex back to his office, Sam realised Tristan had observed their brief intimacy too. He had a sour look on his face, and she bit back laughter. He'd reportedly been playing the martyr since the news had come out (Sam herself had overheard the phrase 'cut my lunch'), but with no Rebecca to encourage his pouting, he didn't have a very supportive audience. It was obvious he resented the older man, but he couldn't do much beyond grumble under his breath. Not when everyone else was obviously so happy for them.

Sam had been worried her promotion would be suspect, their relationship being made public so soon after it. It was hard to argue your success was deserving when you were sleeping with the boss, after all, even when it was camouflaged by the promotion of Dave and several other staff. Surprisingly, it hadn't caused a single hiccup. She hoped it stayed that way.

The only non-Victoria problem remaining was to hire Alex a replacement assistant, a task that had proved more challenging than either of them had expected. Sam had continued doing the duties while they looked, but she'd not expected it to still be the case by now.

Alex put it succinctly as he sat at his desk. 'Back to the drawing board, I guess.'

Sam stared mournfully at the pile of CV's. Most of the applicants so far were totally unsuitable. Today had been their only interview, and her heart had sunk from the outset. Minnie was obviously highly intelligent and experienced, but that didn't cancel out her obvious flaws. She didn't object to a bit of skin, but the outfit the woman wore was completely unprofessional. And the obvious flirting even more so.

Her phone rang before she could respond, and she ducked out of Alex's office to answer it. 'Good afternoon, Sam speaking,' she said, before noticing the number on the caller ID. 'Oh, hi Dad.'

'Sam!' he said jovially. 'Finally, you answer! I was beginning to think you and that fella had locked yourself in his office for some "alone time".'

A smacking noise sounded through the receiver, and Sam heard her mother hiss in the background. 'Gordon! She's at work. You can't say things like that.'

Sam rolled her eyes, smiling. 'You can say it,' she clarified. 'I just can't respond in kind. But to answer the implied question, I was in a meeting. Alex and I were interviewing someone. So, what's up?' she asked, trying to nudge him towards the reason for his call. Her parents tended to waffle.

Her mother said something in the background, but she couldn't make out what it was as her father was shushing her. 'I'm asking her! Just give me a minute,' he said crossly. 'Sam, your mum wants to know if you're still coming for dinner tomorrow night.'

She hid her exasperation as she answered. This was the third time they'd confirmed. 'Yes, I'm still coming for dinner. And bringing Alex and his daughter. If anything changes, I'll let you know.'

Her dad paused, and Sam could practically smell his discomfort.

'Your mother tells me he's a bit older than you,' he said, his voice a blend of concern and sternness. 'Should we be worried?'

She bit back a laugh. It was sweet, really, how they fretted over her. Even if it was also annoying. She'd needed it at one stage. 'It's eight years, Dad,' she said. 'Not eighty. And I'm thirty-eight, not sixteen. You're six years older than Mum. Should I worry about you two?'

He huffed, and she reminded herself to moderate her tone. She hadn't meant it to sound sharp. They weren't to know how much she'd healed in the last few months. She'd been avoiding having honest conversations with them for a while now.

'Well, I'm not your mother's boss!' he said. 'It's all a bit fishy, don't you think? You start bumping uglies with the guy signing your paycheques, then suddenly you get a promotion. And we're not supposed to wonder if he's taking advantage of you?'

Sam had turned while he spoke, and she realised Alex was watching her. He could probably hear her from there. And for once, the desks around her were all empty.

'The promotion was significantly in advance of our "uglies" bumping,' she said drily. 'But thanks for the vote of confidence.'

Alex burst out laughing, and she frantically signalled for him to be quiet. Her dad would be embarrassed if he knew anyone else was privy to even her end of the conversation.

He managed to get the noise level under control, but tears leaked out of his eyes as he bent over his desk and his shoulders quivered. Sam smiled at him and shook her head, while her parents argued in the background.

'Put it on speaker!' said her mother urgently.

'Which button is it?' said her dad.

'The speaker button!'

'I don't know which button that is!'

'Just give me the phone!'

This last demand was accompanied by some muffled cracking, and suddenly her mum's voice was magnified. 'Sam? Sam, can you hear me?' she said.

'Yes, Mum. I can hear you,' Sam answered patiently.

'Darling, it's not that we aren't happy for you,' she said. 'It's just that you've been so quiet since Loga — I mean, over the last few years. It's all happened very suddenly. We just want to be sure you're okay.'

A wave of guilt washed through her as her dad chimed in.

'You were barely leaving the house for a while there, and now there's this boy,' he said. 'Are you sure you're ready for that?'

No wonder they've been so overbearing.

She'd shut herself off from the world for months after Logan died, only seeing her parents. She'd barely spoken, barely even moved. They'd had to coax her to eat. And as soon as she'd started to function at the bare minimum, she'd begun edging them out.

They'd hovered from what they'd obviously considered a respectful distance, but it had annoyed her to no end. She'd just wanted to be alone. And so, she'd pushed them further away. It only occurred to her now how habit-forming that had been. They didn't realise she'd been flirting with the land of the living long since, because she hadn't included them.

'Yes,' she said, blinking back tears. 'But thank you. It means a lot to me that you still look out for me. I know things got a bit dicey after Logan died. You basically had to go back to caring for a toddler. I haven't been appreciative enough of that and I'm sorry.' She grabbed a tissue from the box on her desk, dabbing at her eyes before any real damage could be done to her makeup. 'I don't think I'll ever be quite the same, but you don't need to worry anymore. I've been on the mend for a while now. The day-to-day stuff isn't so hard anymore, and I get out a lot more.

'Alex makes me happy,' she continued, smiling at him while he watched her. 'We didn't rush into this or anything. He's been off the market for a long time too. Neither of us planned this. It just sort of … happened. I promise, this is a good thing. And you're going to like him.'

Her mum was crying now, and Sam swallowed a lump in her throat too. *No need to get that going.* She'd managed to stave off the worst of her emotional response so far, but there must have been something in her face, because the next thing, Alex was there. He knelt beside her while she wrapped up the conversation with her parents, holding her hand.

By the time she finally hung up the phone, she felt wrung out. She purposefully relaxed her shoulders, exhaling slowly. Alex nodded towards his office, and she followed him inside.

He put his arms around her as soon as the door closed. She was surprised that she didn't want to cry anymore. His presence should have left her feeling safe enough to show some vulnerability, but instead it left her just feeling ... home.

'Do they have a point?' Alex asked quietly.

She snorted. 'No,' she answered. 'Absolutely not. I remember how I felt when Logan died. It was like there were holes everywhere. Spaces, where he used to fit. And I was stumbling around in the dark, trying not to fall into them, but I didn't know where they were. The best I could do was stand still and shut everything out.' She leaned back to look up at him. 'I did that for a long time, and I don't think they noticed when I started moving again. Probably because the only direction I walked in for a long time was wherever there weren't any other people.'

He'd let go of her torso during this speech, reaching up to cup her face instead.

'And now?' he asked. 'Are the holes gone?'

The hollow feeling she associated with Logan's loss visited her for a moment, and she knew she couldn't lie to him. 'No,' she whispered. 'I don't think they're going to go anywhere. Even with you ... you're not a replacement. You're a lot of wonderful things, but you aren't a magic heal-all. The holes are still there. I just don't notice them as much. Maybe the edges aren't as jagged.'

He watched her with an unreadable expression, and she felt the need to try and put it in terms he might understand.

'Maybe it's like you with Victoria, in some ways. Nothing I can do will scrub out the past. She'll always have done the things she did. We have the future though, and that's more than I thought I'd get.'

He smiled, jumping when her phone rang outside the door again. She contemplated not answering it, but he let go and stepped away, so she dutifully scampered to her desk.

'Um, I'm not sure what to do,' whispered their new receptionist through the phone. 'Someone has come in to drop off their application for the assistant job, and he's insisting he wants to give it to Alex in person. I've told him he's in a meeting, but he's just sat down in reception to wait him out.'

This was an unusual turn of events. Sam wondered if the persistence was a promising sign or if the man was just even pushier than she herself was. Either way, her curiosity was engaged. Putting the phone down, she quickly conferred with Alex, before requesting he be invited in for them to feel him out.

Her trepidation increased ten-fold when the man was escorted to the door.

It was Isaac, Dimitri's assistant.

Neither Alex nor Sam showed any emotion as the receptionist left, not inviting their visitor to sit or bothering to greet him.

He nodded his acceptance of their wariness and started speaking instead. 'I can explain,' he began, but appeared too nervous to begin doing so.

'What are you doing here?' asked Alex finally.

Isaac dithered for a moment, answering in a pleading tone. 'I want to apply for the assistant job, but I knew you wouldn't consider me if I didn't get to speak to you, so —' he stopped talking as Alex cut him off.

'I was under the impression you were already employed,' he said levelly. 'By my competitor.'

Isaac nodded, still looking anxious. 'Not happily,' he qualified. 'Dimitri isn't an easy man to work for. I've been thinking of getting out for a while now. I could be a real asset to you, already being well informed in your field.'

Alex contemplated this for a moment, sharing a look with Sam. It was true, the man was highly qualified, not to mention competent if

Dimitri tolerated him. If it weren't for the obvious trust issues, it would be an easy decision.

Sam looked back at the nervous man, wondering what would have possessed him to think he had a shot.

Alex voiced her feelings, not hiding his incredulity. 'Why would I trust you?' he asked.

Isaac steeled himself. His knowledge of Dimitri's duplicity had been obvious from the moment he arrived, and Sam realised he'd been building up to this moment since then. He reached into his pocket and pulled out a USB drive, placing it on the desk without giving a verbal answer.

Neither Sam nor Alex touched the drive, instead focusing on Isaac.

'What's on it?' asked Sam finally, her curiosity getting the better of her before Alex's.

Isaac licked his lips, smiling for the first time since he arrived. 'Proof,' he answered.

Chapter 30 – Ding! Round Two

Sam walked into the courtroom with Alex, her eyes immediately finding Victoria. The cruel woman's eyes dropped to their clasped hands, condescending to raise one eyebrow, before turning away. She wasn't sure what to make of the other woman's refusal to meet her gaze, although quite frankly, she didn't care. It didn't matter what she thought. Only the judge.

She caught sight of Isaac's face as she turned to speak to Michael. His look of unease turned to one of resolve as he noticed Dimitri on the other side of the aisle. Sam was glad to see their nemesis was ignoring the younger man. Isaac was potentially in a lot of trouble for the emails he'd stolen. With any luck, they would damn both Victoria and Dimitri. *Two for the price of one.*

Dimitri's appearance on Victoria's witness list had been a surprise. Victoria's new lawyer provided the list before Michael had even had a chance to subpoena the horrible man. Sam had been wondering what he had up his sleeve since she'd learned of this, trying not to let on to Alex that she was concerned. She'd only learned last night that he was as worried as her.

She perked up when a third man entered the courtroom. It appeared Victoria still hadn't left Paul. That was interesting.

'That's a good sign, right?' asked Sam in a low voice. 'Didn't we decide that meant she wasn't confident last time?'

'He's on her witness list,' answered Michael. 'I'd be surprised if she'd given him the boot before he testifies. She doesn't have Rebecca and Tiffany in her pocket this time.'

Sam nodded. It made sense. She just wanted a sign that things were going to go their way. The suspense was killing her.

She gave Alex a quick kiss for good luck, before settling into her seat to wait for the judge. It wouldn't be long now.

Victoria's side went first this time. As her therapist left the stand, Sam involuntarily looked at the other side of the courtroom. She hadn't been surprised when the shrink had gone first. It'd almost been boring, hearing her give much the same testimony as last time. Whoever came next would begin the real show.

She tensed as Paul's name was called. By comparison, he looked relaxed, smiling slightly as he meandered to the witness box and was sworn in.

You'd think he'd be more apprehensive about committing perjury, after Tiffany and Rebecca, thought Sam.

'Mr Fraser,' began Duncan Smith, Victoria's new lawyer. 'When did you first begin to suspect your wife's history of abuse?'

Paul assumed a stony expression, the perfect image of a protective husband.

'Probably around two and a half years prior to her and Alex separating,' he answered. 'A large group was staying at a mutual friend's place for a wedding, and the place was a rabbit warren. I mistook hers and Alex's room for my own and accidentally walked in on her changing. I'd known her for a few years prior to this and always wondered why she seemed so guarded, but it wasn't until I saw the bruises that I became suspicious.' He cleared his throat before continuing. 'I apologised profusely of course, having violated her privacy, but she seemed more concerned that Alex might find out another man had seen her nude and marked than she did about the impropriety. She swore me to secrecy.'

Sam wondered how much truth there was to this story. Had an accidental meeting really been how their affair began? Were they smart enough to have mixed the lies in with some truth?

'And did you keep that promise?' prompted Duncan.

Paul nodded. 'I did, although mostly because I couldn't be sure my suspicions were correct,' he said. 'I did try to do some casual investigating, but I didn't find out much. Not a lot of people knew much about their marriage, beyond that they were rumoured to be unhappy.' He shrugged. 'I saw her a couple more times over the next few months and tried to get to know her better, but she was very hard to pin down. She confirmed later that she was avoiding me, frightened I would unsettle the status quo.'

Nicely done, thought Sam, her lip curling in disgust. *Implant the idea that she was keeping things quiet, so the judge doesn't question why there aren't more witnesses.*

'How were your suspicions confirmed?' asked Duncan.

'I struggled for a bit when I couldn't be sure,' Paul answered. 'I tried to convince myself it was none of my business, but when I heard Alex was interstate for a few days, I knew I had to confront her. I showed up at their home and coaxed it out of her. Alex was abusing her.' His mouth compressed into a grim line after this pronouncement, his expression unchanging as he and Duncan continued their rehearsed false testimony.

Sam noticed there was no mention of their affair. Paul didn't come out and lie about it, but much of what he said could easily be construed as the experience of a concerned friend.

Also conspicuously absent was mention of his own wife, who had been battling cancer for much of the intervening period — and dead for the six months preceding Alex and Victoria's marriage ending. Not until Michael began his questioning did Sam's anger begin to abate.

'At what point did you and Mrs Fraser commence having an affair?' asked Michael bluntly.

Paul's face stayed blank while answering, but a glance at Victoria showed she was annoyed.

What did she expect? That we were just going to roll over and play dead?

'And did your own wife know about your infidelity at the time of her death, or had she been too focused on her illness to notice you were cheating on her for the preceding year and a half?' questioned Michael.

'Objection,' called Duncan. 'Relevance.'

'Sustained,' agreed the judge.

While it did throw a little shade at Paul's character, it would have been a stretch to argue his testimony wasn't credible based on a history of marital dishonesty. Sam suspected Michael knew this and had asked the question knowing the answer didn't matter. He just wanted the judge to have a better understanding of the circumstances.

Her suspicions hardened to certainty when he didn't give up the line of questioning completely.

'Had you engaged in other infidelities during the course of your marriage to Angela Fraser?' asked Michael.

'Objection,' called Duncan again, exasperation colouring his tone. 'Again, relevance. Your honour, the witness is not on trial. His own marriage is not the subject of this case.'

'Sustained,' agreed the judge. 'Mr Davis, please stick to the point.'

Having quite sneakily made his point, Michael appeared to take the admonishment in his stride and smoothly changed the subject. 'To your knowledge, did your current wife ever confide in anyone else about her alleged abuse, both before and after the relationship with Mr Whittaker ended?'

'Objection,' called Duncan again. 'Speculation. Bordering on hearsay, your honour.'

'Your honour, I'm not asking the witness to speculate or to present any of the information Mrs Fraser gave him as fact. I am attempting to gain a clearer picture of *his* knowledge.'

The judge nodded. 'I will allow it, Mr Davis, but you had best have a point,' she said.

Michael turned to the witness box again, waiting for an answer.

Paul waited for Duncan's nod before doing so. 'I was the first to find out,' he stated. 'But I inadvertently informed Dimitri Ivanov during an emotional display several months before she ended their marriage. I was pleading for her to leave Alex, unaware that Dimitri was in earshot.'

So that's why Dimitri is here. Victoria had two people lie to bolster her story last time, and this time would be no different. *Gotta give her some credit,* thought Sam. *This isn't as out of the blue as her last perjurious circus. She's learned her lesson. Make it believable.*

'So,' continued Michael, 'in the nine or so years that your wife was in a relationship with Mr Whittaker, you, a near stranger, were the first and only person she confided in. Why do you think she went to so much trouble to keep it quiet, only to confess everything to one nosy busybody?'

'Objection,' called Duncan again. 'Speculation. Mr Fraser isn't to know what caused Mrs Fraser's talkativeness.'

This was sustained, and the rest of the questions were frustratingly unhelpful. Michael also seemed to realise they were going nowhere, as he soon let Paul leave the stand.

Sam was ambiguous about how things were going so far. The age of the events made it quite difficult for Michael to cast doubt on Paul's claims, and the therapist seemed to truly believe the things she'd testified to. There was still a long way to go, but no tangible hope had appeared on the horizon.

Dimitri was at his most confidently evil as he answered Duncan's questions. Hopefully, the judge was as put off by this as Sam was, but it was difficult to tell.

'How did you come to learn of the abuse Mr Whittaker subjected Mrs Fraser to?' asked Duncan.

It's almost like watching a movie. If she weren't so emotionally invested in the outcome, the web of lies unfurling would have been entertaining.

'I overheard a conversation,' he replied, 'between Paul and Victoria. It was … passionate. I believed him to be greatly saddened by the loss of his wife. When coupled with the pain of knowing his love belonged to another … well, he was pleading with her to leave him, telling her he would protect her and little Anastasia.'

'And you made your presence known at that time? Or did you confront them later?' clarified Duncan.

Dimitri's forehead furrowed. 'I was hesitant to interfere, you understand,' he explained. 'Aleksander is the son of a dear friend. I did not want to believe the things I heard of him in this conversation. But too many things added up, you see.' His expression turned harder, almost scornful. 'The men of their family, they pride themselves on being "womanisers". They have no respect for the fairer sex. Another "notch in the bedpost" is all they wish.'

Erik shifted next to her, perhaps uncomfortable that his and Noah's antics were better characterised by that statement than Alex's has ever been.

'I had heard rumours that Aleksander was unfaithful, and I was not surprised. That his lovely wife was too committed to end things was more mysterious. I could not understand why this woman, who had once been vibrant and laughing, would subject herself to a philandering husband? I hear this, and it makes sense. She is too frightened to leave.' He shook his head sorrowfully. 'And the poor little girl, seeing her father strike her mother; my heart goes out to her. It is not my place, but I could not stay quiet. I went into the room, and I joined my pleas to Paul's. "Leave him", I said. "I will help you". I had overheard that she was frightened to stay with Paul, that Aleksander would be jealous and violent if he thought she had given herself to another, and so I offered to have her and the little girl stay with me. I knew it would kill my friendship with the Whittaker family, but it was the right thing to do. They would not presume she was having an affair with an old man.'

Duncan nodded. 'And what was her response?' he asked.

'She would not,' confirmed Dimitri. 'She said she did not want to come between friends, but I could see fear in her eyes. She was afraid, too afraid to leave him.'

'And did you accept her wishes?' asked Duncan.

'I did,' he said. 'I watched her closely though, much as Paul did, for any sign she may need my help. When I heard she had left him, I was so happy. I went to see her and was shocked to learn that she had left Anastasia with Aleksander's family. I offered to accompany her to go and collect her, but she refused. She had taken the biggest step, but Aleksander's attempt to take his life had paralysed her, I think. If he were so desperate to do something so drastic to himself, what would he do to his daughter if she were taken from him?'

'So, you believed Mr Whittaker was capable of hurting his daughter?' confirmed Duncan.

'Objection,' called Michael, his first for quite some time. 'Leading the witness.'

'Let me rephrase,' said Duncan, before the judge could respond. 'Did you believe Mrs Fraser's fears had merit?'

'Objection,' said Michael again. 'Calls for speculation.'

'Your honour, I am not asking Mr Ivanov to speculate on Mrs Fraser's frame of mind,' argued Duncan. 'I am asking if he agreed with it.'

'You have not successfully established what her frame of mind *was*,' said Michael. 'How could he answer that question without speculating?'

'Your objection is sustained,' ruled the judge.

Duncan tried again. 'Mr Ivanov, what did you fear Mr Whittaker would do had Mrs Fraser taken their daughter while he was hospitalised?'

'Objection!' said Michael again, exasperated. 'Still calling for speculation, your honour.'

'Sustained,' said the judge, nodding. 'Mr Smith, if your witness has testimony as to an actual threat, please ask him straight out. Otherwise, move on.'

Sam thought furiously. There were two issues at stake today: the divorce settlement and the custody agreement. The second would have a large impact on the first. Whoever went home with Stacey would get most of the money. Both sides had accepted that, so both sides would be fighting for her, albeit for different reasons. This line of questioning was supposed to be Victoria's grab for custody. The neglect and emotional abuse Alex planned to bring to light wouldn't hold a candle against a threat of violence to their child.

Her heart lifted as Duncan indicated he had no further questions. *Good work, Michael.* They weren't out of the woods. Not even close. But it was a start.

'Mr Ivanov,' began Michael, 'is it true you have remained friendly with the Whittaker family up until quite recently?'

'Objection,' called Duncan straight away. 'Leading the witness.'

The judge sustained the question, and Michael looked to be fighting an eye roll. That question was easily asked another way.

What a pointless waste of time.

'Were you invited to a party earlier this year, in celebration of Bernard and Eva Whittaker's fiftieth wedding anniversary?' he asked.

'Yes,' agreed Dimitri. 'But I was unable to attend.'

'And did you invite Alex Whittaker to attend your latest product launch party around the same time?'

'Yes,' agreed Dimitri again. 'He was invited as a professional courtesy. He is in a similar line of business.'

You won't be in business for much longer, thought Sam smugly. *The things you and Victoria cooked up prove you're as much of a scheming asshole as she is.*

'And you have been a guest at many other social functions hosted by the Whittaker family, and you regularly invite them to attend your own?' said Michael.

Dimitri agreed again.

'So, it would be safe to assume you did not shun the Whittaker family for what you allege they did to Mrs Fraser.'

It wasn't quite a question, but Dimitri assented anyway. 'Keep your friends close, and your enemies closer,' he quoted. 'I would have happily cut ties; however, Victoria asked me to keep an eye on them. On Aleksander and Anastasia, specifically. She wished to know if her daughter was safe.'

'You were spying?' said Michael interestedly. 'And secretly reporting back to Mrs Fraser. How kind of you.'

Sometimes I think he has as big of a mouth as me, mused Sam. *No wonder Duncan objects so much.*

The comment passed without any interruptions though.

'There was not a lot of reporting,' admitted Dimitri. 'I did not remain in close contact with Victoria or Paul, at their express request. They did not want it to slip that I was a mole.'

'Interesting,' said Michael. 'Then why did you invite them to the same event you also knew Mr Whittaker to be attending at your company? If you intended for them not to see one another, it would have made more sense to keep them separated.'

Sam tensed. They were getting close to the stolen information. She was going to relish the big 'middle finger' that was to come.

'Victoria had already decided she was going to sue for custody by then,' said Dimitri. 'It made no sense to keep them apart. Besides, there were rumours Aleksander was flaunting the morality clause in their custody agreement. It helped her cause to observe him coming to an event with the woman he was dating. And even more so when they enjoyed a romp in my office.'

Eva made a quiet noise of derision, and Sam finally glanced down the row of seats at her. Her teeth were gritted together so hard that she could almost hear them grinding. It occurred to her that this woman was the reason Dimitri was on the stand right now. She'd almost forgotten he had an ulterior motive. Revenge truly was a dish served cold.

For the first time, she wondered if Dimitri knew the true story of what went on between Alex and Victoria. Would he still be so self-serving if he knew about the extent of the violence? She'd vaguely assumed he was just another troublemaker (albeit a high-level one), until now.

Her attention was pulled back to the matter at hand when Michael surprised her.

'No further questions, your honour,' he said.

Chapter 31 – A Spider in the Spotlight

'It'll have a bigger impact if I use it when I question Victoria,' Michael explained during the recess. 'I can always call Dimitri back later and question him about it too if it's needed. I want the upheaval to come during the most damning testimony.'

Alex opened his mouth to argue but shut it without saying anything. It was too late now. And besides, Michael had a point. Victoria was the one who needed to be brought down. The proof Isaac had given them of her manipulations needed to be used strategically.

He let go of his anger with difficulty. Not that it helped much. He was still full of anxiety, hopelessness, fear, and a whole thesaurus of other emotions. Not even Sam's hand in his as they trudged back to the courtroom could summon any good cheer. Time would tell.

The judge took in Victoria's untruths without changing expression. She told the same story as last time, painting Alex as a violently abusive megalomaniac who had manipulated her into giving up custody of her beloved daughter.

'He threatened to kill her if I took her with me,' she said sorrowfully, 'and I believed him. I knew she'd lead a lonely life, but it was the only way to keep her safe. She's his prize possession, you see. Her presence allows him to portray himself as a doting father, to distract from the reality of his narcissism.'

Her lawyer tactfully paused to allow her to collect herself before asking his next question. 'Why did he let you leave then? If his image as a devoted father was so important, why not his image as a loving husband?' he prompted.

Victoria gave a short, bitter laugh before answering. 'He didn't "let" me leave. He threatened to kill himself if I did. He couldn't face a reality in which people knew what he did to me. I left anyway, and that same night, he really did try to kill himself. If Stacey hadn't found him and called the ambulance, he'd have succeeded.'

Duncan nodded, a frown marring his otherwise stoic exterior. 'Why did he think this threat would prevent you from leaving? After all he put you through, why would he think threatening self-harm would stop you?' he asked.

'Because it always had before,' she explained. 'Each time I told him I was leaving, he threw himself down the stairs or hurt himself in some way, telling me he couldn't live without me.' She narrowed her eyes, doing her best to discredit Alex's testimony before he even had a chance to deliver it. 'He threatened to claim it was *me* hurting *him* if I followed through,' she said.

One of his brothers gave a soft, derisive snort from behind him, not heard by the judge. Victoria could surely see his face, but she was too caught up in her performance to be perturbed. 'But still, I never believed he'd go through with his suicide,' she said, sniffing. 'I didn't want him dead. I still loved him in some ways, I just didn't want him in our lives anymore. I thought he was too self-centred to seriously risk his own life. I underestimated how much his image means to him.'

Alex fought an urge to roll his eyes. He should be taking this seriously, and he was, but the things she was saying were so ludicrous it was difficult to keep himself from reacting.

'I should've left the first time he hurt himself,' she sobbed, gaining steam again, 'but I honestly believed he'd carry out his threats to paint me as abusive. He had plenty of evidence to bend in his favour: all those hospital visits where he hurt himself and lied about tripping or falling. And I knew his family would take his side.'

'So why did you leave him, in the end?' asked Duncan.

She clutched her tissue tighter as she answered, gesturing pleadingly.

'In the end, it really came down to what was best for Stacey. I didn't want her growing up seeing what he put me through. I left, preparing for the fight of my life. I convinced myself that if I tried hard enough, I could win a custody battle.' She dabbed her eyes again.

You're not even crying, Alex thought cynically. *You're just trying to garner some sympathy.*

'By the time he recovered from his injuries, I was ready,' she said, calming somewhat.

Alex saw her imagined memory of resolve in the set of her shoulders and the square look on her face, admiring her preparedness. The woman deserved an Oscar.

'I knew how much I wanted, and it wasn't much really. I was willing to take zero of the money if need be, so long as I could get custody of Stacey. I knew he'd probably get visitation rights, but I was prepared to deal with that. I'd have her with me most of the time, and I was determined to mitigate his indifference to her as best I could.'

Duncan nodded along. 'And how did that work out?' he asked.

Victoria's face crumpled again as she lied about her dashed hopes.

'He outfoxed me,' she said, mimicking a brave attempt to hold back her tears. 'Before we even started negotiations, he approached me. That was when he threatened to kill her. I didn't know what to do. How could I prove his threat? In public, he was the very soul of love and devotion. No one would ever suspect the things I knew about him.

'I eventually accepted there was nothing I could do. I had to give him custody. My only hope was that he would slip up. I thought maybe in time, Stacey would grow and become aware of his manipulations, and confide in me something I could use against him.'

Alex was getting annoyed now. How many lies was he going to have to listen to?

'I didn't anticipate how far he was willing to take it. The day we met for mediation … I was gobsmacked at how much money he was willing to give me. I'd assumed he'd give me as little as possible, that he'd use his proposed position as Stacey's primary carer to take the lion's share of our wealth. I didn't realise until the end that it was a bribe. He looked right at me as I learned he meant to deny me visitation rights, and I knew if I protested it would be the end of our daughter.'

'And so, in your state of fear, you agreed to his terms?' asked Duncan. 'How has this affected your life since?'

'I agreed,' Victoria confirmed, an impressive wave of real tears the perfect accessory to her look of hopelessness. 'In the years since, I've thought about Stacey every day, praying she was okay. I remarried, but I couldn't bring myself to have more children. The thought of another child having the love and attention I couldn't lavish on my little girl twisted a knife inside of me every time I considered it. The guilt was a stain on my every happy moment, my every attempt to build a new life.'

'And your financial situation?' he asked. 'You mentioned Mr Whittaker had been generous; how did that work out?'

Having apparently gained control of her weeping, an almost petulant look now crossed Victoria's face. 'It took a few years for me to figure it out,' she said, feigning a sorrowed tone of admission, 'but I eventually understood what he'd done. The value of almost everything he gave me was inflated or steadily dropping. Properties were in a major state of disrepair, or they were situated in locations losing their value. Companies I owned went out of business. Shares were in industries that were failing.'

Alex almost snorted. She'd gotten more than enough to keep her in luxury for the rest of her life — a lot more than him. And even he was wealthier now than the two had been together. If she didn't insist on spending every cent as soon as it touched her palm, she'd be richer still. Stockbrokers, financial advisors … these jobs existed for a reason.

'If I hadn't married a man who was almost as well off as I'd thought myself to be, I'd be bankrupt by now,' she finished forlornly.

'Is this why you're arguing that you deserve a share of his current wealth?' asked the lawyer.

She nodded, her enthusiasm perhaps a shade too obvious, but Alex had to admit his observations were coloured by his knowledge of Victoria's intentions. The money was her real goal. The lies were just tools and screens in her quest to get rich again.

'In part,' qualified Victoria, 'I also believe he should be financially contributing to the life of his daughter, and I intend to gain the custody I should have always had. His child support payments should be of a size to keep Stacey in the best lifestyle he can provide.'

Duncan nodded gravely. 'Thank you, Mrs Fraser,' he said, 'I know it hasn't been easy for you to talk about this today. No further questions, your honour,' he said, giving Victoria a little nod and heading back to his seat.

Alex realised he was leaning forward, so engrossed in Victoria's false testimony that he hadn't noticed his left leg beginning to tingle. He surreptitiously shifted his weight as he sat back, trying to get some blood flowing again.

Michael rose to cross-examine Victoria, beginning his questions without preamble. 'Mrs Fraser,' he began, 'you claim Mr Whittaker was so controlling he used violence to intimidate you. You also claim he never used this against Stacey, a child whose behaviour was much more likely to need reprimanding than yours. How do you explain your certainty he would never raise a hand to your daughter?'

Alex allowed himself some hope in the wake of his question. This was surely a big hole in her testimony.

'He'd never hurt her before,' said Victoria simply. 'And as long as she was "his", he had no reason to begin doing so. He ignored her for most part. She was only useful to him in public.'

'No reason to begin doing so?' pushed Michael. 'You claim he threatened to kill her, but you don't believe he would resort to less drastic measures should the circumstances become unfavourable?'

'He wouldn't,' she said confidentially. 'He's possessive and proud, and he hates me for leaving, but he hates any stain on his image more.

As long as she belonged to him, he'd defend her with the same devotion he would anything he claimed ownership over. I never had any concerns about Stacey's physical safety, so long as she was with him.'

'Mrs Fraser, do you really expect us to believe at no point in the last eleven years has it occurred to you that the man you claim abused you could potentially be mistreating your daughter?' asked Michael incredulously.

'Objection,' called Duncan. 'Asked and answered.'

The judge sustained this objection, and Michael moved on.

'Why aren't you scared he might carry out his alleged threat now?' he asked pointedly.

Obviously prepared by her lawyer to shore up this shaky conjecture in her testimony, Victoria answered smoothly and with a hint of smugness. 'He couldn't get away with it,' she said. 'He knows if he harms her now, the threats are already on record.'

'But you didn't think to report it to begin with?' Michael pressed. 'Surely your opportunity to make these accusations was also present at the time of the original divorce and custody negotiations.'

'I was too scared,' she said, falling back on her frightened victim stance. 'I thought about going to the police, but he already had physical custody during the negotiations. It would have been too easy for him to do it.'

'Yes,' confirmed Michael smugly, pleased she'd led into his next question so neatly. 'Mr Whittaker had physical custody during the negotiations. How did that come to pass? You claim to have left Mr Whittaker because of his abuse, but you didn't think to take your daughter with you?'

A line formed briefly in between Victoria's eyebrows, the only evidence that she was annoyed at being questioned, before smoothing again. She was too used to getting her own way to not be outraged by the scenario.

Shame she's too smart to show it, thought Alex.

'When I made the decision to leave him, I wasn't at the house with them. I called Alex and told him I wasn't coming back, and that's when he threatened to kill himself. In the confusion that followed, I was too scared to do anything. I left her with him until I could get the law behind me.'

Michael looked at her, politely incredulous. 'Mrs Fraser, Mr Whitaker was unconscious for the better part of twenty-four hours after the incident, and in the hospital for several weeks. He physically couldn't care for Stacey during his recovery. Are you claiming you didn't realise custody was yours by default?'

'I knew,' she said quietly, her face convincingly haggard with grief. 'I wasn't even sure whose house she was at though. I psyched myself up to go to the hospital and demand she be given back every couple of days, but I always changed my mind. I was too frightened of making a scene. Anything I did, Alex would've used against me when he was well again.'

Alex realised he was barely breathing. Victoria's performance was mesmerising. To his unease, he could practically feel sincerity oozing from her. He flicked a glance at the judge, but the woman looked much the same as she had since she'd called them to order. Stern. Unflappable. Unreadable.

'And what happened when you did eventually go to the hospital?' enquired Michael.

'I didn't go,' she admitted. 'I was too rattled, too frightened about what would happen if I faced him.'

'So, your husband — whom you earlier claimed to still care for at the time — was grievously injured in a suicide attempt, and you selfishly stayed home,' he mused.

'Objection,' called Duncan. 'Your honour, counsel is testifying. That was not a question.'

'Sustained,' agreed the judge.

Michael nodded, taking the rebuke in his stride. 'Mrs Fraser,' he said. 'What did you do while Mr Whittaker was recovering? Where did you stay? Who did you stay with?'

Victoria lifted her chin slightly, the only evidence she was feeling defensive. 'I was with Paul, my current husband,' she admitted. 'At his home, a few hours away. Dimitri had offered for me to come and stay with him so the family would be less likely to object to my taking Stacey, but I didn't want to live under Alex's yoke anymore. I deserved to be happy.'

'Mr Fraser earlier testified that you were in a romantic relationship for two years prior to the end of your marriage to Mr Whittaker. Do you concur?' clarified Michael.

'Yes,' she answered, her eyes narrowing.

She hadn't wanted to admit to this. He knew it. It'd been conspicuously absent from her original testimony. Her infidelity had some real potential to affect her fiscal share of the settlement. And unlike the unfounded accusations of philandering her side had thrown at him, her affair was proven.

'You claim to have hidden an affair from your allegedly "controlling" and "abusive" husband for two years?' Michael asked, scepticism again peppering his tone. 'Your earlier testimony all but said he outright made you a prisoner in your own home. How could you possibly have had another relationship simultaneously for two years without him noticing?'

'Objection,' called Duncan again. 'Argumentative.'

'Withdrawn,' said Michael quickly. 'Let me rephrase. Mrs Fraser, what steps did you take to hide your two-year long affair from your husband?'

Victoria paused for a moment, collecting her thoughts. Alex hoped it meant Michael had hit upon a line of questioning she wasn't prepared for.

'He wasn't home a lot,' she said. 'He worked long hours, and he was having multiple affairs himself. He was often away for days at a time with other women.'

This seemed weak, and Victoria obviously thought so too. She kept talking, fleshing out her lies properly. 'I knew about the affairs,' she continued. 'He told me if I wasn't going to do the nasty things he likes, he was going to do them with other women. That's why I made sure there was a clause in the custody agreement keeping his sexual partners away from my daughter. I didn't want her growing up with those kinds of bad influences.'

'Ah, yes,' said Michael intently, 'the remarkable clauses in the custody agreement. You claim Mr Whittaker was controlling and manipulative, but somehow you managed to have the morality clause entered, as well as limiting Stacey's time with his family, and premade decisions about everything from her education to her extracurricular activities. How did you manage that with your fear of Mr Whittaker hanging over your head?'

Back on steady ground, Victoria squared her shoulders as she answered.

'I was scared of him, yes,' she said, 'but when I realised that he meant me to have nothing to do with our daughter, I did what I could to ensure she'd have the best opportunities I could manage. I was desperate to give her as much of the life she deserved as possible.' She gestured towards Alex and he almost flinched. 'I believe these restrictions are why he eventually filed for my parental rights to be terminated,' she claimed. 'I did what I could to limit the damage of his influence, but he couldn't live within those constraints forever. He wanted my rights terminated so he could have a more convenient relationship with the woman sitting behind him, whom I suspect to be as immoral as him. They've already been caught getting intimate in a public place. I am genuinely concerned about the environment my daughter has been exposed to.'

Alex saw Michael smile as Victoria extrapolated. Restrained excitement aminated his face. 'You believe it was an eleven-year-old custody agreement that caused Mr Whittaker to file to terminate your parental rights?' he repeated. 'Not your attempts to blackmail him?'

'Objection!' called Duncan again, somewhat more forcefully this time. 'Argumentative, speculative and irrelevant. We are not here to discuss recent events.'

Michael acquiesced, but still made his point. 'I withdraw the question, your honour, but I do not agree with Mr Smith's assertion that recent events are not relevant. We are here today for two decisions to be made, and one of them concerns the living situation of Anastasia Whittaker. Mrs Fraser's character is highly relevant.' He picked up a sheaf of paper as he spoke, holding it up for attention. 'Your honour, I would like to draw Mrs Fraser's attention to exhibit one. May I approach the witness?'

This was it. Now they would see what Isaac's evidence could do. Alex tensed, forcing himself to breathe.

Chapter 32 – A Faint Prayer

'Objection!' called Duncan, standing as well. 'Relevance. Your honour, the exhibit in question contains an illegally obtained series of emails between Mrs Fraser and Dimitri Ivanov and has nothing to do with the eleven-year-old matter we have convened to discuss. The chain doesn't extend back any further than eighteen months ago. I move to disallow it.'

The judge finally spoke, but she gave no quarter to either man. 'The evidence does not need to be obtained legally for it to be relevant, Mr Smith. I am inclined to agree with you about the timeframe though. Mr Davis, how does the exhibit relate to the divorce settlement and custody hearing?'

Michael hadn't managed to make his way out from behind the desk yet, leaning forward over the polished wood to make his point as he answered. Alex could see the tendons in his hands standing out.

'Your honour, the emails reveal Mrs Fraser's plans to blackmail my client, using the original custody agreement to force his hand. Mr Smith has failed to mention that there are also several emails containing confidential information pertaining to Mr Whittaker's business dealings, stolen at Mrs Fraser's behest —'

'The other emails weren't sent by my client!' interrupted Duncan. 'Any mention that Mrs Fraser was involved is hearsay —'

'The emails between Mrs Fraser and her witness clearly indicate that she ordered this!' shot back Michael. 'It's not hearsay when the defendant is evidenced to have incited it!'

'ORDER!' called the judge, banging her gavel, and making Alex jump.

Both men subsided as they took in her frown, but Alex had a sinking feeling. She was staring harder at Michael than she was Duncan.

'Mr Davis, I will remind you that Mrs Fraser is NOT a defendant. She is a petitioner. If you wish to argue that her actions affected Mr Whittaker's company, you will need to do so in another court. We are here to discuss a divorce and custody settlement. Please stick to the point.' She turned to look at Duncan. 'Mr Smith, you will also need to keep your temper.' She finished by giving them both a hard look, and evidently satisfied both men were properly chastised, she turned back to Michael again. 'Mr Davis, you were asked to explain how these recent documents pertained to a situation eleven years in the past but have not yet done so. If you have further comments, make them now, and make them quick, because otherwise I am inclined to agree with Mr Smith.'

Mollified, Michael nodded and began to speak in a less excited tone. 'Yes, your honour,' he began. 'The documents serve three relevant purposes. Firstly, they illustrate the contempt with which Mrs Fraser holds the law. The documents prove that she blackmailed a lawyer into spying on myself, Mr Whittaker and various of his employees, incentivised said employees to spy and steal for her, and also very nearly caused the court to erroneously rule against my client because of the advantage this gave her.' He straightened as he spoke, and Alex allowed himself to hope again. Surely her meddling counted for something.

'Secondly, they prove that she committed similar offences eleven years ago, during the original divorce and custody hearings. This certainly speaks to your insistence that the evidence be timely,' Michael continued.

Duncan harumphed as he sat down but didn't say anything. Alex supposed that meant he didn't have a relevant objection.

'And lastly, they speak volumes about the character of Mrs Fraser, which is highly relevant when considering custody arrangements. The documents prove she is a greedy, unscrupulous liar, who will stop at nothing to get her own way. Anastasia Whittaker should not be placed in her care.'

Duncan's face had gone red. Alex watched him as Michael spoke, mesmerised by the vein pumping rhythmically in his neck. He couldn't look away.

The judge nodded. 'Mr Smith? Any rebuttal?' she asked.

Alex rocked back when Duncan stood, so focused on the man that he hadn't been prepared for the change in their relative stances. He caught himself before he cowered, so tightly strung that he'd viewed the movement as an attack for a split second.

'Yes, your honour,' he was saying. 'Any efforts by my client to win the previous court case are irrelevant. Both petitions were dismissed, and the custody agreement that was the subject of these petitions was invalidated. Her compliance with the law is not the subject of this hearing.' He stabbed his finger on the table as he made his point, the gesture conveying his barely subdued passion. 'Her actions when the dismissed agreement was first conceived aren't relevant, for the same reason. We are convened here today to divide up property and decide custody as if it was the first time. In short, the reset button has been pushed.'

Someone coughed behind Alex, and he jumped, having forgotten that there was anyone else in the courtroom besides the main players.

'As for any relevant commentary on my client's character,' he continued, 'your honour, I've known thieves and murderers who were still capable parents. The desperate actions of a frantic woman aren't evidence she is an unfit parent, and nothing in these documents mentions her time as mother to Anastasia, or even as wife to Mr Whittaker. I say again, they are irrelevant.'

Victoria looked smug, Alex realised. He wondered if anyone else had noticed. He hadn't been paying attention to her while the two lawyers argued, too entranced by Duncan's reactions to take note of hers, but he watched her now.

He tried to be objective about it. Would everyone else be likening her to a cat that fell in the cream, or was it just because he knew her so well?

His eyes had gone funny. She seemed to be quite far away a moment ago, but now she was rushing closer. His peripheral vision had vanished, and her smirk loomed so large he could almost taste it.

'... agree with Mr Smith. The evidence described is not relevant to today's proceedings and will not be admissible. Mr Davis, you may continue your questioning, so long as it does not pertain to recent events.'

Victoria was practically glowing. She'd gone misty, little stars appearing to dance around her. *Why would the devil look so angelic?*

'Alex?' said Michael, appearing between him and Victoria. 'Are you all right? You've gone pale.'

The room tilted sideways as everything faded to black.

Alex sat on the stairs outside the courthouse, a plastic bottle of juice forgotten on the step below him. His family chattered around him, but Sam stayed silent. Her hand rubbed his bicep as he stared at the steps.

On any other day, he'd be mortified. He'd fainted. Him. A grown man. Passed out cold on the floor of the courtroom. His brothers were going to have a field day.

Probably not today though, he thought. They couldn't be that cruel.

Michael sat down on his other side. 'We have to go back inside in fifteen minutes,' he said. 'Do you feel okay? I can have the court date postponed. The judge saw you pass out. She'll approve it.'

And go through this again another day? Not likely.

'No,' he said aloud. 'Let's get it over with. Isaac can still testify, and you can call Dimitri again. It doesn't matter that we can't use the emails.'

Michael looked taken aback, opening and closing his mouth a few times.

'What?' asked Alex.

The lawyer clenched his teeth. It looked like he was preparing himself for a difficult task. 'Alex, I can't use either of them,' he said gently. 'The judge won't allow any testimony about what Victoria's done recently. I don't have anything else relevant to question Dimitri about, and Isaac was probably a kid when you divorced. She'll know it's not relevant as soon as she gets a look at him.'

Alex felt himself nod as if it were someone else moving his head. He certainly didn't feel as calm as he was acting.

'It's not over,' said Michael. 'I still have to finish questioning her. I doubt it'll be hard to cast doubt on all the crap about you inflating her part of the last settlement. If they had evidence, they'd have presented it. And we've still got all your witnesses ...'

He continued to prattle on, reminding Alex about the testimony of his therapist and Stacey's, and of the doctor who'd treated him all those years ago.

He didn't listen. Their help hadn't made this a slam dunk last time, and it was highly doubtful it'd be any different this time.

'Can we just pay her?' he said quietly, interrupting Michael. He broke off, and Sam's hand on his arm tensed.

'We can offer a settlement,' Michael finally said, 'but the judge will want to sign off on it. Whoever gets primary custody of Stacey will be who she'll expect the lion's share of cash to go to. I get the feeling Victoria won't accept anything low enough that'll keep the judge happy and Stacey with you.'

Alex had begun fiddling with the juice bottle during that speech, running his finger around the grooves in the lid. 'So, it's too late,' he summarised. 'Either we win big, or we lose big.' The bottle tipped over as he jerked. 'I should have just paid her to start with,' he murmured.

Sam obviously heard him, as her hand closed reflexively, squeezing his elbow.

He reached over with his opposite hand to rub hers absentmindedly. 'It's not your fault,' he said. 'I knew what she was like. I should've done it to begin with.' He took a deep breath and turned to look at Michael. 'Give it to me straight,' he said. 'What are our chances?'

Michael waved his hand in the air indecisively. 'Depends on how convincing your witnesses are,' he said. 'And you. I'll admit it — having someone with no financial or emotional stake testify was a stroke of brilliance on their part. A dangerous one, considering it's a flat out lie, but as a "Hail Mary", it worked. The emails were supposed to be yours, and now we don't have any surprises up our sleeves.'

Hail Mary, recited Alex, *full of grace ...*

He looked over at Sam for a long moment. She looked back, lifting her hand to stroke across his cheek. 'I might have one,' he said, kissing her palm.

Chapter 33 – A Fateful Night

Alex closed the door to Stacey's bedroom, his guilty conscience almost causing him to go back inside. The little girl had her Nintendo DS hidden under her pillow, and she would probably pull it out after she was certain he was gone. He conveniently 'forgot' about it most nights, allowing her to use it in lieu of the nightlight Victoria denied her.

His wife had left early that morning, not bothering to give them any indication of when she would be back, or to even say goodbye. She hadn't given them any further information when she called this afternoon to remind Alex of something unimportant, but he'd caught a fleeting glimpse of her as she left. She was toting a small suitcase, suggesting she wouldn't be home tonight. Probably not for two or three nights if she followed her usual pattern.

Remembering this, he had a small moment of rebellion and left the hall light on for Stacey. The golden glow would leak under her door, giving her some comfort amid the darkness she was so afraid of.

He concentrated on this satisfying small victory, shying away from his knowledge of where Victoria was when she disappeared for her little trips. She'd begun pretending to seduce him on her return lately, knowing the long-term erosion of his confidence had resulted in his inability to perform. She bolstered her resulting derision with detailed descriptions of what she'd allowed her boyfriend to do to her, leaving him an empty shell of a man.

But tonight, he didn't need to worry about her. He and Stacey had spent an enjoyable afternoon at the park, before a quiet dinner together. Now his daughter was in bed, Alex was planning a relaxing, Victoria-free night of TV in his room before going to sleep himself.

His peace was shattered a little under an hour later when he heard the front door open downstairs. Victoria was home.

His first reaction was panic. Why was she back so soon? Had something gone wrong? He hoped she hadn't fought with Paul. She was likely to take her anger out on him.

Motionless and defensive as a hunted animal, Alex huddled in bed, waiting to see if she would come to his room. His heart rate increased exponentially as she climbed the stairs. He was waiting to hear her footsteps, either coming for his room, or walking past to her own. Curiously, after the last stair creaked, he didn't hear anything for a long while. Was she waiting outside the door? She must have wanted him good and nervous.

By the time he finally heard footsteps again, it took him a moment to understand there were two sets. As Victoria stepped into his room, Paul entered with her. Still scared, but also a little confused, Alex watched warily while they closed the door behind them. She'd never brought her lover to the house before.

'Hi, Alex,' Victoria said, a friendly smile unconvincingly pasted across her face. 'How has your night been? Watching some TV?'

After a pause, Alex managed to croak out an answer, too wary to do anything but play along with her small talk. She kept it up for a while, chatting about this and that, but not bringing up anything of consequence. Paul sporadically joined in their conversation, and the two of them laughed occasionally. They acted as if this was the most natural thing in the world.

He suspected they were trying to probe for information, keeping the banter casual so as not to alarm him. He cautiously responded to Victoria's latest innocently delivered enquiry, confirming he had no plans to see or speak to anyone tonight, wondering when her intentions would be made clear.

There was an immediate change in her demeanour after he answered. She and Paul exchanged a long look before she nodded and turned back to Alex. 'Alex,' she began sweetly. 'Darling, we haven't been happy together for a long time.'

That was an understatement. Their relationship, his entire life really, was a steaming pile of horse manure. Where was she going with this topic?

'You know Paul and I have been seeing each other for a while now,' she said apologetically, 'and we've been talking about the future. We'd both been considering ending our respective marriages before Angie got sick,' she said, referring to Paul's late wife. 'But of course, Paul couldn't leave her when she had cancer. That would be too cruel.'

Too cruel? He hadn't realised she had a threshold.

'It was a relief when she finally passed,' Victoria said callously. 'It meant Paul could move on from his unhappy marriage.'

Alex wondered if Paul was as brutal to Angie as Victoria was to him. He felt a moment's sympathy for the poor woman. Her death had come unexpectedly quick, but if she'd been similarly treated, perhaps it'd been a blessed release.

'And now our only barrier to being together properly is you,' his wife said conversationally, tracing the pattern on the bedspread with one manicured talon.

If Victoria wanted a divorce, he wouldn't stand in her way. He said as much out loud, a thrilling feeling of excitement coupled with fear of the unknown rising inside him. Was this the conversation that would free him?

'I thought about that,' she admitted, 'but I'm not sure. Obviously, I want as much money as possible, but there's no way I can get it all. Especially if I'm leaving the girl with you. No judge will sign off on the kind of settlement I'm looking for.'

He'd give her every cent if it meant she was out of his and Stacey's lives. Thinking quickly, Alex offered what he could to reassure her. 'I'm sure we could work something out,' he said cautiously. 'Even if we have to make another, more private agreement outside of the court.'

Victoria shook her head. 'It wouldn't work,' she said. 'The kind of cash we're talking about will always leave a trail, and I don't want it coming back to bite me in a few years when you've reconsidered.' She flicked a look at Paul again, and he nodded encouragingly.

Alex was shocked when he deduced Victoria was nervous.

'The thing is,' she complained agitatedly, 'it was so much easier for Paul. Angie died, her will was in order, and everything just smoothly went from joint ownership to his alone.' She sighed wistfully, and the hair on the back of his neck pricked up. 'Wistful' wasn't in her nature. 'So, I was thinking,' she said, her eyes narrowing as she licked her lips mid-sentence, 'how much easier it would be … if you died.'

Alex's mind went deliberately blank as he avoided drawing the obvious conclusion. He struggled for a bit, trying to find another path to tread, but couldn't stop the pieces from falling into place.

Victoria had bought Paul, her large, strong lover, to the house for the first time. Questioning Alex closely, she'd discerned they were in no danger of being interrupted tonight. She'd never had any qualms about causing him physical harm.

And she wanted him dead.

He scrambled backwards under the covers, away from where she was seated at the edge of the bed, his wide eyes searching for a weapon to defend himself. He'd never retaliated to her violence before, but he wasn't about to placidly let her end his life.

'Shhh,' Victoria soothed, raising her hands in a placating gesture, 'it's okay, we're not going to hurt you. You don't need to be afraid.'

The reassurance was so out of place coming from her that he didn't believe it for one second. His brain had started to catch up with his emotions though, and he had questions. If they wanted to kill him, why warn him? Why bother trying to keep him calm? This didn't make sense. Surely it would be easier to cut his throat as he slept or something.

'It's not that I want you to die,' she assured him, 'it's just that I'll get a much bigger payday with a lot less legal hassle as a widow, rather than a divorcee.'

'We've come here to discuss your options,' said Paul, finding his voice after his long silence.

Victoria smiled encouragingly; an expression Alex wasn't used to seeing on her face. This was all beyond strange. His thoughts and emotions were ricocheting around his head like a pinball machine, but he was frightened of what clarity would look like.

'The way we see it,' she began, the kind smile out of place on her face, 'you have two options. Option one: you take all those sleeping pills in the drawer of your nightstand,' she said conversationally, belying the sociopathic nature of the request. 'I counted them this morning, and there's plenty there. You'll go peacefully in your sleep. I'll let your family raise Stacey, so you don't have to worry about her. They'll take good care of her.'

Alex broke into a sweat. The sweet reassurance in her tone finally convinced him of what he'd known all along. This woman was a literal psychopath.

'The other option,' Victoria continued, her tone turning to poorly feigned regret, 'is less serene.' She looked over at Paul, who pulled something from his pocket.

A flash crossed Alex's vision as the lamp light reflected in Paul's flick knife. The shocked silence accompanying this big reveal was punctuated only by the creaking of the house.

'A robbery gone wrong,' his wife explained with mock regret. 'You'll put up a fight, obviously, but multiple stab wounds will get anyone in the end. Paul knows where to aim for, so you'll make the least noise,' she said fondly, giving the would-be attacker a smile over her shoulder. 'Stacey's throat will be cut,' Victoria said as she turned back, her conversational tone at odds with her plans to murder her own child. 'Even if you don't make enough noise to attract her while we're attending to you, it'll be easy enough to get her into the room with your corpse before we kill her. That way it'll look like the intruder surprised you both in your bedroom.' She stopped talking, looking at Alex expectantly.

He had stopped breathing. Words wouldn't be forthcoming until he could draw some air back into his lungs. A frown marred Victoria's smooth face as the seconds grew longer, and she tapped her finger on the bed impatiently.

This was madness. She couldn't possibly be giving him this ultimatum. Kill himself, or subject both him and Stacey to their murder? How had she convinced Paul to do this? It was insane.

Alex's eyes flickered over to the other man now, taking in his emotionless face and relaxed stance. It occurred to him they were perhaps as deranged as each other. He'd always known Paul to be quite 'cutthroat'; however, he hadn't considered the epigram to be literal. Fleetingly, he wondered if Angie's speedy demise had been entirely natural, chastising himself for getting off track. That was a problem for another day. If he had one.

'I'm waiting, Alex,' said Victoria irritably.

Irritability was a mundane emotion to be conveying when the subject at hand was literally life or death. Or more to the point: death or death. If these were truly his only options, life wasn't on the cards. Alex shied away from that absolute.

'You can't be serious,' he whispered finally, frightened by the uncertainty in his voice. There had to be a way out of this. He kept repeating this mantra in his head as Victoria's frown deepened and she answered him.

'Am I in the habit of making jokes with you?' she asked.

No, she most definitely was not. If this were a prank, it would be a first. He didn't hold out a lot of hope for that. She was cruel enough, but humour wasn't her style.

Victoria obviously thought this was a reasonable offer. He'd developed an amateur understanding of her twisted mind over the years, and he could appreciate it probably made a sick sort of sense to her. She wanted the money, and he was the obstacle to that. Ergo, he had to be eliminated. She didn't bear him any ill will in particular; she just had an inflated sense of entitlement that allowed her to rationalise this course of action to get what she wanted.

Stacey would be collateral damage.

Assuming he fought them, anyway. And therein lay the rub. Stacey was the bargaining chip; Victoria's one chance to ensure Alex went quietly. His wife understood love to a point. She didn't feel it so could never quite comprehend the all-encompassing wonder of it, but she understood enough to use it to her advantage.

For years she'd mocked him for his weakness, his attachment to people, places, and objects of sentiment. His affection gave her power over him, made him compliant as she slowly broke him down.

To her, this was an easy choice. Either Alex died by his own hand, leaving her with the money and Stacey safe, or they both died, and she got the money anyway.

Victoria sighed impatiently again. 'Alex, we're not going to wait much longer. Either you take the pills, or we do it the hard way. It seems like a no-brainer to me.'

When he still didn't respond, other to open and close his mouth like a fish, she gestured to the pen and pad on his nightstand. 'Let's take this in baby steps,' she said, soothing him like she would a frightened child. 'We'll get your suicide note written first.'

Alex glanced involuntarily at the pen and paper beside him, before fearfully looking back at Victoria sitting at the end of his bed, and Paul standing stoically behind her. He'd been afraid they would use his distraction as an opportunity to lunge, but they were unmoved.

Victoria's eyes narrowed, her pleasant, soothing mask slipping. He knew the effort it'd be taking her to fake a kind attitude. It certainly didn't come naturally. At her gesture, Paul lifted the knife so Alex could get a better look at it.

He picked up the pen and paper beside him, his hands shaking so badly he dropped the pen on the coverlet twice. Victoria smiled her satisfaction as he poised himself to begin writing. He blanked as he struggled to think of something acceptable to write. What should a suicide note say?

'I'll dictate,' said Victoria cheerily, mitigating the least of his worries with her helpful pronouncement. 'I can't do this anymore,' she began, her voice taking on the singsong quality of something long committed to memory.

Alex was sickened to realise she'd already composed it before she arrived tonight. How long had she been planning this?

Victoria droned on for a while, occasionally pausing so his mechanical scribbling could catch up, before finishing with a cliché. 'I know this is a selfish way out, but I don't know what else to do. I'll be at peace now. Please try not to be angry. Love, Alex.'

As he finished signing his name, Alex's trembling reached a crescendo and tears formed in his eyes. The pen slid limply from his hand as Victoria walked around the bed to take the pad from him. She ran a critical eye over his work, checking he'd copied her dictation to the letter.

Satisfied, she threw it carelessly onto the nightstand and opened the drawer underneath. The heartless woman rifled through the collection of odds and ends, finally emerging with her prize. Unscrewing the top of the little bottle, she indicated for Alex to hold out his hand.

When he hesitated, she looked imperiously at Paul. He obliged without changing expression, joining her at the side of the bed and waving the knife back and forth a foot or so from Alex's face.

A tear leaked out as Alex slowly uncurled his hand, leaving it lying in his lap. He couldn't bring himself to offer it up to her any more diligently, but this seemed to satisfy her. She poured the whole bottle into his large hand; the innocuous little pile belying its true power.

Victoria looked pleased at how far they'd come. She motioned to the glass of water sitting beside him, and he reluctantly picked it up. All that was left now was for him to start swallowing.

His throat had become parched and constricted in his state of high anxiety, and he took a sip of the water to lubricate it. He baulked when Victoria spoke, excitement evident in her voice. 'Now, the pills,' she instructed.

When he remained still, she impatiently swapped positions with her lover. Paul lazily moved the knife towards him, causing Alex to cringe backwards.

'Gently,' cautioned Victoria, and Alex understood she was talking to Paul, not him. 'He just needs a little encouragement.'

Paul nodded, placing the bared steel against Alex's throat almost lovingly. The blade wasn't pressed hard enough to cause him any physical discomfort, but the vulnerability he felt at its presence was intense. He understood all too well how little effort would be required for the hulking man to slice through the skin and sinew, piercing his jugular and opening his windpipe.

He was paralysed by his terror. He sat, his breathing close to hyperventilation, desperately trying to think of a way out of this. 'You can have all of it,' he croaked. 'Everything, just leave me Stacey. I'll even give you alimony. Just please …' His voice broke on the last word, scared his desperate plea wouldn't be enough to stop this madness.

'I wonder if your little girl will look as scared as you do,' said Paul conversationally, 'when I hold the knife to her throat.' He grinned down at Alex, a little maniacal around the eyes.

Alex whimpered, unable to look away. Thinking of Stacey, he bitterly resolved to do what needed to be done.

He let the pills fall into his lap, all but one, bringing it to his lips and swallowing it down with some water.

Victoria frowned over Paul's shoulder. 'You can do more than one at a time,' she commented, exasperated.

His trembling hands picked up two, and she shook her head at him, a stern look on her face. He hesitantly doubled it, Victoria nodding her acceptance as he placed the four pills in his mouth, swallowing again before he could chicken out and spit them on the bed.

The pile gradually emptied as he repeated the damning ritual. The whole process had taken less than a minute. As he swallowed the last three, Paul took the knife from his throat and sauntered past Victoria to stand in his original position on the opposite side of the bed again.

'There, there,' said Victoria comfortingly as she followed him. 'It'll all be over soon.'

Her and Paul shared an elated look, and he pulled her in for a brief kiss. Victoria turned to face Alex as Paul closed the knife, storing it back in his pocket. Paul put his arms around her as they settled in to watch her husband expectantly, waiting for the inevitable.

Paul appeared to quickly grow bored. Within a minute of their vigil beginning, he moved his hands from Victoria's waist to lewdly squeeze her breasts.

'Paul,' she admonished, her playful tone contradicting her protest, 'we're not alone.'

His crazed grin flashed again before he answered. 'Wouldn't be the first time I fucked you in front of a corpse,' he said, pushing her forwards a step.

She giggled as she bent over, placing her hands on the bed. Alex's quiet sobs turned to shocked silence as he saw Paul lift her skirt and lower her panties to her knees. Victoria's eyes bored into Alex's with a lust he'd never been able to inspire.

Paul quickly undid his pants and, evidently finding her ready for him, pushed himself inside Alex's waiting wife. He grunted with satisfaction, before winking at Alex and beginning to thrust rhythmically.

Victoria moaned, and Alex began to cry again, harder this time. He was hardly able to believe his death would be accompanied by the humiliation of witnessing his wife cuckold him. He couldn't summon the strength to look away, never having felt this mortified, this helpless.

The taboo situation obviously held a special excitement for Victoria as she neared her climax within a few minutes, going down onto an elbow as she reached her other hand underneath to stroke herself.

Alex was crying so hard by now he struggled to breathe. He felt himself start to convulse at the same time as Victoria did.

As she cried out …

He vomited.

He'd swallowed the pills less than ten minutes ago, and they came up mostly still intact, just starting to dissolve in his bile. He stared at this foul miracle on his bedcovers for one disbelieving moment, before leaping out of the bed to take advantage of his second chance. It was only a few short steps to the balcony door, and he had no thought in his head other than to get out of this room.

Victoria was knocked onto the bed as her lover struggled to lunge after Alex with his pants around his ankles. Paul's fumbles would have been comical if the situation hadn't been so desperate.

He managed to get his pants up enough to barrel into Alex just as he opened the stubborn balcony door. They both flew outside into the cold night, Paul pushing Alex to the ground and winding him. His attacker quickly pulled Alex to his feet, ignoring his weight and frantic struggles, and wrapping an arm around his throat in the process.

Alex was in imminent danger of suffocating. He hadn't managed to get any air back after his fall before Paul began choking him. Victoria caught up to them, helping to contain the thrashing, desperate man.

Dark spots appeared in Alex's vision as his struggles grew feebler. He noticed peripherally that they were moving him to the edge of the balcony.

This observation had no meaning until Paul finally let go of his throat. The two assailants desperately pushed his upper body beyond the barrier, fighting to get his centre of gravity to the point of no return.

Welcome air rushed into Alex's lungs, and he gulped two breaths before they achieved their goal. He used it to scream as he fell.

Chapter 34 – Oops

'We were only one story up, so it was a leap of faith on their part,' continued Alex, pale and sweating as he told the terrible tale. 'If there hadn't been any obstacles, I had a fair chance of survival. I think they were counting on the fence.' He took a deep breath, and Sam's whole body twitched. She wished she were up there with him, holding his hand while he relived the terror of that night. 'It was one of those fancy wrought iron barriers, dividing the house from the garden,' he explained. 'It was topped with sharp spikes, and I think the idea was to impale me. I got lucky though. I missed the points facing upwards, but I hit one of the points facing outwards instead.' He removed his tie as he spoke, hands shaking, before unbuttoning his shirt.

'It ripped me open, starting at my thigh and running up my whole torso, grazing my neck, and then doing more damage from my chin to my temple,' he explained, tracing the line of the scar, now almost visible in its entirety. 'I blacked out almost immediately, so I don't know exactly what happened next. Stacey must have heard something as it was her that called the ambulance. I'm guessing I made enough noise to spook Victoria and Paul, or they'd have checked on me before they left.' His hands stilled, holding his shirt open to illustrate his injuries as he spoke, and Sam felt sick. She could imagine how it must have looked before it healed. 'It's a miracle I didn't die,' he said, much closer to his normal colouring and tone of voice.

Now the worst of the story was over, he seemed to be coping better, but Sam's concern was slow to ease.

'As it was, I lost a large amount of blood, shattered several bones, sustained damage to my stomach, liver and lungs, and also damaged muscles in my leg, abdomen, pectoral and shoulder,' he said clinically. 'You can see I have quite a large, deep scar, starting mid-thigh and finishing on my face.'

The courtroom was dead silent.

Michael had paused after Alex's conclusion. Sam had noticed he had a flair for the dramatic, and this did tend to heighten the tension when used correctly.

The judge broke the silence when it became clear Alex had finished speaking. 'That's quite a serious accusation,' she noted to Alex, who nodded grimly.

'It's preposterous, your honour,' Victoria declared, standing. 'I have already informed the court what happened that day. I was not at home the night of his suicide attempt.'

The judge looked taken aback at her presumption.

Was Victoria really so narcissistic as to think she could interrupt the proceedings whenever she felt like it, with no consequences?

Paul stood next to her, perhaps to add his protests, perhaps to confess (probably the former), but was stalled when another voice sounded instead.

'Yes, you were,' it said, a strange mix of timidity and certainty in the voice coming from the back of the court.

A rustling sounded as everyone turned in the direction of the unexpected participant.

'I heard you,' stated Stacey. Her shoulders were hunched, but the look on her face was pure stubbornness. She had come to state her case.

Sam wondered how long she'd been sitting there without them noticing.

'Stacey!' exclaimed Alex. 'What are you doing here?' Still on the witness stand with his shirt undone, he hovered, half-seated, half-standing, obviously wanting to go to her, but unsure if he were permitted to leave.

Sam went to her instead, and she saw Alex sit cautiously and jerkily begin doing up buttons as she put an arm around the fragile-looking girl.

'Stacey Whittaker, I presume?' asked the judge, not unkindly.

Stacey squared her shoulders and nodded as she visibly gulped, perhaps swallowing her fear.

'Mr Whittaker, you may step down,' instructed the judge, suddenly decisive. 'I would like to hear from Miss Whittaker.'

Hope flared in Sam so quickly that she had to swallow a squeak.

'Your honour, I am yet to question Mr Whittaker!' exclaimed Duncan, his knuckles white where they rested on the table.

'You can question him after,' said the woman dismissively.

Alex looked sick again. He hadn't moved after the judge spoke, just opening and closing his mouth, his shirt half buttoned, while Stacey moved towards the front of the courtroom. 'Your honour,' he said faintly. 'I don't want … she's too young. To testify, I mean. You're just going to traumatise her …'

Sam cringed. This sounded weak. If Stacey didn't testify now, it would look like he was trying to keep her off the stand to avoid damning himself.

'Step down, Mr Whittaker,' repeated the judge.

Alex dithered, only capitulating when Michael motioned urgently. Now was not the time to get on the judge's bad side. Not when Stacey had potentially thrown them a lifeline.

She was quickly sworn in as Alex sat, and to Sam's surprise, the judge began to question her herself. The two lawyers were redundant by this stage, apparently. 'What was it you heard?' she asked gently.

Stacey began her damning speech, perhaps had been rehearsing it for some time now. 'I heard Mama,' she began, unconsciously using the diminutives she had as a child, 'and a man, but mostly Mama, in Daddy's bedroom. They were talking for a long time.' Her eyes flickered between Victoria and Paul. 'I wanted to come in,' she explained, 'because I was frightened, but then Mama said …' Tears had begun forming in the young girl's eyes as she spoke, and her voice broke as she struggled to finish her sentence. She took a deep breath and tried again. 'Mama said the man was going to kill us!' she sobbed, breaking down.

Alex rocked forward, and Sam almost stood to put a calming hand on his shoulder.

Stacey took a shaky breath, her face twitching as she fought to get herself under control. Clearly determined to say her piece, she soon spoke again. 'They kept going quiet, and I hoped they'd gone, but then they'd start talking again. After a long time, Daddy started crying. Mama and the man were quiet, and then Mama made a funny noise. I was really happy because I thought maybe Daddy had hurt her back for once,' she said, blushing as she added defensively that she hadn't known what sex was when she was five to understand what it really meant. 'And then Daddy threw up. There was lots of banging and thumping after that, and then he screamed.'

Victoria had been sitting with her mouth hanging open as she listened to Stacey speak, Paul gripping her arm tightly. She stood as she voiced her protests, Sam watching with incredulity.

'Your honour, this is ridiculous!' she began angrily. 'Alex has obviously coached her to lie, or maybe brainwashed her or something.' She drew herself a little taller as she spoke, ignoring the judge's frown as she spoke out of turn, her words rolling together as she tried to talk her way out of the corner her daughter had backed her into. 'Her bedroom wouldn't have been close enough to hear these things even if it had happened! The story makes no logical —'

She broke off as Stacey interrupted her. 'I wasn't in my room, I was in Daddy's bathroom,' she clarified.

Victoria spat back her damning response without pausing to consider her words.

'Don't be absurd, you were in bed! I checked on you myself!' she said sternly.

A red flush crept its way up her neck and over her face as she realised the implications of her statement. It was quickly chased by a white so sickly it was almost grey.

A sheen of sweat broke out on her face, and Paul stood to shake her so hard that Sam practically heard her bones rattle. He let go before anyone could react to this violence, running for the back of the courtroom.

He was tackled by a triumphantly grinning Noah, who was quickly squashed under James and Erik. Christian was not able to join in as his mother and Sam were in the way, and the grim satisfaction in his face looked slightly tarnished at his exclusion. The bailiff quickly intervened, but Paul did end up with a bleeding lip for his trouble. Predictably, all three of the brothers would later claim responsibility.

After order had been restored, the judge motioned for Stacey to explain. Sam suspected she was curious more than anything. Victoria had already basically confessed.

'I went through the hole,' explained Stacey, talking directly to her father. Impossible to see his face from behind him, Sam did notice the tension in his shoulders ease.

'I'd accidentally knocked a decent-sized hole in the wall of her wardrobe shortly before all this,' he explained to the judge, taking the woman's interested look as permission to speak out of turn. 'I was afraid Victoria would be angry, so I'd been waiting for her to leave for a few days before I called someone to fix it. It was low to the ground so I could hide it behind some of Stacey's toys.'

'The other side went into the cupboard under his bathroom sink,' added Stacey helpfully.

The judge nodded, displaying the most positive reaction Sam had seen from her all day. 'When did you wake up during the alleged events?' she asked Stacey.

She flashed a guilty look at Alex before answering. 'I was never asleep,' she explained. 'I was pretending when she came in. I thought she was Daddy, checking to make sure I wasn't playing my video game. I heard someone outside the door and put it under my pillow, and I didn't know it was her until I smelled her perfume.'

The judge nodded decisively, thanking her for her testimony. She had evidently heard enough, and she straightened authoritatively to give the verdict, briefly pausing to give Stacey permission to leave the stand.

'Victoria Fraser and Paul Fraser, you are both to be remanded in custody pending your trial for attempted murder. I am also ordering an inquiry into the death of Angela Fraser. I am awarding sole legal and physical custody of Anastasia Whittaker to her father, Aleksander Whittaker. No visitation rights are awarded to her mother; however, I recognise Stacey is mature enough to decide herself if she wishes to arrange something more informal for the benefit of her mental health.'

Stacey screwed up her face at this. Sam doubted she'd exercise that right.

'Regarding the divorce settlement,' she said with a frown. 'If Mrs Fraser is found guilty of the crimes she is charged with, I have no doubt the worth of the full joint estate she and Mr Whittaker shared will be awarded to Mr Whittaker. Until such time as this is assessed, all her assets are hereby frozen. Mr Whittaker, you are free to continue managing your money, investments and property as you wish.'

On this joyful note, court was dismissed.

Later that night, Alex finally shooed his family out and saw Stacey off to bed. He was with her a long time, and Sam deduced they were probably talking about the secrets they'd kept from one another. She suspected there were multiple reasons why Stacey had never spoken up before. For one, no one had thought to ask her what happened before she found Alex on that fateful night.

It was always just assumed she'd been woken by the fall. Everyone had been too busy praising her bravery and quick-thinking to question her closely. Even her therapist concentrated only on how she'd felt when she found him, confessing her oversight as they left the courthouse.

Sam also wondered if Stacey had similar reservations to those Alex felt. They'd talked about it several times since his original confession. Finally opening up to a trusted confidant had allowed him to analyse his reasons for keeping quiet. He and Sam had deduced that in not talking about it, he'd managed to relegate it to a world of fairy tale. The whole experience had been incredibly surreal, and the resulting injuries had worked to distract him from his emotions for too long while he physically recovered.

Quite simply, even thinking about it made the situation too 'real' for him, so he'd shied away from it. Stacey, a frightened little girl at the time, would have had an even bigger aversion to speaking. Lending the event the credibility of her voice would have given her nowhere to hide. Her actions today had been incredibly brave.

Alex came down the stairs as Sam pondered this, and she smiled while he reached for her.

'How is our little heroine?' she asked him, searching his face for clues to his emotional state.

'Exhausted, exhilarated and emotional,' he answered with a small smile. 'I think it was a bigger day for her than it was for me.'

'It was a massive day for both of you,' corrected Sam, 'and pretty much everyone, truth be told,' she added. *Especially Victoria and Paul,* she thought privately.

Alex's hands strayed down the curve of her hips, kneading her buttocks while a wicked grin grew on his face. 'Let's forget about it for a little while,' he suggested.

Not waiting for an answer, he threw the laughing woman over his shoulder in a fireman's hold, making for his bedroom. Sam struggled to keep her mirth quiet for Stacey's sake, only losing the urge to laugh when Alex kissed her deeply.

He was different tonight. The time since their first night had seen him grow in confidence during their lovemaking, but he always held back, an invisible force staying his hand.

Tonight, all his restraints had been loosed. His touch was no longer hesitant, hands and mouth finally certain of their actions. Overwhelmed, Sam could do nothing but let him pleasure her as he wished. It was a heady ride, and she marvelled at how perfectly they fit together.

Not just in the physical sense, either. Their imperfect pasts had left wounds that few people would have the sensitivity to soothe. The pathways they had taken to get to where they were today had been fraught with painful lessons, but the thing they had both learned most keenly was compassion. Sam would never wish such an excruciating schooling on anyone, but if it had to be endured, finding love at the end was a perfect salve.

About the Author

Holly Carr was born in Geelong, Victoria, where she still lives today with her husband and a cat with no sense of personal space. She graduated from Deakin University in 2010 with a Bachelor of Arts (Public Relations), majoring in Literary Studies.

Holly first began writing creatively while she was at university, only setting aside her incomplete manuscript due to time constraints. It took ten years before she finally sat down to write again, and her first completed novel 'IMPERFECT' practically wrote itself. She enjoyed the experience so much she has already begun work on another.

When she takes a break from writing, she enjoys occasional visits from her grown-up son, pole dancing, eating far too much Mexican food, and pretending to know a lot about wine.

You can get all the latest info about her books at her website www.hollycarr.com.au, or on Facebook @hollycarrauthor.